Solving,
Resolving,
and Dissolving
Philosophical Problems

Solving, Resolving, and Dissolving Philosophical Problems

Essays in Connective, Contrastive and Contextual Analysis

P. M. S. Hacker

WILEY Blackwell

Registered Offices
John Wiley & Sons, Inc., 111 River Street, Hoboken, NJ 07030, USA
John Wiley & Sons Ltd, New Era House, 8 Oldlands Way, Bognor Regis, West Sussex, PO22 9NQ, UK

For details of our global editorial offices, customer services, and more information about Wiley products visit us at www.wiley.com.

Wiley also publishes its books in a variety of electronic formats and by print-on-demand. Some content that appears in standard print versions of this book may not be available in other formats.

Library of Congress Cataloging-in-Publication Data
Names: Hacker, P. M. S. (Peter Michael Stephan), author. | John Wiley & Sons, publisher.
Title: Solving, resolving, and dissolving philosophical problems : on the methodology of connective, contrastive, and contextual analysis / P. M. S. Hacker.
Description: Hoboken, NJ : Wiley-Blackwell, 2025. | Includes bibliographical references and index.
Identifiers: LCCN 2024034639 (print) | LCCN 2024034640 (ebook) | ISBN 9781394278817 (paperback) | ISBN 9781394278831 (adobe pdf) | ISBN 9781394278824 (epub)
Subjects: LCSH: Analysis (Philosophy). | Philosophy–Methodology.
Classification: LCC B808.5 .H27 2025 (print) | LCC B808.5 (ebook) | DDC 146/.4–dc23/eng/20240905
LC record available at https://lccn.loc.gov/2024034639
LC ebook record available at https://lccn.loc.gov/2024034640

Cover Design and Image: Nina Hacker

Set in 10.5/12.5pt SabonLTStd by Straive, Pondicherry, India

For

Hans Oberdiek

and

Claire Parker

Contents

Contents

Introduction

At some stage in their lives, most thoughtful people wonder about philosophical problems. Can one arrive at adulthood without questioning whether God exists, whether there is life after death, or what our existence on earth is good for? A reflective young adult can hardly fail to ask whether human life has a purpose, and if so, what it is, or to query what a good life is and how it should be lived. Many people are liable, at some time or other, to wonder what truth is, and if they succumb to the deceptive appeal of the excesses of postmodernism, they may take perverse comfort in thinking that there is no absolute truth, only your truth and my truth and the truth of the ruling classes. We are singularly ill-equipped to handle such deep questions and to confront such dogmatic and intellectually pernicious relativism without assistance.

Great philosophers throughout the ages have struggled with them. It is not the purpose of this short book to give an account of their struggles. Such accounts are to be found in fine histories of philosophy such as Anthony Kenny's *New History of Western Philosophy*. The great philosophers of the past adopted a wide variety of methods of philosophical enquiry. These different methods have been well surveyed in numerous publications and another such survey will not be essayed here, even though this is a book concerned with methodology. Indeed, it is written to advocate a particular method or interconnected set of methods for solving, resolving, or dissolving problems in philosophy. But it is a method or methods altogether distinct from the those practiced in most current university departments. This book presupposes little philosophical knowledge, but only curiosity and an open mind. It demands only a willingness to learn not doctrine but method, and the courage to suspend judgement and to challenge received ideas.

Given that we are going to be deeply concerned with method in philosophical enquiry, it might seem that we should start our investigations with a brief and uncontroversial statement of what philosophy is, as one might start a book on methodology in biochemistry with a clear, brief characterization of what exactly biochemistry is. But to try to characterize philosophical problems on the first page of a book concerned with philosophical method would be to rush in prematurely, leaving the angels behind. There are few problems more controversial in philosophy than the problem of what precisely philosophy is and what exactly a philosophical problem is. That itself is an interesting fact, for no other academic subject suffers from such omphaloskepsis (navel-gazing). Physicists do not write lengthy and controversial papers on what physics is. Chemists and biologists do not write passion-provoking books on what chemistry or biology are. Nor do economists or experimental psychologists quarrel over what their subject is, as opposed to how to do it. But what philosophy is, is a perennial philosophical problem. It will not be confronted now, although by the end of this book something of an answer will have emerged.

My purpose in this book is not only to try, by considered argument, to demonstrate to readers *what* they should think on some deep philosophical problems, but also to show them *how* they should think productively. Indeed, my intent is to do the former by means of the latter. I have selected fifteen perennial philosophical topics for scrutiny (Essays 1–15). Many alternatives might well have been chosen, but these struck me as particularly revealing. They should be of concern to any thinking person, and the results of the methods of enquiry are often both striking and unexpected. The essays fall into three groups: (i) the nature of the mind, the mind/body problem and the nature of consciousness, our knowledge of other people; (ii) epistemological problems concerning knowledge, belief, memory, imagination, thinking and dreaming; (iii) the roots of value, the nature of moral goodness, and the differentiation between the bad, the wicked, and the evil; and so as not to end on so grim a subject: the characterization of human happiness.

Each of these essays (with the exception of the one on dreaming) gives a highly compressed overview (between 11 and 13 pages) of a very much longer and far more comprehensive discussion of these topics in a tetralogy on human nature that I published with Wiley/Blackwell between 2007 and 2021: *Human Nature: The Categorial*

Framework (2007), *The Intellectual Powers* (2013), *The Passions* (2018), and *The Moral Powers* (2021). My purpose in the tetralogy was to provide a comprehensive survey of all the characterizing conceptual connections of the salient features of human nature that I had come across in fifty years of philosophical study. It was intended to be, among other things, a repository of logico-grammatical truths pertinent to the philosophical investigation of human nature (what Kant called 'philosophical anthropology' and the British called 'the moral sciences'). For it seemed to me absurd that these should be lost from generation to generation and have to be laboriously discovered afresh. To be sure, philosophy is not a progressive subject: there are advances and regresses, but that does not mean that we cannot salvage enduring insights from the wreckage and pass them on to future generations. The tetralogy employed the methods I had learnt from my betters and from decades of study and writing, but it was not a treatise on method. It was a treatise on human nature.

This short book, however, *is* a treatise on method. But method before practice is like recipes before dinner. The strategy of the book is to display the methods in practice before examining the theory of the practice. But as the various logico-linguistic techniques are employed in the essays, their use and the fruitfulness of their use are recurrently emphasized. There is a degree of deliberate repetition in the methodological comments – one cannot teach a technique, such as playing the piano, without reiteration. A comprehensive *overview* and systematic *defence* of the methods of connective, contrastive, and contextual analysis is given only in the long concluding Essay 16. There, criticisms are rebutted, misconstruals are corrected, and misunderstandings are clarified.

It will quickly be noticed that this book lacks all the usual critical apparatus characteristic of academia. There are hardly any footnotes sprouting at the bottom of the page, very few *contemporary* philosophers are mentioned and fewer still are explicitly confronted in the thrust and riposte of debate. This is no coincidence. Everything has been pared away in the interests of clarity of ideas and transparency of argument. Who actually holds the ideas among our contemporaries and how many *variations on a given idea* can be found in what goes by the name of the 'literature' is of little moment for my purposes. What matters are the ideas, *perspicuously displayed*. Any competent philosopher can build yet more epicycles on erroneous orbits of misplaced planets – but these are of mere scholastic, not substantive, interest. Similarly, *who* advances a given misguided argument in the bustle of today's philosophical bourse is irrelevant to the display of its invalidity or inadequacy in a book on methodology (a *Prioritätstreit* [priority dispute] over truth may be forgivable, but surely not over error). One consequence of this economy of expression is that the discussions are often extremely condensed. Each essay should be read slowly and more than once.

The methods advocated are at odds with much philosophical practice in the Anglophone world today. It is perhaps an exaggeration to assert that contemporary students of philosophy, both undergraduates and graduates, are instructed to approach any given philosophical problem by reading the last decade of journal publications that discuss it, and perhaps a handful of chapters or extracts from current books. But it is not far from the truth, as is exhibited in current philosophical journals, companions to philosophy and philosophical handbooks, Wikipedia, and encyclopedias of the Internet beloved by students of philosophy and philosophical journalists. Are these not the official repositories of human knowledge in the twenty-first century? This popular pedagogic principle of economy of effort is not arbitrary, only parochial, cleaving to passing fashions that will be obsolete within a decade or two. It is based on the natural sciences, the general form of which is progress. No physicist is likely to be told to read Galileo or Copernicus for an essay, and no biologist is instructed to read Galen or Vesalius for a tutorial. Teamwork, led by a powerful professoriate, with incessant bureaucratic demands for immediate research results characterizes contemporary methods of scientific research at universities. Following this example is eroding philosophical excellence in the academy.

The pedagogical emulation of the sciences in philosophical method guarantees:

(i) the domination of current philosophical doctrines and the reinforcing of current preconceptions and prejudices

(ii) proliferation of -isms and -ists

(iii) the relative neglect of twenty-five centuries of struggle by philosophers of genius with problems many of which differ but little from those with which we currently engage.

(iv) the assimilation into philosophy of methods of research alien to the nature of the subject and inimical to the achievement of its intellectual goals – no matter how satisfactory for university bureaucracies and international measures of quality control in terms of publications and citations.

The domination of current philosophical practices and products is a consequence of two features. The first is the increasing centralization of education both at governmental level and at the level of university administration, and the growth of power of the university professoriate and pedagogical bureaucracies. This corporatism penalizes independent thought by students and junior faculty alike. It ensures that few will have the desire, let alone the courage, to cut across the grain of current prejudices. The student of philosophy, from undergraduate to faculty, is not guided by the problems, but by current thinking on the problems with all its preconceptions.

The second is the belief in philosophical progress on the model of scientific progress. Philosophy is seen as a battleground of doctrines. Only time (and perhaps science), it is thought, will tell which ones will triumph.

It is this, in part, that leads to the proliferation of -isms and -ists. It is they that guarantee blinkered thought. For -isms and -ists are ready-mades designed to save one the trouble of thinking for oneself and to prevent one from reading a text with an open mind. It makes teaching easy, for one need not teach students how to think for themselves and how to confront a question by themselves, but only to opt for a party. The primary question then becomes: what sort of -ist should I be: a functionalist or a reductionist, a realist or an anti-realist, an internalist or an externalist, a representationalist or an idealist ... or some other -ist?

Because the mainstream of anglophone philosophy today is mesmerized by science and intoxicated by theory, and because it conceives of philosophy as progressive on the model of the natural sciences, history of philosophy (with the exception of ancient philosophy) is to a large extent relegated to the sidelines. This is the obverse face of the science-emulating assumption that the research of the last decade already incorporates all that is currently known, and therefore this alone is worth studying. But philosophical problems are not akin to problems in the empirical sciences that are to be solved by observation, theory construction and confirmation or infirmation. There is much more to be learnt from studying the great thinkers of the past who tussled with problems similar to, if not identical with, those we engage with than from reading all the articles written on a given problem in the last decade. No one writing in current philosophy journals is as deep a thinker as Plato or Aristotle, Aquinas or Scotus, Descartes or Spinoza, Hobbes or Locke, Hume or Kant. The distinctions they drew, for example between *psuchē* and body, may still be of value to us.

Their lack of some of our distinctions, for example, between the voluntary and the intentional, may illuminate the value of our distinctions. Distinctions they drew that are fundamentally different from ours, for example between form and matter, may free us from the prejudice that our current distinctions are the only correct ones, or are the best ones.

Studying the way past geniuses engaged with problems similar to ours helps to give us a measured distance from the way we currently handle the problems, and so a sharpened awareness of our own parochialism. The distance of centuries between their works and ours makes it easier to pin down their fundamental presuppositions and to question them. That in turn makes it easier for us to lay bare our own presuppositions and to challenge them. If it is sometimes relatively easy for us to apprehend what is awry with widely accepted ideas among philosophers of the past, that should not encourage us to pass them by with a sense of superiority. On the contrary, it should drive us to investigate, for example, how great thinkers such as Descartes, Spinoza, Leibniz, Locke, Berkeley, or Hume could have been so taken with their New Way of Ideas that the philosophical vision of their culture was, as it were, mesmerized for one hundred and fifty years. Only by discovering this can we learn anything from their great mistakes. We can rest assured that had we, *per impossibile*, been philosophers during their times, we too would have walked blindly along the Way of Ideas without any awareness of its irremediable defects. This investigation into the deep roots of their errors may in turn make it easier for us to search for similarly unquestioned philosophical presuppositions of our times.

Philosophers should greet each other, Wittgenstein suggested, with the exclamation, 'Take your time!' Faced with a philosophical problem, we are prone to rush to answer it. And if we are blinkered by current -isms and -ists, we shall expend much effort elaborating how a realist would answer the question and how an anti-realist would do so, how an absolutist would handle it and how a relativist would, how an internalist would cope with it and how an externalist. But that is futile. One must rather take things slowly. First, investigate the question: how does the problem arise in the first place? What needs would an answer serve? What is the point and purpose of asking the question? What are its presuppositions? Is it a good question at all? In short, challenge the question, rather than rushing to answer it.

Some fundamental philosophical controversies persist for many centuries. A wise methodological principle is that when faced by a perennial debate between two different schools of philosophy with respect to some great matter, one should not examine the arguments on both sides and plumb for the strongest. If that could have solved matters, they would have been solved many a century ago. Rather, *one should investigate what is agreed upon by all participants in the debate, and challenge that.* It is the agreed presuppositions, very often the unmentioned agreed presuppositions, that may hold the key to the solution.

Many striking and unexpected conclusions result from the use of the manifold methods and techniques of connective, contrastive, and contextual logico-linguistic analysis. These conclusions stand in diametric opposition to many contemporary views, doctrines, and theories. I hope that they will be sufficiently convincing and appealing to encourage readers to eschew the colourful banners waving in the marketplace of ideas and to fend for themselves. Equipped with the methods, they will be able to follow Kant's advice, *Sapere aude,* and have the courage to think for themselves.

Acknowledgements

I am indebted to many dear friends and colleagues who encouraged me in the writing of this book. Their moral support has been heart-warming and their judicious criticisms have saved me from many an error. Hanoch Ben-Yami, John Cottingham, Lassi Jakola, Anthony Kenny, Juan Pascual, Severin Schroeder, and Gabriele Taylor all read one or more of the essays. Their comments were invaluable.

I am grateful to attendants at my final two courses of lectures at Oxford University on Wednesday afternoons in the Radcliffe Philosophy Department lecture room in Michaelmas Term 2023 and Hilary Term 2024. Their questions were stimulating and challenging.

I owe a special debt of gratitude to Hans Oberdiek and Claire Parker who read and commented in detail on every essay. Their demand for clarity was exemplary, their criticisms invaluable, and their suggestions unfailingly constructive. The very idea of the book was Hans's. I would not have been able to bring it to fruition but for Claire's constant support and enthusiasm.

PART I
Philosophical Psychology

1

The Nature of the Mind

"The genuine philosophy of the human mind, is in so low a state, and has so many enemies, that, I apprehend those who would make any improvement in it must, for a time, build with one hand and hold a weapon with the other."

Thomas Reid, Correspondence, letter to
James Gregory, 6 August 1783

1.   That human beings have a mind is news from nowhere, but what it is that one has when one has a mind is perplexing. Am I identical with my mind or is the mind a part of me – the thinking part, perhaps? When I speak of my mind, am I speaking of myself or of my *self*? The mind is something I have and so, it seems, is the self, for am I not required to be true to mine own self? Is the mind identical to the self or distinct from it? Where does the soul stand? Do human beings have a soul, or is that an obsolete theological notion? If not, is the soul identical to the mind or distinct from it? And how is the soul related to the self? Of course, I also have a brain. If I have a mind, a soul, a self, and a brain, what is this 'I' that has these things?

Some of these items, things or entities can be readily disposed of. Their entitative claims are altogether bogus. Incidentally, beware of the pretentious term 'entity' – it sounds impressive, but it is merely an Anglicized cognate of the Latin *ens*, which means no more than the humble Anglo-Saxon 'thing'. So, what sort of thing is a self? Indeed, is

Solving, Resolving, and Dissolving Philosophical Problems: Essays in Connective, Contrastive and Contextual Analysis, First Edition. P. M. S. Hacker.
© 2025 John Wiley & Sons Ltd. Published 2025 by John Wiley & Sons Ltd.

it *a thing* at all? How should we investigate the matter? Certainly not by surveying all the pronouncements of philosophers on the self nor by scrutinizing all their philosophical theories. Philosophers have the difficult task of exploring the bounds of sense, of clarifying the manifold distinctions between sense and nonsense, of showing the multiple forms of nonsense – and by 'nonsense' I do not mean rubbish, I mean forms of words and utterance that for one reason or another do not make sense, that transgress the bounds of sense even though they do not seem to do so. Since philosophers, or at any rate analytic philosophers, spend much of their time crawling, with a magnifying glass, along the boundaries that separate sense from nonsense, it is not surprising that they often find themselves, the descriptions they offer, and the theories they advance, on the wrong side of the boundary. When faced with a problematic notion, such as the self, the I, the soul, the mind, we should not begin our investigations with a survey of the prevalent philosophical theories and their argumentative support and then endeavour to choose the most plausible one or, perhaps, more radically, come to repudiate the very idea of *theory* in philosophy as a deep misconception. That can come much later, when we have found our own way. Only then may we be in a position critically to evaluate the doctrines and theories of past and present philosophers. We should start by wiping the board clean and examining the raw data.

What are the raw data for a philosophical problem or puzzle if not the past theories? Philosophical problems and puzzles, as we shall show again and again in the course of these essays, are conceptual problems and puzzles. They are rooted in our conceptual scheme, in the ways in which we conceive of things and features of things in the world we inhabit, in our experiences of them and in our thoughts about them. Our conceptual scheme is expressed by the language we employ in our discourse and articulate reflections. Indeed, our language is inextricably implicated in the creation and moulding of our concepts. So the raw data for critical reflection are the uses of words, and they are tabulated in our dictionaries. So our first stop of call is the complete *Oxford English Dictionary*, with its itemization of usage and plethora of examples of each use, as well as lexicographical history and etymology. This will not give us any answers to our conceptual questions, but it will provide us with the raw data upon which to work.

2.   If we look to the *Oxford English Dictionary* for elaboration of meanings, we find that the noun 'mind' is said to signify the faculty of consciousness and thought which enables human beings to be aware

of the world and of their experiences. This connection between the mind and consciousness was Cartesian. The concept of consciousness was of seventeenth-century origin and defining the mind in terms of being conscious *of* something (transitive consciousness) was a radical innovation that, as is patent from the *Oxford English Dictionary*, is with us to this day. But the concept of mind is very much older than the seventeenth century and had previously been conceived in terms of the capacity for rationality. Only philosophical investigation can disclose which is the more coherent and illuminating conception of the mind and of human nature.

A first step towards elucidation is to examine English usage, perspicuously laid out in the *Oxford English Dictionary*, to see what light it sheds on our concept of mind. What is most striking is the multitude of English idioms that make use of the word 'mind', for example, to have a keen mind, an open mind, to close one's mind to, to clear one's mind, to call to mind, for something to slip out of one's mind, to have a mind to do something, to be in half a mind to do something, to be in two minds whether to do something, to make up one's mind, to change one's mind, to have something in mind, and many more. Rather than dismissing this as language-local idiom, which it is, and dismissing it as of no philosophical importance, which it isn't, we should seek for patterns in usage that illuminate our concept of mind and provide grounds for connective and contrastive analysis.

3.   The manifold idioms are evident in daily discourse. To get an overall picture of their point and purpose will be illuminating for elucidating the concept of mind. For it is easy to arrange the various idioms in six clusters or focal points, although they are not neat, non-overlapping clusters and they are not exhaustive either. It is also easy to paraphrase each 'mind'-incorporating idiom into an equivalent phrase in which the word 'mind' does not occur. One cluster is focused on memory and remembering. To hold or keep something in mind is to ensure that one won't overlook it; to bear something in mind is to remember it so that one will be able to take it into account. To call or bring something to mind is to recollect it. For something to be, go, pass out of, or slip out of mind is for it to be forgotten. To cast one's mind back is to try to remember, and to be absent-minded is to be forgetful or inattentive.

A second focal point is thought and thinking. To have a thought cross one's mind or for an idea to come to mind is for something to occur to one. For something to lurk at the back of one's mind is to be trying without success to think of something. To turn one's mind to something is to start thinking about it. To have something on one's mind is to be preoccupied with it. To have a load taken off one's mind is to be relieved of anxiously thinking about it. One's mind is in a turmoil when one doesn't know what to do or to think. One's mind wanders when one cannot concentrate or attend. One's mind goes blank when one does not know what to say and is at a loss. One has an original cast of mind when one displays originality in thought, discourse, and action.

A third cluster concerns opinion and opining. To know one's mind is to have formed one's opinion, and to tell or speak one's mind is to express it. To be of one mind with another is to agree in opinion or judgement. To give someone a piece of one's mind is to tell him harshly one's opinion of him.

A fourth focal point is intention and intending. To be minded or to have it in mind to do something is to be inclined or to intend to do it. To have half a mind to do something is to be tempted to do it and to be in two minds whether to do something is to be undecided. To make up one's mind is to decide and to change one's mind is to reverse one's decision. To have a mind of one's own is to be independent in judgement and decision.

A further focal point is the characterization of a person's intellect: one may have a powerful, agile, subtle, or devious mind if one is skilful, quick, and ingenious at problem solving or if one's solutions, plans, and projects display subtlety and cunning. Other characterizations are linked to intellectual virtues and faults. One may have a tenacious, idle, judicious, indecisive mind according to the manner in which one grapples with problems.

Another cluster concerns rationality: one is of sound mind if one retains one's rational faculties and one is out of one's mind if one thinks, proposes, and acts irrationally. One is not in one's right mind if one is distraught and one has lost one's mind if one is bereft of one's rational faculties. One may be small or petty minded if one makes a fuss over trivialities of behaviour of others, one is broad or narrow minded according to one's receptivity to unconventional ideas and behaviour. One may have a mind like a razor or a dirty mind; one may possess peace of mind and have presence of mind.

4.   Here then we can see the concept of mind at work. From this ordering of raw data one may draw important conclusions about the use of the expression 'the mind' in English. Of course, other

languages may not have a word that corresponds exactly with 'the mind': German and French have to make do with a pair of expressions, namely 'Geist' and 'Seele' and 'l'âme' and l'esprit' where English has the triplet 'mind', 'soul', and 'spirit'. So their concepts are somewhat different from ours. Few languages have as wide a range of mind-associated prepositional idioms, which may mean that English is fortunate in being able to draw distinctions absent in other languages. There is much that a philosopher can learn from the wealth of 'mind'-associated idioms.

First, each idiom is paraphrasable into a different equivalent expression in which the word 'mind' does not occur. What does this imply? It does not mean that all our talk of the mind is peculiar 'as if' talk of a 'pretend entity' or 'pretend agent'. Our use of 'the mind' is not at all like our use of 'Father Christmas' or even 'unicorn' and 'dragon'. This does not mean that our use of 'mind'-incorporating expressions is but a *façon de parler*. That would suggest that it is just a manner of speaking, akin to signing one's letters 'yours truly', 'yours faithfully', or 'yours sincerely', and that would imply that in fact people don't have minds. But, to be sure, decisive people have minds of their own, stupid people are mindless, and people who have lost their mind have lost their rational faculties. So what should we conclude? Surely this: that our idiomatic talk of human minds is *a form of representation* – a way of presenting human intellectual powers and their exercise in thought, volition, and action. We present possession of a wide range of intellectual powers and their exercise in the *form* of possession of an object, namely: the mind.

From this we can draw further conclusions. The mind is not an object, not a kind of thing or, more pretentiously, not an *entity* of any kind. The mind, we might say, is not a something, but it is not a nothing either. So taking the mind to be a kind of substance, as Descartes (1596–1650) did, is a mistake. The mind is neither a material substance nor an immaterial substance because it is not a substance at all. To say (correctly) that *human beings have minds* is a conceptual truth that characterizes human nature. It is, in effect, the expression of a rule for the use of 'mind' and 'human being' that signifies that it *makes sense* to ask with respect to any human being what sort of mind he has, whether he has anything on his mind, or whether he has made up his mind, and so forth. A further consequence that flows from the possibility of paraphrastic de-reification is that when we say that that NN has a dirty mind, that he has turned his mind to such-and-such, and that he has changed his mind, we are not talking of one thing that is dirty, has been turned, and has changed. We are talking of one human being who tends to think sordid thoughts, who has taken up a fresh subject for reflection and concentration and has reversed a prior decision. Another important consequence is the repudiation of Thomas Reid (1710–96), who argued that the mind is 'that in [man] which thinks, imagines, reasons, wills', and John Stuart Mill (1806–73) who held the mind to be 'a mysterious something that thinks and feels'. For the mind is not a something, and we don't, by and large, speak of the mind as agential. It is not my mind that thinks, imagines, reasons or wills – it is I, this living human being. Curiously, we do speak of the mind as a patient in as much as my mind may go blank, be in a turmoil, wander – these not being acts or activities of an agent. But, to be sure, my mind does not make up its mind or change its mind since it has no mind.

5.   A further consequence of our investigation thus far is that the contemporary tendency to identify the mind with the brain is mistaken. For the mind is not a kind of thing, but the brain certainly is. It is a bodily organ, about seven inches high and three pounds in weight consisting of billions of neurons and synapses. But a material object cannot be identical with something that is neither material nor an object.

In response to this objection, philosophers may shift ground and advance the idea that psychological attributes are in fact identical with brain states, processes, or events. Knowing and believing, understanding, being frightened and being cheerful, desiring and intending are all, according to some philosophers, states of mind. They are contingently identical with states of the brain.

This cannot be right. Cortical states are states of the brain, mental states are states of a human being and a human being is not a brain but has a brain. A brain may be in a sclerotic state, a human being cannot; a human being may be in an anxious state, but a brain can't be anxious about anything. Knowing, believing, and understanding are not mental states comparable to feeling frightened, being cheerful or anxious. The latter do not persist during periods of sleep or unconsciousness (which is why 'sleep knits up the ravell'd sleeve of care'). But one does not cease to know, believe, or understand things when one falls asleep (and one does not have to learn them afresh when one awakes). There is no such thing as being in a state of knowing (as one may be in a state of anxiety), let alone such a thing as being in a believing state or in a mental state of understanding (for further elaboration, see Essays 6 and 7). Something that is not a state cannot be identical with a state.

6. Since Descartes philosophers have struggled with the question 'What is the mind?' Some, like Descartes, have held that the mind ('anima', 'l'âme', 'l'esprit') is a substance – a persistent immaterial entity annexed to the body, but which can survive the demise of the body. Others like Locke (1632–1704) have held that the mind is a collection of perceptions and ideas unified by consciousness, connected to a human body. Yet others, like Berkeley (1685–1753), agreed with Descartes that the mind is a spiritual substance but denied that it is annexed to a material body, since he denied that there are any bodies at all. Hume agreed that there are no material substances, but argued that there are no spiritual substances either: the mind is merely a bundle of perceptions held together by causation and memory – but left it opaque how perceptions can be tied in bundles, and how causation and memory can function as binding string. To such incoherences have great thinkers been driven.

When philosophers have been struggling with a question over many centuries, giving increasingly bizarre conclusions, it seems appropriate not to add yet another theory but to challenge the question. Perhaps the question 'What is the mind?' is just a bad question. Why so? In part, because *What is* questions invite *It is an* answers and as our linguistic investigations suggest, the mind is not *an anything*. We should reject the question and replace it by another one: *What has to be true of a creature for us to say of it that it has a mind?* This question is more manageable.

To have a mind a creature has to be a sentient animal that has and exercises a wide range of powers to do or refrain from doing something, and the ability to acquire further powers through experience and learning. More specifically, it must acquire and then possess and exercise powers of rationality and reasonableness. A creature with a mind has the ability to reason, correctly or incorrectly, from premises to conclusions and to be sensitive (reactive) to reasons, which may be good, poor, or perverse, for thinking, feeling, and acting. Such abilities presuppose possession of a language.

Our linguistic analysis showed that talk of the mind focuses on mnemonic powers that stretch far wider than merely remembering *how* to do things, *where* certain things are, *when* certain events regularly occur, and so forth. It includes memory *that* certain things are so, that certain things happened or *are going to happen* (e.g. the time of the opera next week), personal memory (possession of a history and 'autobiography'), memory of general truths (all // some // many // much // most // X-s are Y-s), and timeless truths (of logic or mathematics). It is patent that this requires mastery of a language incorporating logical connectives ('not', 'and', 'or', 'if … then …') and quantifiers ('all', 'some', 'many', 'a few'), devices for temporal indexing and reference (now/then; earlier/later; yesterday/today/tomorrow; last year/next year), names of kinds of things, place-referring expressions, and pronouns. This will be further discussed in Essay 8.

Possession of a mind was linked with the ability to think, correctly or incorrectly, and to form opinions, reasonable or unreasonable. A creature with a mind has the ability to reason, correctly or incorrectly, from premises to conclusion, from evidence to what it allegedly supports, to acquire information or opinion from reasoning and to retain it for future use. This too is a prerogative of language-using creatures. Possession of a mind is equally closely connected to intention-formation on the basis of thought and opinion. To have a mind implies possession of the powers of practical reasoning: to form intentions on the basis of what one knows and remembers and of opinions and convictions, which may be enlightened or prejudiced and bigoted. Creatures with a mind not only pursue purposes and have immediate goals, but are able to form intentions, both good and evil, long in advance of action, to modify them on the basis of new information or changing plans.

To have a mind is to possess and use powers of intellect manifest in thought, feeling and action. These are powers not of minds, but of creatures with a mind. They are not powers of brains, since brains have no intellect and there is no such thing as a brain acting for a good or poor reason, or harbouring and defending an opinion, let alone making inferences and weighing evidence. *Of course*, creatures with minds also have brains without which they would not have the constitutive features of having a mind. A brain is indeed necessary for any creature to have a mind, but it does not follow that the mind *is* the brain.

7.   We have not examined the variety of theories of mind produced by philosophers throughout the ages. Plato's Socrates (470–399 BC) is a primary font of dualism of mind and body. According to his Orphic views, a person's soul pre-existed its bodily incarnation and survives the death of the body – a doctrine known as metempsychosis. A different kind of dualism was advanced by Christianity and powerfully articulated by Augustine (354–430 AD). In the hands of Descartes, the primary source of substance dualism, the boundary of the mind was redrawn and the nature of the mental was transformed. Biology was

reduced to physics, which concerned itself with the study of the laws of matter in motion. The limits of physics lay at the portals of the mind. The mind was conceived to be a persistent immaterial object defined by the unique attribute of thought, in an extended sense of the term that incorporates all conscious experience. It is distinct from the body, although intimately united with it in human life. The mind is in two-way interaction with the body. It was redefined not as the rational part of human beings, but as consciousness of all thought and experience. It was held to be identical with the self or person, and to be transparent to its subject – there was nothing in the mind of which the self was unaware, and everything one was conscious of was as one was conscious of it as being. Moreover, the thoughts or experiences of which the mind consists were indubitable. The subject alone has direct knowledge of his own thoughts or experiences, which are uniquely owned by him. This conception is still with us in the contemporary idea that to have a mind is to have experience, and that to have experience is for there to be something that it is like for the subject to enjoy or undergo it. These ideas will be investigated in Essay 4.

From the point of view of the current investigation, the most important of the ancient philosophers who investigated the nature of man is Aristotle. He rejected Plato's dualism and advanced a form of non-reductive monism. While Plato (428/7–348/7 BC), like his teacher Socrates, conceived of the mind or soul as being embodied but surviving the death of the body, Aristotle (384–322 BC), his pupil, conceived of *psuchē* as a biological concept (it is commonly mistranslated as 'soul' which is a moral or theological concept). The *psuchē* is constituted by the powers of living things. All living things have a vegetative *psuchē*, namely the powers of metabolism, growth, and reproduction. Animals have a sensitive *psuchē*, since over and above their vegetative powers they have powers of sensation, perception and locomotion, desire, and aversion, as well as susceptibilities to pain, pleasure, and emotion. The rational *psuchē* that is distinctive of man consists, in addition to the vegetative and sensitive powers, in the further abilities to reason and to act for reasons. To have the rational *psuchē* is to have an intellect and will (ratiocinated desire). It is to be able to reason, to apprehend and act for reasons, to deliberate and decide on the basis of reasons for what to think, feel, and do. The Aristotelian *psuchē* is not a substance. It is neither identical with the animal body nor distinct from it. The *psuchē* stands to the body as the form of a statue to the statue of which it is the form. It makes no sense to ask whether they are one or two. Accordingly, the *psuchē* is not a part of a human being nor is it embodied in the human being or human body. Rather, the human body is *empsuchos*: informed by the *psuchē*. It is not causally related to the living animal, since powers are not causes of their exercise. The human *psuchē* is not essentially private, since I may express my thoughts and then you will know what I think, and I may share my thoughts with you. It is not transparent to its subject, since I may not realize that I know or understand something and may think I know or understand something but be mistaken. Its deliverances are not indubitable, since I may doubt whether I remember something and be unsure whether I love someone. It is not an agent, for the *psuchē* does not do anything, rather we do things with our *psuchē*, not as we do things with our hands but as we do things *with our talents*. Nor is the *psuchē* the subject of psychological attributes, since capacities, abilities and liabilities do not think, perceive, feel or form intentions.

Why is this so important? Because it shows that there is another way of conceptualizing mind-associated phenomena that dispenses with the reification characteristic of early modern European culture and later. In this Aristotelian form of representation, the functions the concept of mind fulfils in our languages are taken over by biological powers, in particular by the sensitive and rational powers (the latter, when considered independently of the vegetative and sensitive powers, being *nous*). This could not be more different from the dualist form of representation and its various degenerate offspring. What is most striking, however, is that our ordinary English idiom of the mind is far closer to the Aristotelian model of the *psuchē* than to the Cartesian and empiricist conceptions of the mind and to contemporary psychological and neuroscientific models of the mind/brain.

8.   In the opening remarks, it was noted that I can be said to have a soul, a self, and mind and a body. We have explained how to construe possession of a mind. We must now turn to demythologization and say something about the notions of the self and the I or ego.

Let us turn first to the notion of a self. The expression is indeed an ancient one. Its earliest use was simply to emphasize a nominal, as in *'se selfa man'* which meant 'the *very* man who' or 'the *same* man who'. This is the ancestor of the emphatic pronoun 'itself' (as in 'the thing itself'), the reflexive pronoun 'my (your, him, her, it) self', and it survives in the modern adjectival use 'the selfsame ...'. It was altogether natural that the reflexive pronoun should evolve into an independent nominal and also become used to signify aspects of a person, hence someone's nature, character, physical constitution or appearance at different times. Hence: 'one's former (or 'later') self', 'being or looking one's old self again' (after illness). Side by side with this diachronic use emerged a use to signify synchronic aspects of a person, as in 'his better self', 'her true self', 'one's natural self'. But it was an egregious error of seventeenth-century philosophers to start using this harmless four-letter word to signify some *thing* within a human being which a person essentially is, namely 'a self'. For it is a logical truth that nothing can be identical with a part of itself or an aspect of itself. I should indeed be true to mine own self, to the better and most fundamental aspects of myself, but I am not a self and I don't *have* a *thing* within me that is called 'a self'.

Similar arguments apply to talk of 'the "I"'. The confusion that this grammatical aberration generates is only masked, but not reduced by Latinization into 'the Ego'. 'I' is a first-person pronoun. It is not a noun and cannot licitly take either a definite or indefinite article. There is no such thing as 'an I', any more than there is such a thing as 'a he', 'a she', or 'an it'. It was a misfortune, and an unnecessary one to boot, that Freud used these malformed expressions ('das Ich' and 'das es' (unfortunately translated as 'the Ego' and 'the Id')) to speak of aspects of the human personality. 'I' is a pronoun. Unlike the pronouns 'he', 'she', and 'it', *it is not a referring expression*. In this respect, it is more akin to 'now' and 'here', rather than to 'then' and 'there'. Construed as a referring expression, it seems to be a miraculous one, for it seems immune to referential failure and to misidentification. But this is an illusion. It is not like an arrow that always hits its target, but like an arrow stuck in the wall around which one can always draw a circle. It is akin to the point of origin of our system of pointing (our deictic system) and not akin to points on the graph that are indicated by the other personal pronouns. *Its primary role is to index an utterance.* One commonly uses it to speak about oneself, but one does not thereby identify oneself – rather it enables one's audience to identify of whom one is speaking. Unlike the other singular personal pronouns, it has no anaphoric use to refer to someone already mentioned. It is not a referring expression, and it certainly does not refer to something called 'a self'. That it can be used in silent soliloquy does not show that it refers to a self, but only that one is thinking about oneself. Of course, it is used by human beings who are subjects of experience. It has a use in ascribing experiences to oneself, but not to ascribe experiences to one's self. It is used in speaking *of* oneself, but not in speaking of one's self.

2

The Nature of Our Body
and the Mind/Body Relation

1. In the previous essay the Aristotelian notion of the *psuchē* –
misleadingly translated as 'soul' – was introduced. It is a biological
concept, not a theological or moral concept. It signifies the distinctive
powers of macro-biological living things. It differentiates the characteristic powers of the plant kingdom, of the kingdom of living animals, and of mankind. Hence Aristotle writes of the vegetative *psuchē*
of plants, the sensitive (animate) *psuchē* of non-human animals, and
the rational *psuchē* that is unique to human beings. Plants have *only*
a vegetative *psuchē*. Their distinctive powers are to metabolize, to
grow, to produce seed and multiply. Animals likewise have a vegetative *psuchē*, but in addition to their powers of metabolizing, growth,
and reproduction, they have a sensitive *psuchē*, that is to say: senses
by means of which they can apprehend their environment and feel
sensations in their body, they have desires, they are self-moving and
pursue goals. Human beings alone also possess a rational *psuchē*, that
is: the power to reason from premises to a conclusion and sensitivity
to reasons for thinking, feeling, and acting. Human beings alone have
the species-characteristic of possession of an intellect (to which
Aristotle refers as *nous*). Note that the *psuchē* is not an agent that
acts, any more than a human being's ability to read is an agent. But a
reader exercises his ability to read whenever he reads a text. So too, a
living being uses its *psuchē* whenever it exercises its characteristic

*Solving, Resolving, and Dissolving Philosophical Problems: Essays in Connective,
Contrastive and Contextual Analysis*, First Edition. P. M. S. Hacker.
© 2025 John Wiley & Sons Ltd. Published 2025 by John Wiley & Sons Ltd.

powers and abilities. One uses one's *psuchē* not in the sense in which one uses one's legs to walk, but in the sense in which one uses one's talents to do skilful things.

One important aspect of the Aristotelian form of representation of human powers is that the relation between the *psuchē* and the human body is not problematized. How my *psuchē* is related to my body is no more puzzling than the question of how my height or weight are related to my body. They are, as Aristotle might put it, *of* the body, not relations *to* the body. The *psuchē*, being an array of distinctive animate powers, is not a relatum in a binary relation. My ability to metabolize, to perceive and to move, to think and to act for reasons, do not stand in a *relation* to me: they are attributes *of* mine. This puts Aristotle in firm opposition to the dualist views of his teacher Plato, who conceived of the mind or soul as an enduring being that is embodied in a living human but pre-existed its embodiment and survives after death. It also put Aristotle in opposition to the subsequent Christian view of a human being as a composite of body and soul, whose soul survives death. For Christian Platonists, such as St Augustine, the soul stands in a *relation* to the body, in as much as it is *embodied*. By contrast, according to Aristotle, the body is, as it were, 'ensouled' or *empsuchos*, that is, endowed with distinctive powers, abilities, and capacities. How the mind or soul and the body are related is pivotal for the European Christian tradition and has been debated for the best part of two millennia. Note also that Aristotle's conception of human nature is articulated in terms of human powers – potentialities, not actualities. Moreover, the identity of potentialities is determined by their actualization – by what they are potentialities to become, to be, and to do.

2.   In the history of the modern debate, it is by and large assumed that the problematic relatum in the mind/body relation is the mind, the concept of the human body being thought to be relatively unproblematic. According to Cartesian dualist theories, my mind is a thinking substance in a two-way causal relation to my body. How an immaterial substance, the self or ego could cause changes to my material body by exercise of the will remained opaque, and how the impact of light, sound, and touch upon the body could produce impressions, ideas and experiences in the mind was problematic. According to Descartes, the point of interaction lies in the brain, in the pineal gland. But how an immaterial mind could interact causally with a material object like the pineal gland and move the animal spirits within it

remained an unsolved and insoluble mystery, as Descartes himself confessed in his correspondence with Princess Elizabeth of Bohemia (1618–80).

One seventeenth-century response (from so-called Occasionalists such as Malebranche (1638–1715)) was to argue that there is no interaction at all – rather a change in the one provides an occasion for God to cause a change in the other. A related doctrine advanced by Leibniz (1646–1716) argued that the mind and the body are like two clocks showing the same time. They were so created that any change in one is from birth programmed to coincide with a change in the other. In the nineteenth century, epiphenomenalists such as Thomas Huxley (1825–95) held it to be intelligible that a change in the body should cause a change in the mind, but altogether unintelligible that a mental event should have any causal power over matter – that would be a case of telekinesis. All changes to bodies are caused by physical substances or events. So attributes of the mind are epiphenomenal – mere froth on the surface of matter in motion. These are surely desperate expedients.

An alternative line was to reject the idea that human beings are two substances. Locke rejected mental substances in favour of the idea that we are a bundle of ideas annexed to a material object, namely the body. But how ideas can be bundled was left opaque, as was the concept of *being annexed* to matter. (How does one annex an idea or thought to a human being?) Berkeley took the opposite route, arguing that there are no material things and that matter is an illusion. So we are mental or spiritual substances *owning* ideas of thought, feeling and perception. Hume (1711–76), however, thought that the idea of a purely spiritual substance was incoherent, lacking any principle of individuation and identification. So we are no more than a bundle of ideas related to each other by ties of causality and memory. This was, to be sure, a *reductio ad absurdum* of solutions to the question of the mind/body relation and a sign that something was deeply wrong and that a new start was needed. This Kant (1724–1804) essayed. His critique of the various doctrines of the soul or mind in the 'Paralogisms of Pure Reason' (*Critique of Pure Reason* A 341–405/B 399–432) was brilliant, but his constructive attempt to replace them with an acceptable alternative in the 'Transcendental Deduction' was a failure.

3.   We do indeed need to start afresh. Our discussion of the mind in Essay1 brought a broom and shovel to the Augean Stables of

mistaken philosophical theories of the mind. Now we need to do the same with respect to the concept of the body a human being has. Once the concept of the human body has been clarified, we may confront the puzzle of the relation between mind and body with confidence.

A good point of departure is Descartes's characterization of his body:

> The first thought to come to mind was that I had a face, hands, arms, and the whole mechanical structure of limbs, which can be seen in a corpse, and which I called the body … by a body I understand whatever has determinable shape and definable location and can occupy space in such a way as to exclude any other body; it can be perceived by touch, sight, hearing, taste or smell, and can be moved in various ways, not by itself but by whatever it comes into contact with it. For, according to my judgement, the power of self-movement, like the power of sensation or thought, was quite foreign to the nature of a body. (*Meditations* 2 (AT VII, 261))

Descartes, a physicist and mathematician, held biology to be reducible to physics and argued that the only explanatory principles for matter in motion were mechanical. Accordingly, mere brutes, as he put it, have no mind, since they do not speak or think and are not conscious subjects of experience. No special biological principles need be invoked for scientific investigations into living animals. By contrast, Aristotle, being a biologist, had held that all the sciences of life: botany, zoology, and the sciences of man, have their own distinctive constitutive vocabularies and explanatory principles.

Descartes was right that the whole mechanical (anatomical) structure of limbs can be seen in a corpse. But the living human body is not an animated corpse. One studies anatomy in the autopsy theatre, but not physiology, not the frenetic activity of the billions of living cells that maintain the dynamic equilibrium between the organism and its environment, nor the ceaseless action of the internal organs that enable the living animal to function and engage in its characteristic forms of behaviour. Descartes sought to eliminate teleology from nature. Hence he did not conceive of animal motion as goal-directed and purpose-guided, nor of animals as having a good any more than machines have a welfare. Only human beings have the power of self-movement, generated by the volitional powers of the mind. Human action is indeed a form of telekinesis, since it is the causation of the movements of the body by the mind.

4.   In many respects we are not, in our natural forms of thought and talk, Cartesians. When *we* contrast mind and matter, when we admire the *triumph of mind over matter*, we are not speaking of the power of the mind to move the body and limbs by acts of will. Rather, we are concerned with heroic resistance to exhaustion and pain – with the triumph of the will over *physical suffering*. Pain is felt in the body, not in the brain, let alone in the mind. It is my back that aches, my feet that are sore, my shoulder hurts and my arm is injured. Our body, contrary to the mechanist Cartesian conception, is sensitive. But I am not an animated body; my mind does not dwell in my body; and it does not own my body either. Nor do I.

It is time we turned to elucidating our concept of the human body.

5.   The English word 'body' has many different meanings that in philosophical investigation are commonly confused. 'Body' may mean

  (i)   a spatio-temporal continuant consisting of matter: as in 'A body of cold air' or 'A body of land'
  (ii)   a movable spatio-temporal continuant consisting of matter with determinate boundaries, that is, a material object;
  (iii) a living organism: in this sense *all* organisms *are* living bodies;
  (iv)   what living organisms, especially but not only human beings, are said to *have*: as in 'She has a beautiful body';
  (v)   the corpse or dead body an organism leaves behind on death. (It is noteworthy that many languages do not use the same word for the living organism as for the corpse.)
  (vi)   a human person: as in 'She's a nice old body', now obsolete save in Scottish English but with a distinctive residue in 'somebody' and 'nobody'.

We handle this proliferation of meanings, as well as many others, such as 'the body of a document (as opposed to the appendices)', 'the body of a church' (as opposed to the ambulatory), or 'the body of a car' (as opposed to the wheels), that are philosophically irrelevant, perfectly satisfactorily, but they can lead to puzzlement.

Conceptual puzzles flourish alongside the paths of good sense. In a quasi-technical (Newtonian) sense, human beings *are* bodies (see ii); they are also living, sentient, self-moving organisms (see iii) and as such *are* bodies. They also *have bodies* (see iv). But how can what *is* a body also *have* a body? How is *the body I am* related to *the body I have*? When human beings die, they leave a dead body (see v) behind. So how is the body I am related to the body I shall leave behind – to my corpse? Is it the same body or a different one? And since I patently have a mind, how is the body I have related to my mind? We must find conceptual order in this lexical confusion if we are to clarify the mind/body relation.

Human beings *are* bodies, as are plants and animals. They all differ from inanimate (mere) material bodies in virtue of being alive. This marks a qualitative difference, as Aristotle emphasized and Descartes denied. It goes with a manifestly enriched vocabulary, not because our language-using ancestors were so sapient, but because our instinctive reactions to what is alive and what is dead or inanimate are so different. The animate body a human being is, is the human organism that he is. The human organism has parts: head, torso and limbs, which are parts of the human being. In a different principle of division, a human being has a brain, a heart, liver, pancreas, as well as nerves, arteries, and veins, that are its internal constitutive parts. Some of these are organs, others are not.

The vocabulary of death is equally distinctive, especially with regard to human beings. We speak of someone's body being cremated or of a battlefield as being strewn with the bodies of the dead. It is moot what kinds of creature can be said to leave a body (i.e. a corpse) behind. Plants and trees do not *have* bodies (although they *are* bodies). They do not leave bodies behind when they die. A copse of dead trees is not a copse of corpses of trees. What of animals? Dead fish at the fishmongers are not corpses of fish. A dead cow is not a corpse but a carcass of a cow. So, what has to be true of an animal for it to be said to leave a corpse behind when it dies? The boundaries of the expression are indeterminate, but if we have to draw a line, it surely has to be that an animal leaves a corpse behind on death if and only if it is an animal that can be said to have a mind.

We are inclined to assent to such remarks as 'When I die, I shall no longer exist, but my body will persist for a while' or 'When I die, my body will cease to be me, and I will no longer exist'. Extra-philosophically, these are harmless, but in trying to elucidate the nature of the body, they are misleading. For, as we shall see in a moment, the body I have is not me, and the body I leave behind, my corpse, is not the (living) body I was. ('King Henry is lying in state' means 'King Henry's body/corpse is lying in state', since King Henry no longer exists and when we say solemnly 'King Henry is making his last journey', referring to the cortege to interment, we mean that his corpse is being taken for burial, since the king's last journey occurred *before* he died.) A living body is not the same *anything* as a corpse (the body that is left behind): no common concrete substance noun (a count noun that names a kind of thing associated with a criterion of identity, like 'cat' or 'cabbage') subsumes both. Of course, the living organism N is the same *spatio-temporal continuant* as the corpse N will leave behind when he dies, but 'spatio-temporal continuant' is not a concrete substance noun. A corpse is a dead human being and a dead human being is no more a human being than a fake five-pound note is a five-pound note. It is the human being that dies, not his body. When a human being is killed fighting valiantly, it is he, not his body – the body he has, that is killed. Nor can one say, as one stands by his coffin 'That is the body he had', since he never had a corpse.

So, what can be attributed to the body a human being has? What can someone's body be?

First, properties pertaining to the physique and fitness of a person: as in 'a supple / athletic / powerful / muscular / flabby / body'.

Second, properties pertaining to health: as when we say that one should have a healthy mind in a healthy body. Such attributions are sometimes used to draw a contrast with a person's mind, as in 'His body is frail, but his mind is as sharp as ever' or 'Her body is recovering, but her mind is sorely damaged'.

Third, surface properties: one's body may be sunburnt all over or nicely tanned; it may be painted blue all over, or gleam with oil; it may be covered with dust and sweat, mud or blood. It may be badly lacerated or covered with insect bites.

Fourth, aesthetic appearances: as when someone's body is beautiful / attractive / alluring / sexy / sensual / dumpy / ugly / fat / gangly.

Fifth, as already noted, my body is sensitive: *verbs* of sensation, but not nouns, may licitly be predicated of the body one has and of its parts. My body may ache all over, it may itch all over, my hand may hurt, my feet may be sore. However, my hand does not have a pain, my head does not have an ache, and whereas I may have a stomach-ache, my stomach does not.

6.   Is all this mere linguistic idiom? It is linguistic idiom all right, but there is no 'mere' about it, for it is pregnant with conceptual implications. A Socratic midwife can bring them to light. But we should not be surprised at anomalies – natural language was not designed on a drawing board and the discernible patterns may be incomplete and irregular.

It is evident that whatever is true of the body a human being has is true of the body a human being is. Or, to put things less opaquely, everything attributable to my body is attributable to me. If my body is muscular, if I have a muscular body, then I am muscular. If my body is frail, then I am frail. Equally, if his body is covered with dust and sweat, then he is covered with dust and sweat. If her body is lithe and graceful, then she is lithe and graceful. If her body is beautiful, then she is beautiful (unless we are using 'body' to the exclusion of her face, for she may have a beautiful body but not a beautiful face). If my body aches all over, then I ache all over. If my head aches, then I have a headache, but my head does not have an ache. If I have hurt my hand, then I have hurt myself, but my hand has not hurt itself. My body may be racked with pain, but it is not my body that cries out, even if I cry out inadvertently.

What else *cannot* be said of the body a living human being has? A human being's body is not the subject of voluntary and intentional predicates. My body may tremble or be paralysed, but it does not move itself, it doesn't walk, jump, or run. Nor is it the subject of perceptual, cogitative, or affective predicates. It doesn't see or hear, know, believe, or think, feel cheerful or angry. It may drip with sweat, but it cannot weep. It may be unfit, but it cannot take exercise. Since people's bodies are logically excluded from being the subject of these predicates, we are inclined to think that something other than their body must be their subject, namely: their mind. But it is the *human being*, not the *mind*, that is the subject of experience and the agent of action. My body cannot chat to the neighbours, go shopping, cash cheques, get married or divorced, stand for parliament, or get elected. Nor, to be sure, can the mind. Evidently, one's mind and one's body do not between them collect all the attributes that can be ascribed to the human being one is. That is one reason why Peter Strawson's (1919–2006) account of persons in *Individuals* (1959) is mistaken. The correct contrast to somatic attributes (and the predicates that signify them) is not psychological or mental attributes (and predicates) – that merely recapitulates Cartesian substance dualism in the form of predicate dualism. The right contrast is with non-somatic attributes (and predicates), which include not just perceiving, feeling, believing, desiring, and intending, but also giving lectures, writing books, doing the shopping, and playing cricket (which are not something minds do).

7.   It is clear from our survey thus far that our talk of the body one has is not talk of a further item in addition to the body one is. It is

rather a way of speaking of the *corporeal* or *somatic* characteristics of a human being in contrast with non-somatic characteristics. That is why everything that is true of my body is true of me, but there are indefinitely many things true of me that are not true of the body I have. One might say that talk of 'my / his / her/ body' is the *form* in which we present the somatic characteristics of human beings.

Unclarity about the fact that our talk of the body we have is a form of representation of our corporeal characteristics may itself produce puzzlement. One may wonder whether the body I am and the body I have occupy the same space. Indeed, they may seem to compete for the same parts, for surely I have two legs and two arms and my body has two legs and two arms? This is confused. *Having* two limbs can be said to be a somatic characteristic, but it generates confusion to speak of one's limbs as parts of the body one has, since one's limbs are not somatic characteristics. No one speaks of the legs of my body, but only of my legs. But one can intelligibly speak thus of the corpse (the dead body) one leaves behind – it would be a way of remarking that the corpse (the dead body) has not been mutilated.

A different account has been suggested. The relation between a human being and his body, it was averred by David Wiggins (b. 1933), is the same as that between a statue and the piece of marble that constitutes it. But this is mistaken. A marble statue is not constituted by *a piece of marble* nor is it *a piece* of marble, any more than a cake is constituted by a piece of cake or is a piece of cake. Michelangelo's *David* was *made out* of a large piece of marble, but it does not consist of a *piece of marble* – rather, it consists of *marble* (more than a ton of it). Nor is the *David* constituted by a piece of marble, any more than Rodin's *Balzac* is constituted by a chunk of bronze. A human being does not consist of a piece of flesh and blood, rather, he is made of flesh and blood, although not made out of flesh and blood. He is not *constituted* by his body.

Another conception, advanced by Peter Strawson, is vehicular. He argued that my body is the vehicle of my agency in the world. It is the body the arms of which rise when I raise my arms, the legs of which move when I walk, and with the eyes of which I see when I open my eyes. But this too is mistaken. First, my relation to my body is not that of a driver to his car. My car is indeed the car the wheels of which turn left or right when I turn the steering wheel. When the driver turns the steering wheel, he makes it go round; but when he raises his arm he does not make it rise or cause it to rise. When he turns the steering wheel with his hands, he brings it about that the car changes course; but when he raises his arm he does not *bring it about* that his arm rises or that he touches the ceiling. Second, I see with my eyes and walk with my legs, but I do not see with my body's eyes or walk with my body's legs – these are forms of words that lack sense. My legs may be bruised, but no one would say that my body's legs are bruised unless they are speaking of my corpse.

A different but related account of the relation between a human being and his body capitalizes upon the dependence of perceptual experience upon facts about the body. Whether one sees anything at all depends upon whether one's eyes are open. What is visible to one is said to depend on where one's body is located, on the direction in which one's head is turned and how one's eyes are oriented. Such facts of experience-dependence allegedly explain why the possession of a particular body should be ascribed to the same thing, a human person, as states of consciousness. They are said to explain, Peter Strawson averred,

> Why a subject of experience should have a very special regard for just one body, why he should think of it as unique and perhaps most impor-tant than any other … they might even be said to explain why, granted that I am going to speak of one body as *mine*, I should speak of *this* body as mine. (*Individuals*, p. 93)

But this is mistaken. True, visual experiences depend on where one is, the state of one's eyes, and the direction in which one is looking. But this does not explain why a particular body should be spoken of 'as standing in some special relation' – called 'being possessed by' – to one. For, as we have seen, the body a human being *has* is not a body he possesses, any more than the wife, birthday, or mind he has are his possessions. Of course, one can sell one's body, but that is to sell sex-ual services and selling one's body does not leave one bodiless. One may sell a kidney and have it removed, leaving one short of a kidney. One may lose an arm or a leg, but to lose a limb is not to misplace it but to have it amputated or lost in an explosion. But one cannot lose one's body. To be sure, someone may find my body, but then he needn't return it to me. One might insist, as Strawson does, that the relation between a human being and his body is indeed one of owner-ship but that it is *inalienable* ownership. But that would be mistaken: only what *can be* alienated can be inalienable – to be inalienable it must *make sense* for it to be alienated. But it makes no sense to alienate either the body one is or the body one has, for there is no such thing as alienating the living organism one is or one's somatic characteristics. The idea that one owns one's body is therefore incoherent.

So much for other attempts to explain the idea of having a body. They are all flawed. Our analysis of English idiom suggested that our talk of a human being's body is a way of presenting the corporeal characteristics of human beings. One might wonder why this peculiar form of representation has been so successful. The answer is not difficult to come by. We have a wide variety of attitudes to our corporeal features. We may be proud of our body, if it is fit and beautiful, or we may be ashamed of it if it is fat, flabby, and ugly. We admire the bodies of the young and are horrified by the mutilated bodies of the injured. We may feel comfortable with our body or ill at ease with it. Being self-conscious creatures, much preoccupied with sexual attraction and given to degrees of hypochondria, it is hardly surprising that we should think a great deal about our physique, aesthetic appearance, attractiveness, and physical condition. It is not at all surprising that the idiom of the body we have, that is, of our somatic characteristics, should appeal to us.

8.   What then is the relationship between the mind and the body? The question is ancient. It has plagued Christian culture since its inception. The problem of the mind/body relation, one might say, is insoluble. It cannot be solved, but it can be *dissolved*. Our investigation has shown that the mind is not an item that could literally stand in a relation to other kinds of thing – to have a mind is to have an array of powers of intellect and will. It is the living human organism – the body one *is* – that has and exercises these powers. But the body a human being *has* – the somatic characteristics he has – is not the kind of thing that *could* stand in a relation to one's intellectual powers. My body does not have a mind – what, one might wonder, would corporeal characteristics do with a mind. Similarly, my mind does not have a body – what could powers of intellect and will do with corporeal characteristics? As we have shown, the mind cannot own its corporeal characteristics, nor can it reside in them. It is the living human being that has a mind and a body.

The so-called mind/body relation disappears on analysis. The mind/body problem simply evaporates, like a mist across a landscape that lifts once illuminated by the sun.

3

What Is Consciousness?

"Consciousness is a fascinating but elusive phenomenon; it is impossible to specify what it is, what it does, or why it evolved."

Stuart Sutherland

1. 'What is consciousness?' is a singularly intractable question. It is difficult to know how to engage with it. Where should one begin? Confronted by this bland interrogative, one is inclined to batter against it, like a butterfly against a windowpane. Leading neuroscientists declare that the analysis of consciousness is perhaps the greatest unsolved problem in all of biology. Eminent cognitive scientists aver that no one knows what consciousness is or whether it serves any purpose or that it is impossible to specify what it is, what it does or why it evolved. Famous psychologists are equally baffled: despite much progress, it is held, consciousness remains as elusive as ever; it is and always has been a great mystery. One eminent philosopher has gone so far as to say that our ignorance about consciousness may be the largest outstanding obstacle to a scientific understanding of the universe, another has asserted that it is the most mysterious feature of our minds, and a third has despaired, declaring that there is reason to suppose that the problem of consciousness is a problem which is beyond our cognitive capacity to resolve.

Solving, Resolving, and Dissolving Philosophical Problems: Essays in Connective, Contrastive and Contextual Analysis, First Edition. P. M. S. Hacker.
© 2025 John Wiley & Sons Ltd. Published 2025 by John Wiley & Sons Ltd.

Something must be going wrong. For to be sure, we can see perfectly well that other people in the room are wide awake and fully conscious, even though someone over there has fallen asleep and another, imbibing to excess, is becoming comatose. So too we can see, in the Accident & Emergency Department at the hospital, that some patients have lost consciousness and are unconscious. There is nothing unfamiliar about the phenomena. We can equally see someone in a rainstorm becoming, and then being, conscious that he is getting soaked through, and similarly, we may note from their behaviour and demeanour that someone receiving formal recognition from the monarch for achievement is conscious of the honour being done them. Wherefor the puzzle and whence the mystery?

We have already noted the analytic principle: when baffled by a conceptual question, replace abstract nouns by verbs or other parts of speech, for nominals are substantive hungry. 'What is consciousness?' invites an answer of the form 'Consciousness is ...' and no such answer is forthcoming. Better by far to begin with 'What is it to be conscious?' – a question that fruitfully drags in its wake the further question: 'Do you mean just "being conscious" as opposed to being unconscious, or do you mean "being conscious *of* something?"' And that immediately invites a distinction between *intransitive* and *transitive* consciousness.

2.   Intransitive consciousness is simply *being conscious* by contrast with *being conscious of* something or *being conscious that* something is so. It takes two primary forms: *being awake* as opposed to *being asleep* and *being conscious* as opposed to *being unconscious*. The waking/sleeping contrast belongs at home, the conscious/ unconscious contrast belongs in the hospital. Consciousness is something one may lose when one faints, is knocked out, or has a high fever. One recovers it when one regains consciousness. Responsiveness during sleep is far greater than during periods of unconsciousness (one may toss off the blanket, stop snoring when shaken, cover one's eyes to shade them – all without waking), and one is relatively readily woken from sleep. There are intermediate states between waking and sleeping (half-asleep, half-awake, just dozing off) and manifold levels between being conscious and being unconscious. The Glasgow Coma Scale used since the 1970s determines different levels of unconsciousness/consciousness according to the responsiveness of the subject. Three different categories of response are tested (eye, verbal, and motor), each one differentiated

into four to six levels. So, for example, eye responses range from not opening eyes at all, to opening eyes in response to a peripheral pain stimulus, to opening eyes in response to a voice, and opening eyes spontaneously. Verbal responses range from making no sounds, making incomprehensible sounds, emitting inappropriate words, manifesting verbal confusion and disorientation in response to questions, to oriented normal discourse. Comparable distinctions are drawn for control of movement.

Being conscious and being unconscious are states of a creature, although not mental states. Rather, *being conscious is a condition for being in any occurrent mental state*. One can normally see whether a person is conscious from their responsiveness to stimuli: for, to be sure, one can pretend not to be conscious or to be asleep, and one can pretend to be semi-conscious or intoxicated, but there is no such thing as pretending to be conscious or awake.

Despite what has sometimes been averred to the contrary, one's consciousness is not an object of experience for one. There are and could be no *grounds* on which one might say 'I am awake', 'I am conscious', or 'I have regained consciousness'. That one is conscious or awake is not something evident to one by 'introspection'. Nor is it information one might acquire by having 'access' to one's consciousness. I may become and then be conscious of your regaining consciousness or waking up, but I cannot become and then be conscious of my regaining consciousness, although I may become conscious of a nurse moving around the room as I regain consciousness. *There is no such thing* as being conscious of my consciousness – this is a meaningless concatenation of words. My own intransitive consciousness is not an object of possible experience for me, but *a precondition of my having any experiences at all*. Of course, as I regain consciousness in the hospital bed, I may say 'I am conscious' or 'I have regained consciousness', but *not on any grounds*. That I am conscious is not a piece of information I have acquired *on the basis of evidence or experience*, which I then convey to others in my exclamation. My utterance is not a report for others, but a signal: I could just as well have said, 'Hello'.

3.   Philosophers and psychologists, psychiatrists and cognitive neuroscientists also speak of *conscious states* or *states of consciousness*. This notion too belongs among the forms of intransitive consciousness. A conscious state or state of consciousness is not a state that is conscious any more than a happy outcome is an outcome that is

happy (but an outcome that makes someone happy) or a passionate belief is a belief that is passionate (but a belief that someone cleaves to passionately). Many speak, seemingly pleonastically, of conscious mental states. That one is in a so-called *conscious mental state* does not imply that one is conscious of the state one is in. One may be in a state of intense concentration in which all one's attention is being given to the task at hand. In such cases, one is not conscious of one's state of concentration, although one may later realize how intensely one was concentrating since one did not hear the doorbell ringing.

A *state of consciousness* is a mental state one is in *while one is conscious* (for example, a state of concentration, of joy or elation, excitement or trepidation). It does not persist through periods of sleep or loss of consciousness. For my pangs of anxiety do not persist during sleep, which mercifully 'knits up the ravell'd sleeve of care', even though one may sleep less soundly for having been acutely anxious when awake. States of consciousness thus contrast with *dispositional mental states*, such as persistent depression that may last for weeks, lasting jealousy or envy that do not lapse with sleep or loss of consciousness. Dispositional mental states in turn contrast with *dispositions of character or temperament*, such as cheerfulness or timidity.

These distinctions will prove invaluable. For it is common to characterize numerous psychological attributes as being mental states which are no such thing. It is widely asserted that belief is a mental state, but whereas one may be in a state of disbelief, one cannot be in a state of believing or a state of belief. I may visit someone and find them in a state of anxiety, but not in a state of believing that war is immanent. Similarly, one may be in a state of ignorance, but not in a state of knowing that the government has fallen. These striking conceptual features will be explored and explained in Essays 6 and 7.

It has also been suggested that a conscious belief is a belief one is currently thinking about or entertaining – otherwise our beliefs are unconscious. On this account, most of the beliefs we harbour are unconscious ones. This is mistaken. It is true that we distinguish between:

(i)   bearing in mind something one believes to be so
(ii)   something one believes crossing one's mind
(iii) thinking about one's belief that things are so
(iv)   thinking about one's believing things to be so

But these are cannot reasonably be characterized as 'conscious beliefs'. One may believe that Hannibal should have assailed Rome after his great victory at the battle of Cannae, but when I am not thinking on this, it does not lapse into being an unconscious belief any more than all the things I know and am not thinking about are unconscious knowledge. It is perfectly acceptable to speak of unconscious beliefs, as long as one does not think that a belief that is unconscious stands to a belief that is not unconscious as an occluded chair stands to a visible chair. An unconscious belief is not just like a conscious one only not conscious. Rather, an unconscious belief is a belief that colours one's emotional states or attitudes and informs one's actions, but which one is unwilling to acknowledge, either to oneself or to others, *as* something one believes.

4.   Transitive consciousness: the syntactical forms of transitive consciousness are *conscious that*, and *conscious of*. The moot question that we must resolve is the range of possible objects of transitive consciousness. Clearly, one may be conscious of perceptibilia – of the man standing by the door, of the sound of bells in the distance, of the smell of fried bacon wafting in from the kitchen. One may be perceptually conscious of people or objects, of features of people or objects, of states of affairs that obtain, processes that are going on, or events that occur. We may dub this *perceptual consciousness*. But we must not jump to conclusions – although we may be conscious of perceptibilia, not all instances of perceiving something imply perceptual consciousness. If I am intentionally attending to something I am looking at, I cannot be said to be either conscious of it or not conscious of it. For one cannot voluntarily or intentionally be perceptually conscious of anything. The 'cannot' here is logical – there is no such thing as being voluntarily or intentionally perceptually conscious of something. Hence too, no such thing as being involuntarily or unintentionally perceptually conscious of something. That is why it makes no sense to order someone to be conscious of something: 'Be conscious of the weather!' or 'Be conscious of the scent of the roses!' are not intelligible orders, whereas 'Pay attention to the approaching storm' is. This striking feature will be explained subsequently.

A different form of transitive consciousness consists of *consciousness of facts already known*. This form of consciousness may itself take three different forms. Known information may

  (i)   occupy one's mind
 (ii)   weigh with one in one's deliberations
(iii)   colour one's thoughts and manner of behaviour

One may be painfully conscious of having been snubbed and dwell on it, as one may be arrogantly conscious of one social superiority (like Mr Darcy in *Pride and Prejudice*) if it is currently and recurrently before one's mind, if it *occupies one's thoughts*, that is, if it something one is *persistently aware of*. Similarly, one may be in possession of information that is directly relevant to a matter under deliberation (ii), as when one chairs a committee and knows that such-and-such facts must be borne in mind in coming to a decision. So, in the course of the deliberations, one is *acutely conscious of those facts*. A third kind of case is when information one possesses gives one reason for modulating one's behaviour, mien, and tone of voice (iii), as when one is conscious that one's dear friend has just lost their spouse and one changes one's behaviour in response to the information of which one is conscious.

Yet another form of consciousness is consciousness of one's own actions, which may in turn take two different forms:

 (i)   qua actor or agent
(ii)   qua spectator

In the first kind of case, one can be said to *consciously and deliberately* crack a joke in the course of one's lecture or insult an adversary in one's speech in the House ('the Right Honourable Gentleman is intoxicated by the exuberance of his own verbosity'). Here the agent knows what he is doing and is attending to the doing of it. This use stands in diametric contrast to cases of perceptual consciousness. In the second kind of case, what one becomes conscious of is typically *not* something one is intentionally doing, as when a lecturer realizes with dismay that he is repeating last week's lecture or repeating a joke he has already told earlier in today's lecture. Here he becomes *embarrassingly conscious* of what he is *inadvertently* doing.

A further form that consciousness may take is *self-consciousness*. This is not, contrary to a long and misguided philosophical tradition, a matter of being able to say how things are subjectively with one. When little Tommy says, 'Mummy, I want a banana', he is not manifesting any burgeoning self-consciousness, but merely expressing his desire. Self-consciousness, properly speaking, may take various forms.

An artist may be self-conscious as opposed to spontaneous. In this sense, Leonardo was a highly self-conscious artist, who might spend a whole day scrutinizing his painting, before adding another brush stroke. By contrast, Jackson Pollock was a highly spontaneous and intuitive artist, whose drip-painting was a response to the moment. Similarly, Flaubert was a highly self-conscious, reflective author, by contrast with Balzac or Trollope.

In a quite different sense of 'self-consciousness', someone is said to be self-conscious when they are aware of being looked at by others and feel embarrassed or moderate their behaviour in response to the scrutiny of others, as when young women, aware of being the subject of attention by young men, may laugh a little stridently, sway their hips a little markedly, toss their hair a little provocatively.

There is a further sense of 'self-conscious', which is justifiably used when characterizing human nature. We are correctly said to be self-conscious creatures, unlike other animals, in as much as we possess *the capacity to reflect on our reasons and motives*, the power to think about our attitudes, our tendencies and pronenesses, to evaluate them and to change them in the light of reasons. This is a prerogative of language-using creatures.

Yet another form of transitive consciousness has been the salient pre-occupation of the philosophical tradition since Descartes and Locke, namely *consciousness of the operations of one's mind*. Contrary to the philosophical tradition, one is not, or not normally, conscious of seeing, hearing, smelling, or tasting anything, as opposed to being conscious of *what* one saw, heard, tasted, or smelled – if appropriate perceptibilia caught and held one's attention. Exceptionally, one might become and then be conscious of the fact that one can see or hear something when one's sense faculty is restored after loss. One is not conscious of thinking, believing, knowing, or remembering something whenever one thinks, believes, knows, or remembers. True enough, we *can say* that we are thinking, and we are able to say *what* we are thinking – but this ability does not rest on being conscious of anything. If one were to say, 'I think the battle of Zama was in 202 BC' (an expression of tentative judgement) or 'I think your roses are beautiful' (an expression of first-hand opinion based on observation, unlike 'I believe your roses are beautiful' that is based on hearsay) and were asked 'Were you conscious of thinking that?', one would be bewildered. Of course, one might say, 'Yes!', but only because if one said 'No!', it might seem that one was *not* conscious of thinking what one was thinking – that one was *ignorant* of so thinking. And *that* one would not wish to say. To be sure, what one would probably say is, 'What *do* you mean?'

There is such a thing as consciousness of the operations of our minds, but it is by and large restricted to *being conscious of one's feelings*. In this context, 'one's feelings' incorporate sensations, moods, attitudes, occurrent emotions, and intimations. One may be conscious or aware of the increasing pain in one's tooth, of the tickling sensation between one's shoulder blades, of the itch in one's neck. One may be conscious or aware of one's posture and the disposition of one's limbs. One may become conscious of one's feeling of weariness or of well-being, if and when such feelings impress themselves upon one – catch one's attention. One may also become conscious of one's increasing irritation or excitement, or of one's inclination to do something, as well as of one's misgivings about some matter or other.

So, we now have an overview of the different kinds of objects of transitive consciousness. This survey can teach us some important methodological lessons.

First, the data for conceptual analysis and elucidation are provided by meticulous scrutiny of linguistic usage. The large *Oxford English Dictionary* is an invaluable repository of information and of innumerable examples of usage stretching over many centuries.

Secondly, the linguistic data is mere raw material. It has to be *ordered* before it can be used to delineate the logical character of the concept or concepts under investigation – as we have ordered the linguistic data on consciousness to yield the varieties of transitive consciousness.

Thirdly, our ordering of the data makes it obvious that no analytic definition could serve any fruitful purpose in shedding light on the concept of consciousness. It is evident that the concept is far too multifaceted to be caught in so primitive a web as an analytic definition in terms of necessary and sufficient conditions of application. What we are faced with here is a concept that has a multiplicity of centres of variation, linked together by complex strands. This will become evident as we proceed to the next stage of our connective analysis.

5.   A distinct idea of transitive consciousness is to be obtained by distinguishing between being conscious of something or conscious that something is so and other psychological attributes with which it is liable to be confused. To become and then be conscious of something or other is not an act or activity. One *cannot* – there is no such thing as – *deliberately, voluntarily,* or *on purpose,* becoming or being conscious of something. This stands in contrast to paying attention to something, for one can deliberately attend to something and one can decide in advance to attend to something. Similarly, one *cannot decide* or *refuse* to be or become conscious of something. Unsurprisingly, one

cannot have a reason for becoming or being conscious of anything, whereas one may have good reasons for attending to something. Consequently, contrary to what has sometimes been suggested, to *think about* one's thoughts or 'mental operations' is not to be conscious of them (nor yet to be unconscious or non-conscious of them). Moreover, becoming or being conscious of something is not an activity either. One cannot be engaged in being conscious of something, nor can one be interrupted in the middle of being conscious of something as one can be interrupted in the middle of attending to something. Not being an act or activity and not being subject to the will, it should not be surprising that *there are no means or methods* of becoming and then being conscious of something. To be conscious of something is neither to possess nor to exercise a skill. For one cannot be trained to be conscious of things but only to take note of things, and one cannot take consciousness lessons to improve one's transitive consciousness, only be trained to have a more sensitive receptivity. Although philosophers of the early modern era presented consciousness as an inner sense, transitive consciousness is neither an inner nor an outer sense since it is not a sense-faculty at all. For not only is there no organ of consciousness comparable to sense organs that subserve sense-faculties, but there is no such thing as exercising one's consciousness in exploratory activities as one can exercise one sense-faculties in exploratory activities. To become conscious of something or that something is so is *an occurrence* at a time, but not something one *does* at a time. It is something that *happens* to one.

6.   A clear idea of consciousness can be attained by exploring the connective analysis of the concept – its place within the conceptual network. The concept of consciousness lies at the confluence of the concepts of knowledge, receptivity, realization, awareness, attention, taking cognizance of something, being affected by knowledge already possessed. Let us explore this thought.

That transitive consciousness is a cognitive concept is patent: if one is conscious of NN standing by the table, then NN is indeed standing by the table. If one is conscious that it is time to go, then it is indeed time to go. So, consciousness is a *factive verb*. If one is conscious of something, or conscious that something is so, then it follows that things are as one is conscious of them as being. If they are not, then one is not conscious of them being so, but it only seemed to one that they were.

Although 'to be conscious of' and 'to be conscious that' are cognitive verbs in this sense, they are very specialized kinds of cognitive verbs. They are *result verbs* not *achievement verbs*. Achievement verbs mark the successful upshot of trying, but one cannot try to become or be conscious of something or make an effort to be conscious that something is so. One cannot try because to become conscious of something is not a voluntary or intentional act or activity. That 'to be conscious of' is a cognitive result verb gives us a pivotal clue. Transitive consciousness is a form of *cognitive receptivity* – it is not knowledge achieved but knowledge thrust upon one.

'To be conscious of' and 'to be conscious that' belong to a small class of verbs of cognitive receptivity that are intimately interwoven. Other members of this class are 'to be aware that' and 'to be aware of', 'to notice', and 'to realize'. Put figuratively, to notice X is to be struck by it; to be aware of X is for it to sink in; to realize X is for it to dawn on one; and to be conscious of X is for it to be before one's mind. Each of these concepts subserves a special purpose.

One may notice something momentary, such as a sudden flash or noise, but one cannot become and then be conscious of something momentary. For since being conscious of something is preceded by becoming conscious of it, what one is conscious of must persist for at least a short time. (To notice must not be confused with taking note of something. I cannot order you to notice something, but I may order you to take note, pay attention and register, something. 'To notice' is a verb of cognitive receptivity, but 'to take note of' is not.)

'To be aware' is a first cousin of 'to be conscious of'. Everything that I am conscious of I am also aware of, but there is much that I am aware of that I am no longer conscious of. Moreover, there is much that I am aware of that I was never conscious of, if becoming conscious of it was not the cognitive route to my awareness of it. Let me explain. I may become and then be conscious of something if it catches and holds my attention, and I thereby receive knowledge of how things are. My attention will duly lapse, but the knowledge received will not, unless I forget what I came to know. I will remain aware that things were so or that such-and-such happened as long as I call it to mind with reasonable frequency, advert to it from time to time, bear it in mind when relevant. Of course, much of what I know was not knowledge achieved by my attention being caught and held by something, but by being taught and by learning (where my attention was voluntarily given). If items thus known are borne in mind and adverted to with moderate frequency, then I am aware of them, for example: that Aunt Jemima is in hospital, that I must go to visit her sometime next week, that the Second World War broke out in 1939, that Bologna University is the oldest university in Europe, that deadly nightshade is poisonous. I cannot be reminded of what I am currently conscious of, but you may need to remind me of something that I am aware of, since what I am conscious of is before my mind whereas what I am aware of is something I bear in mind.

Realizing is exclusively of facts, whereas consciousness is also of things, features of things, events, states of affairs, and so forth. That is no coincidence, since realizing results from 'putting things together'. What one realizes is the upshot of knowledge already possessed – of facts that are already at one's disposal. Sudden realization is the sudden dawning of an implication of what one already knows. Like the other verbs of cognitive receptivity, one cannot voluntarily or intentionally realize something. Hence too, one cannot intend to realize something or order someone to realize something. Realization is interwoven with perceptual consciousness, since one becomes and then is perceptually conscious of something that captures one's attention, but one must realize what it is. If one fails to realize that it is a man standing in the shadows of the bushes and thinks it is a cow, then one is not conscious of a man in the bushes or of a cow either.

The nexus of perceptual consciousness with attention caught and held determines its conceptual boundaries. One can attend to an object or to features of an object, to an event or a state of affairs. One cannot be conscious of many things at the same time precisely because one cannot attend to many things at the same time. This contrasts with awareness, for one may be aware of many things at the same time, since one can bear many things in mind simultaneously. One cannot remain conscious of what no longer holds one's attention, although one may remain aware of it. It is important to note that one cannot become or be conscious of what one is *deliberately* attending to, any more than one can involuntarily lie, discover something one already knows, or detect something one has already found out. Of course, it does not follow that one is not conscious of something one is deliberately attending to – rather, the question *cannot sensibly arise*. It is not surprising that perceptual consciousness is largely restricted to peripheral attention.

7.   The results of our investigation are dramatic. The early modern idea that consciousness is constitutive of the mental is completely mistaken. The objects of consciousness range far wider than current mental states. The thought that the deliverances of consciousness are infallible and indubitable is misconceived. That to be conscious of something implies that things are as one is conscious of them as being does not imply that consciousness is infallible. It means

only that if what one is holds is false, then one is not conscious of things being thus. Similarly, the supposition that the deliverances of consciousness cannot be mistaken is a grievous distortion of the humble fact that 'to be conscious of' is a factive verb. The restriction of the objects of consciousness to the current operations of the mind has no warrant at all. From the seventeenth century onwards, it was generally held that consciousness is a faculty for knowledge of one's subjective mental operations. But that is profoundly mistaken. Consciousness is not a faculty. Our ability to say that we are in pain, that we believe this-or-that, that we want such-and-such, does not depend on being consciousness of anything. The ultimate irony of the tale is that our declarations that we are in pain, that we think this or want that are not objects of knowledge in the sense in which our declarations that other people are in pain, think this or want that are. This will be explored in Essay 6.

4

Consciousness and Experience or 'What It Is Like to Be a Bat' Revisited

1. Philosophical problems are like eddies and whirlpools in the stream of our culture. They arise at a given time, with multiple sources – in our languages, in our purely intellectual advances (geometry, mathematics, formal logic), in theology (Catholicism, Lutheran Protestantism, Calvinism), in our scientific discoveries and innovations (Newtonian dynamics, relativity theory, quantum mechanics, neuroscience), in our technical inventions (clocks, computers), and in our natural dispositions of reasoning. Some persist for many generations, indeed sometimes for millennia, others fade away (see Essay 16).

Our philosophical concerns are with the concepts we now have, not with concepts and conceptual frameworks that have sunk into the mists of history and are studied only by historians of ideas. But precisely because our concepts arose at certain times and places, evolved in response to certain needs and within given cultural, scientific, and social contexts, it is often philosophically fruitful to examine the historical roots of a problematic concept and the manner in which it evolved over generations to form the concept we have today. Conceptual history and etymological investigation are not only interesting in their own right, they are also often a source of philosophical insight. This is nowhere more marked than in the case

Solving, Resolving, and Dissolving Philosophical Problems: Essays in Connective, Contrastive and Contextual Analysis, First Edition. P. M. S. Hacker.
© 2025 John Wiley & Sons Ltd. Published 2025 by John Wiley & Sons Ltd.

of the concept of consciousness, the connective, contrastive, and contextual analysis of which was explored in the previous essay.

2.   It is striking that the ancients had no word for consciousness and that unlike the moderns did not characterize the mind as the domain of consciousness, even though they raised questions about our own knowledge of our perceptions and thoughts and misguidedly introduced the idea of an inner sense to explain the possibility of such knowledge. The mediaeval use of the Latin noun *conscientia* had nothing to do with our modern concept of consciousness. Rather it signified *shared knowledge* or *being privy to* information about something or someone. This notion later drifted into that of private, *unshared knowledge* about something or someone, including oneself, and thence into having private guilty knowledge about oneself. It was but a short step from this to the notion of *conscience* and *guilty conscience*. It is no coincidence that the French, to this day, have only the one noun *la conscience* to do service for both *conscience* and *consciousness*. It comes as something of a surprise to find out that the word 'consciousness' and its cognates are relative newcomers to English. One will look for them in vain in Shakespeare. The expression 'to be conscious of' is first recorded by the *Oxford English Dictionary* as occurring in the first decade of the seventeenth century. To be conscious of something, like its Latin root *conscius* (from *scio*, 'I know', and *cum*, 'together with'), initially meant *shared knowledge* or *being in the know*, a use that persisted into the nineteenth century and is still to be found in the novels of Jane Austen. Side by side with this use, 'to be conscious of' evolved, in the seventeenth and eighteenth centuries, into a first cousin of 'to be aware of'. What one might be conscious of was not limited to one's own states of mind or mental operations. One could be conscious of one's surroundings, of past, present, or future facts, of other people and their moods and feelings.

What emerged over time was the modern concept of consciousness that we examined in the previous essay, that is, a complex and ramifying form of cognitive receptivity – an extremely useful, if specialised, tool in our conceptual toolbox that belongs together with *being aware of, realizing*, and *noticing* that are likewise forms of cognitive receptivity. The emergence of the idea of intransitive consciousness that stands in contrast to being unconscious is a mid-nineteenth-century coinage. Prior to this *regaining* or *losing one's senses* served this purpose.

3. It was an intellectual misfortune that the term 'consciousness' and its cognates ever fell into the hands of philosophers. It was Descartes who introduced the term into philosophical discourse in the middle of the seventeenth century. He employed the term *conscientia* in order to account for what he conceived to be the knowledge we have of the contents of our own minds, which he termed 'thoughts' – an expression which he stretched to include not merely cogitations, but subjective perceptions, feelings, and desires, in short everything that could be thought of as 'operations of the mind'. In the wake of Descartes, consciousness became a mark of the mental and the salient characteristic of the human mind. Whatever is 'in the mind', it was argued, is an object of consciousness and whatever is an object of consciousness is known infallibly and indubitable.

While it was Descartes who set the ball of consciousness rolling in philosophy, it was John Locke, fifty years later, who gave it a pivotal position in philosophical attempts to render human nature and our sense of our own identity perspicuous and intelligible. We are who we are because we are conscious of our past experiences and can call them to mind. Consciousness, in the hands of late seventeenth- and eighteenth-century philosophers, became 'inner sense' – the means whereby we know immediately of the operations of our minds, the perception of all our perceptions. Indeed, this special philosophical sense of 'consciousness' became known as 'apperception'. Whether it was a special philosophical sense or a special philosophical confusion is debatable. For, as we have seen, to think about one's past experiences is not to be conscious of them and to be able to say what experiences one is currently undergoing is not to be able to see or apperceive one's experiences.

4. The centrality of consciousness or apperception to human nature and to our understanding of human nature characterizes eighteenth- and nineteenth-century philosophical reflections. With the early twentieth-century shift away from philosophy of psychology towards logic and philosophy of language, debates about consciousness and its nature sank to the bottom of the philosophical agenda. Indeed, with the rise of behaviourism in the early twentieth century (John Watson (1878–1958) in the United States), doubts were cast on the very existence of consciousness. The concept, it was alleged, belongs on the rubbish heap of history together with concepts like witches and hobgoblins. However, even assuming that consciousness exists, scepticism was expressed about its relevance to empirical psychology. For whatever

consciousness may be, it is something profoundly subjective. Only I, it was held, have 'access' to my own consciousness. Hence consciousness of one's own mental operations, not being intersubjectively verifiable, was methodologically excluded from respectable empirical and experimental psychology. A sea-change occurred in the 1970s. Suddenly consciousness moved to the top of the agenda, not only for philosophy, but also for psychology, cognitive science, and cognitive neuroscience. Whole university departments sprang up dedicated to consciousness studies. Suddenly we find distinguished scientists and philosophers declaring that consciousness is the deepest of all problems in biology, that it is an impenetrable mystery, that it is the last barrier to our achieving a fully scientific understanding of the universe, that no one knows what consciousness is or what it is for. How did this transvaluation of values take place? The story of this transformation sheds light upon philosophy and philosophical method. It is an exemplary instance of how not to do philosophy.

5.   Gilbert Ryle (1900–76), in his 1949 masterpiece *The Concept of Mind*, argued that numerous psychological attributes, such as understanding, knowing, believing, wanting, are not *mental states* to be known to their subject by introspection, but are to be understood as dispositions and tendencies, susceptibilities and liabilities, achievements and endeavours. However, he did not extend this analysis to pain and other occurrent sensations (tickles and itches) or to emotional agitations (twinges of fear or anxiety, thrills of excitement, or shocks of surprise). Other, more materialist-inclined philosophers such as U. T. Place (1924–2000) stepped into the breach, eager to eliminate all traces of Cartesian and Lockean consciousness and introspective knowledge of the mental. Place argued for the identity of sensations and agitations with brain states. This, he thought, would remove the last Ryleian residue of a Cartesian ghost in the human machine, retaining Ryle's sophisticated dispositionalist analyses of such concepts as understanding, knowing, believing, wanting, and so forth. This modesty was rapidly swept aside by a much more ambitious doctrine, Central State Materialism, advanced by David Armstrong (1926–2014), an eminent Australian philosopher. If itches, tickles, and other agitations can be identified with states of the brain, Central State Materialists argued, why stop there? Why not sweep away Ryle's painstaking and refined analyses of understanding, knowing, believing, wanting, etc., and identify *all* mental attributes with states of the brain?

It was in response to this hard-nosed materialism that *functionalism* developed in the United States. Different animals doubtless have significantly different brains and have markedly different brain states, but they surely are subject to feelings of fear and anger, desire and satisfaction, pleasure and pain. So mental states must surely be capable of *multiple realization* in very different biological systems. Moreover, with the rise of artificial intelligence (AI) and the invention of AI systems such as Deep Blue that beat the world chess master Garry Kasparov in 1997 and AlphaGo that beat Go Master Lee Sedol in 2016 relying on neural networks and reinforcement machine learning, it seemed plausible to suppose that purely mechanical, non-biological systems, such as computers, neural networks, and robots, can think and reason.

Central State Materialism had argued for the identity of the mind and the brain. Brain states were identical with mental states. If pain and pleasure, hope and fear, knowledge and belief are to be identified with brain states, then they had better be *states*. For only a state can be identical with a state. Distinguishing between objects, events, and processes, let alone further refinements such as distinguishing between states, powers, abilities, capacities, susceptibilities, and liabilities, could be left until later. The notion of a mental state was never subjected to critical scrutiny and analysis but taken for granted as a conceptually innocent catch-all. Functionalism took over this seemingly innocuous move. In fact, it was anything but innocent. The essential error was already made before the first moves in the game were even ventured. The concept of a mental state commits one to a certain way of looking at things. If something is a mental state, then one can safely ascribe to it any of the logically defining features of mental states. But there is no such thing as a mental state of knowing (by contrast with being in a state of ignorance), no such thing as being in a mental state of believing (by contrast with being in a state of disbelief or incredulity), and no such thing as being in a mental state of intending (see Essays 6 and 7).

Machine-state functionalists such as Hilary Putnam (1926–2016) argued that what makes a mental state such as a pain, an intention, a desire, a thought, or a memory the mental state it is depends only on its function in the system of which it is a part. The identity of a mental state is fixed by its sensory inputs, its causal relations to other mental states, themselves defined exclusively in terms of causal relations, and its behavioural outputs. So, for example, pain was held to be a mental state typically caused by injury, that produces beliefs, desires, and agitations, themselves defined not intrinsically but purely causally, and that generates a behavioural output of pain behaviour (grimaces, groans, winces, etc.). So mental states are not identified by introspection or inner sense, but exclusively by input, output, and other interacting mental states functionally defined.

All this chimed nicely with the idea of a Turing machine, namely a computer provided with a program, that is, a finite table of causally efficacious instructions, designed to respond to questions from a human being in a manner that would persuade the interrogator that a human being was giving the answers. Turing too identified thoughts with states of a system defined solely by their roles in producing other states and verbal outputs on the computer screen. On this background, it was not surprising that American functionalists held that any creature with a mind could be regarded as a Turing machine.

6.   It was not surprising either that it was widely held that this whole doctrine reduced human beings to machines. Mental states, it seemed, had no intrinsic character – only causal interactions with other mental states. The mind, it seemed, had disappeared, if not into a black hole then at any rate into a black box. Something crucial had been left out. What was missing from this tale? Why, the most important thing of all – Life itself, felt human experience, consciousness, the qualitative character of experience. In 1974, the American philosopher Thomas Nagel (b. 1937) wrote one of the most influential papers of the last fifty years. It was entitled 'What is it like to be a bat?' and it was designed to save our humanity from the theoretical predations of science. Let us examine the argument and its consequences. It had three pivotal theses.

First, an organism has conscious mental states if and only if there is something it is like to *be* that organism – something it is like *for* the organism. There is not anything it is like to be a brick wall or to be an ink-jet printer, but there is something it is like to be a human being, just as there is something it is like to be a bat. We must not confuse what something is like, which is a question concerning similarity, with what it is like for an organism to be the organism it is and to experience the experiences it enjoys or suffers. It is the latter that is denominated 'the subjective character of experience' or 'subjectivity' and (in the fulness of time) 'the what-its-likeness of experience'. It is this that is the essence of consciousness. It is the deepest mystery in the known universe and the greatest obstacle to a purely scientific understanding of the world.

Second, subjectivity is essentially connected to the notion of a *subjective point of view*, by contrast with scientific facts that are objective. It is inevitable that an objective physical theory about the objective world will be unable to account for facts of subjectivity. The idea of a point of view is species specific. Because the experience of humans is broadly similar in its qualitative character, we can grasp the subjective character of other human beings' experience. But what it is like to be a bat (that senses space and movement and objects by echolocation) is essentially beyond our ken. For facts of experience, facts about what it is like for the experiencing organism are fully accessible and hence fully comprehensible only from a generic point of view. We know that *there is something it is like* to be a bat and that there is something it is like to experience echolocation, but we can have no idea of *what* it is like because we do not share the point of view of bats.

Third, *every* experience of a conscious creature is such that there is something it is like to have it. Experience (like Cartesian thoughts) encompasses not only feelings, perceptions, and desires, but also thinking thoughts, having beliefs, knowing and believing, wanting and intending. There is something that it is like to think that *p*, and something quite different that it is like to think that *q*. So what it is like to think that 2 + 2 = 4 is altogether different from what it is like to think that 2 + 3 = 5, and what it is like to see the top button on one's shirt is quite different from what it is like to see the second button.

7.   One of the most dramatic consequences of the conjunction of functionalism and this conception of felt experience is that in principle the world might be exactly as it is, only without consciousness. It might consist not of human beings, but of zombies who behave just as we do, only lack subjective experience or 'subjectivity'. Of course, we know that we ourselves have experience and we know what it is like to be us, but are others really humans and not zombies? The problem of other minds suddenly acquires a desperate urgency. Moreover, the question of what consciousness is for seems to assume an intelligibility it would otherwise lack. Distinguishing intransitive from transitive consciousness as we have done in the previous essay does not generate a mystery concerning what being awake or being conscious is for (if there is any mystery it concerns what being asleep is for). Identifying transitive perceptual consciousness does not produce any deep puzzles concerning what peripheral perception is for. Unless humans

were liable to having their attention caught and held by items on the periphery of their perceptual field, they never would have survived. But the question of why nature came up with subjectivity is altogether different. Would it not have been more economical from an evolutionary point of view to generate zombies? Numerous cognitive neuroscientists and biologists held this to be a pressing question. For what *is* the evolutionary warrant of consciousness?

8.   The three pivotal theses are mistaken and need to be refuted. The account of consciousness is radically confused and needs to be uprooted. The most fundamental mistake was to respond to functionalism rather than challenging it. Functionalism should have been exposed for the nonsense it is and the board wiped clean in order to start afresh with the conceptual analysis of consciousness. Instead, a mythology of consciousness and subjectivity was conjured up. In fact, functionalism was not the last (threatening) word of science, but merely another altogether typical word of scientism. It seems that we cannot resist the temptation of construing ourselves on the model of our machines. Our humanity does indeed need saving, but not from philosophical absurdities such as the claim that we are all Turing machines. We shall not dissect functionalism here, but only the what-its-likeness of experience and its misconceptions, subjectivity and its incoherences. It is from these that philosophers and gullible scientists need saving. For Thomas Nagel's paper swept cognitive neuroscientists, psychologists, psychiatrists, biologists, and zoologists off their feet and provided a rich seedbed for the growth of nonsense. It reinstated among philosophers a pernicious neo-Cartesian conception of consciousness in which the domain of the mental was yet again identified with the sphere of consciousness. This stood in the way of a proper connective, contrastive, and contextual analysis of consciousness that is set forth in the previous essay. Moreover, it carried with it a cascade of unnoticed conceptual incoherences that entered philosophical and scientific discourse.

9.   It is true that the question 'What is it like for a brick wall to be a brick wall?' makes no sense. This a question that can be asked only with respect to living creatures who enjoy and suffer diverse experiences. For the questions 'What is (or was) it like for you (or for a person of some category) to be a so-and-so? / to do such-and-such?' are requests for positive or negative hedonic or attitudinal responses. The kinds of answers that are apt are: 'It was wonderful/awful/

marvellous/terrifying/enjoyable/boring/exciting'. Six capital points should be noted.

First, experiences are not generally identified by their hedonic tone or 'qualitative character', but by what they are experiences of. Smelling lilac may be just as pleasant as smelling roses, but what identifies the experiences and distinguishes them from one another is that the one is a sensory experience of lilac and the other is of roses. Seeing the Sistine Chapel and listening to Beethoven's Ninth may be equally wonderful, but *what* experiences they are is not *identified* by their qualitative character.

Secondly, while every experience is a *possible* subject of attitudinal predicates (pleasant, unpleasant, interesting, boring, attractive, repulsive) most experiences have *no actual* hedonic tone or qualitative character at all. This is just as well, since otherwise we should be emotionally swamped. 'What was it like for you to see the lamp posts in the street / see the button on your shirt / cross your legs?' would *normally* not be asked, and if it were asked one would normally respond 'What *do* you mean?'. For normally these experiences are *hedonically indifferent* (the exceptions are, for example, when vision is restored after an operation and the first thing one sees is the button on one's shirt, or when one has been paralysed and the first movement one makes is to cross one's legs – *then* one might be asked 'What was it like to cross your legs?')

Thirdly, while 'experience' is a sloppy portmanteau word, it is misguided to stretch it to include thinking, let alone knowing, believing, and understanding. These are not mental states and these verbal nouns are not phenomenological nouns. One cannot intelligibly ask what it is like to know that 25×25 is 625, or to believe that the Battle of Hastings was fought in 1066, or to understand the sentence *Ich bin müde*. These are not experiences.

Fourth, in those cases where someone's experience did have a hedonic tone or qualitative character and there is an answer to the question 'what is (or was) it like for you to be a so-and-so (a doctor, mother, soldier, ballerina) / to do such-and-such (see the Sistine Chapel, climb Everest, meet the King)?', for example: it was fascinating, fulfilling, wonderful, interesting, rewarding – it does not follow that there was something that it is (or was) like to be or to do it. Indeed, the form of words 'there was something it was like for me to climb Everest' in fact makes no sense. What seems to be an English phrase is no more than latent nonsense: a grammatically ill-formed phrase – as will now be shown.

The question 'What was it like for you to do such-and-such?' (where doing such-and-such *can* be said to be an experience) will get a hedonic or attitudinal answer, for example, 'It was wonderful.' It follows that there was something *that it was* to do such-and-such, namely wonderful. But it was *not* 'like wonderful' (except perhaps in California and among the British illiterati). The experience *was* wonderful, but it was not *like wonderful*. The insertion of a 'like' is a result of a miscegenous crossing of the question 'What is it like to do X?' which may be answered 'It is rather like doing Y', with the question 'What is it like for you to do X?', which demands an attitudinal, hedonic answer such as 'It was wonderful'.

For those with some familiarity with formal logic (the second-order predicate calculus), all this can be couched technically [others may skip this paragraph]. There is nothing awry with second-level quantification over hedonic and anti-hedonic properties such as 'wonderful', 'charming', 'delightful', 'repulsive', 'disgusting'. The form of such quantification, however, is not 'There was something *it was like* for me (or 'for NN') to V', namely wonderful', but rather, "There was something that *it was* for me (or 'for NN') to V, namely wonderful.' That is, existential generalization requires the dropping of the 'like', for the experience was not *like wonderful*, it *was* wonderful. This should be obvious from consideration of the question, 'What was it like for you to V?'. For the answer is not 'To V was like wonderful', but 'To V was wonderful'. And the existential generalization of the latter sentence cannot yield the form of words 'There is something which it is like to V, namely wonderful'. The latter aberration is the result of a miscegenous crossing of the existential generalization of a judgement of similarity ('What is V-ing like?') with the existential generalization of a judgement of the affective character of an experience ('What was it like for you to V?'). The result is a sequence of words that looks like a well-formed English sentence but is not. It is latent nonsense, which has now been rendered patent nonsense.

Fifth, there are determinate logico-grammatical constraints on the formation of questions of the form 'What is it like for a Y to be an X?' as well as on the question of 'What is it like for you to be an X?' These logical constraints preclude the formation of the questions, 'What is it like for a bat to be a bat?' as well as 'What is it like for a human being to be a human being?' no less than the questions, 'What is it like for you (me) to be a human being?' and 'What is it like for me (you) to be me (you)?'

We often ask, 'What is it like to be an X?' (a tinker, tailor, soldier, sailor) without specifying *for whom*. Sometimes the subject class is obvious: 'What is it like to be pregnant?' is limited to women. Often it is the addressee, as in, 'What was it like to fight in the war, Dad?' But sometimes the subject class needs specifying: 'What is it like for a man/ woman/ a soldier/ a sailor, etc. to be an X?' In all such cases the subject term Y differs from the object term X, and two principles of contrast are involved, that is, what is it like for a Y *as opposed to* a Z to be an X, and what is it like for a Y to be an X *as opposed to* being a Z. But one cannot intelligibly ask 'What is it like for an X to be an X?' (we might call this 'the non-reiteration principle). One cannot ask 'What is it like for a doctor to be a doctor' as *opposed* to someone who is not a doctor being a doctor, for that makes no sense. Someone who is not a doctor cannot also be a doctor, although they may *become* one. The interpolation of the phrase 'for a doctor' here is illicit and adds nothing to the question 'What is it like to be a doctor?' which is a simple request about the form of life of doctors. It follows that the questions 'What is it like for a bat to be a bat?', 'What is it like for a human being to be a human being?' and 'What is it like for me to be me?' are nonsense. For they violate the condition of non-reiteration and transgress the two contrast principles. A bat cannot be anything but a bat, just as a human cannot be anything other than a human, and I cannot be anyone other than myself. So there isn't anything that it is like to be a bat, since this form of words makes no sense. 'What is it like to be a human being / bat?' amounts to no more than a question about the generic character of human (bat) life. There is nothing mysterious or ineffable about it. One may answer 'Nasty, brutish and short' or 'Full of hope and fear'. And any chiropterologist can give us a good description of the life of bats.

Finally, there is a radical misuse of the concept of a point of view in the claim that what characterizes subjectivity is that it essentially involves a generic point of view. One may see something from a viewpoint, but not from a point of view. And anyone may look at what I see from the same viewpoint if I vacate it. But although pain can be said to be something 'subjective' (an attribute of a sentient subject), I don't experience pain from my point of view or indeed from any point of view. Nor do I perceive whatever I perceive from a point of view but from a position in space. I may *pass judgement* or *give an opinion* from a political, economic, or strategic point of view, or *from my point of view*, that is: from the point of view of my interests, preferences, or concerns. Although a judgement given from the point of view of my interests or concerns may be said to be 'subjective', there is nothing subjective about a judgement made from a political, economic, or strategic point of view. It is muddled to claim that I and only I have 'access to my subjectivity', for I don't *have access* to my pain at all, I just have it. I don't have access to my thoughts – I think them. But if I tell you what I think, *you* have access to my thoughts. The idea that we cannot observe another person's 'subjectivity', but only their behaviour is mistaken. We can and do observe other people perceiving things, we can and do observe their moods and emotions, and we can and do observe and commiserate with their suffering.

So, what emerges from all the excitement about the ineffability of what it's like to be a bat, what it's like to be me, and the what-its-likeness of experience? What, after careful analysis emerged from all the mystification? Only this: one can ask a person what it is like to fulfil the various roles they fulfil and to do the various things they do, and they can normally tell one. One cannot ask a brick what it is like to fill a hole in the wall or an ink-jet printer what it is like to run off twenty copies of a paper. For only sentient creatures have roles and have experiences, enjoying some, disliking others, and being indifferent to most. A meagre result for so much noise.

5

Other Minds and Other People

"There seems to be an unalterable contradiction between the human mind and its employments. How can a soul be a merchant? What relation to an immortal being have the price of linseed, the tare on tallow or the brokerage on hemp? Can an undying creature debit *petty expenses* and charge for *carriage paid*? The soul ties its shoes, the mind washes its hands in a basin. All is incongruous."

Walter Bagehot

1.   Failure to apprehend that our talk of the mind is the form in which we present our ascriptions of cognitive, cogitative, and volitional powers of human beings and their exercise (see Essay 1) led and continues to lead us into dire confusion. One kind of confusion that has dogged European thought for many centuries is whether and how we can know anything about other minds, what is passing within them, what they are thinking, what they are feeling, and what they want or intend to do. The questions were raised in the early fifth century by St Augustine and have never been put to rest. It is still a pressing issue today, not only among philosophers but also among cognitive neuroscientists, psychologists, and psychiatrists. It is likely to remain problematic as long as we continue to think of the mind, rather than the human being, as the agent of thought and subject of consciousness or assimilate the mind to the brain and conceive of the brain as that in us that thinks and reasons, perceives and desires. Each generation

Solving, Resolving, and Dissolving Philosophical Problems: Essays in Connective, Contrastive and Contextual Analysis, First Edition. P. M. S. Hacker.
© 2025 John Wiley & Sons Ltd. Published 2025 by John Wiley & Sons Ltd.

will have to disentangle itself from the knotted skein of threads that form the network of our thought about ourselves, our distinctive powers, and their exercise.

The confusion is not inconsequential. It is sometimes claimed that for a child to apprehend other human beings as subjects of thought and experience and to attribute mental states to them, the child must form a *theory of mind*. For, it is argued, mental states are not directly observable. What is observable are mere bodily movements. So a system of inferences is needed in order to make predictions about the mental states and consequent behaviour of others. The idea of a facilitating theory of mind caught on and was duly invoked to explain the deficiencies and limitations of autistic children. It was argued that the problems of autistic children are to be explained in terms of their inability to construct a theory of mind in the early years of their lives. *This* claim guides therapeutic treatment down very specific lines, which may well be irrelevant or even defective if the doctrine is misconceived, that is, if the very idea of a young child constructing theories is as unintelligible as the idea of a baby remembering that before it was born it reflected on the origin of life and the existence of God.

Philosophers have been no less enmeshed in confusion. Really to know what passes in another man's mind, John Locke argued, we would have to *pass into their mind to perceive what ideas were before him*. But this is a meaningless form of words, since there is no such thing as passing into another man's mind, any more than there is checkmate in draughts. Later generations argued that the existence of other minds is a hypothetical conjecture – an inference to the best explanation of the observable behaviour of others. A person's behaviour was alleged to be best explained by reference to an unobservable mental state that causes it. But inferences to the best explanation in science, as when the existence of an unobserved planet is postulated to explain deviations in the orbit of an observable planet, are verifiable by further observations. By contrast, the existence of other minds and other's states of mind are, *ex hypothesi*, not observable.

The most common philosophical account, originating with Augustine, was that we know of the existence of other minds and other people's states of mind *by analogy with our own case*. For if I injure my foot, it hurts and I cry out in pain. I can observe other people injuring their body and crying out. I infer that by analogy with my own case, they suffer pain. But this seems a singularly thin and feeble basis for the construction of analogical hypotheses. Just because *I* have hurt myself, feel pain, and cry out, can I infer that all the teeming millions of mankind who injure themselves and then cry out also feel pain between the injury and the subsequent cry, as I do? By any scientific standards of analogical hypotheses, that seems an irresponsible inference from far too narrow a base.

Scientists themselves are equally bewildered. By the final third of the twentieth century, neuroscientists had come to think that the mind, conceived as an immaterial object in liaison with the brain by means of the pyramidal cells in the motor cortex (as had been thought by John Eccles (1903–97), and his colleague, the renowned philosopher Karl Popper (1902–94), was a dualist fiction. From this correct thought they jumped to the misguided conclusion that either the mind does not exist, or the mind just is the brain. (Buridan's ass, in eradicating one bundle of hay so that only one is left, is no less of an ass.) But if the mind is the brain, or if thinking and reasoning, perceiving and having sensations, deciding and forming intentions are activities of brains, how is it possible for us to know whether others are thinking and what they are thinking? The problem of other minds was transformed at a stroke into the problem of other brains. Since brains are enclosed in skulls, how can one brain achieve knowledge of the mental states of other brains? It is hardly surprising that many concluded that the brain must construct a theory of other mind/brains. One's brain, it was argued by distinguished psychiatrists, creates models of the physical world by combining signals from the senses and prior expectations. A human being is non-consciously aware of these models in navigating a route through the physical environment. It is in the same way that we acquire our knowledge of the minds of others – using cues from one's senses and prior experience of the behaviour of others, one's brain creates models of the minds of others.

The confusions of scientists are mirrored by the confusions of speakers on radio and television, of journalists in the press, and of the educated public. It is common to hear such people say, 'One can't really know the feelings of others' or 'One can never really know what other people are thinking'. It is tempting to suppose (as Locke did) that in order *really* to know what other people's mental states are, one would have to be able to 'enter their mind' and perceive there what they are experiencing and thinking. So *real* knowledge is not attainable. And if real knowledge is not available, our beliefs about the mental states of others are anything but certain. They lack the certainty we have regarding our own thoughts and experiences. For such beliefs rest on probabilistic inferences from outer behaviour to inner states of mind.

But something must be wrong. When a woman in childbirth is screaming in agony, no one can say 'It is probable that she is in pain' or 'We can't be certain that she is suffering'. When someone sincerely tells us what they think, we can't say 'That is mere behaviour, mere words – we can't really know what he thinks.' When someone is bereaved and weeping with unbearable grief, no one can say 'We don't know whether he is grieving'. One cannot defend such sceptical claims by arguing that behaviour may all be pretence. For there are practical and conceptual limits to pretence. Someone in a traffic accident, lying in a pool of blood with a patently broken leg and screaming in pain, cannot be said to be pretending. A baby's cries of pain cannot be pretence, since it has not yet learnt to pretend, that is, to model its behaviour on that of others who have hurt themselves. Moreover, the suggestion that ascribing psychological attributes to others presupposes possession of a theory of mind must surely be awry. How could a small child construct anything that could warrant the name of 'theory'? If the theory of electricity, relativity theory, and the theory of evolution are paradigms of different kinds of scientific theories, then what could be meant by asserting that a child who has barely mastered a language is in the process of constructing a theory of anything? Even worse is the suggestion that a brain, which cannot intelligibly be said to have mastered or not to have mastered a language, constructs a theory of other brains (or of other mind/brains).

It should strengthen our suspicions to learn that the very idea of a theory of mind or of a mind/brain has rotten roots. One root lies in an explanatory conceit. Wilfred Sellars (1912–89), a distinguished and influential American philosopher) defending a naturalistic, anti-Cartesian, philosophy of psychology, adopted an expository myth of the existence of proto-humans called 'Ryleans' who had a behaviourist language without concepts of mental states. He argued that they would improve their explanatory and predictive resources if they postulated the existence of unobservable inner states that modify their behaviour. It was unfortunate that of this fictitious myth others made a factitious doctrine. The second root lies in a joint study of chimpanzees published in 1978 by a primatologist and a psychologist who had been pupil of Wilfred Sellars. Chimpanzees pay attention to alpha males who observe them hoarding food and they change the hiding place of their cache as soon as they see that they are unobserved. This, it was suggested, could be rendered intelligible only on the assumption that chimpanzees attribute beliefs both to themselves and to others. Because mental states of chimpanzees are not observable (since, it was claimed, only behaviour is observable) chimps have to construct a theory of mind to make predictions about the behaviour of alpha males seeking to steal their food. For the hoarding chimps must surely impute beliefs and desires both to themselves and to the alpha male who is seeking to steal their cache of food. Otherwise, how could the hoarding chimps make predictions about the behaviour of the alpha male (e.g. where it will look for the cache)? This, it should be obvious, was an unwarranted intellectualization of animal behaviour. Differential responses to conspecifics do not imply recognition of the beliefs and desires of others but only intelligent associative responsiveness to their behaviour. The question of how a languageless chimpanzee might impute beliefs and desires both to itself and to others was not raised. Misconception descended to farce when psychologists, reading about the putative theories of mind of chimpanzees, decided that it would be equally illuminating to ascribe theories of mind to human children. If chimpanzees have a theory of mind, why should human children not have one too!

2.　Puzzlement about other minds seems endemic. Among those who have become entrapped in this part of the web of our conceptual scheme are thinkers of towering stature. The question of how they could have talked themselves into such nonsense is pressing and anything but trivial. For the errors of great thinkers are sources of enlightenment when they are clarified. Great errors are beacons of illumination when they are laid bare. That is why the study of *dialectic*, that is to say: the logic of conceptual illusion, is such an important part of philosophical enquiry.

What then led so many outstanding philosophers and scientists into such dire straits? We should seek not for one misguided reason, but for a whole battery of mutually supporting misguided reasons. For deep and persistent philosophical confusions are hardly ever held in place by one overriding argument, but by a multiplicity of arguments. That is why it is so common to find that a single refutation of one salient point has so little effect.

So let me tabulate the arguments.

(i)　One deep confusion was already noted in a previous discussion. It is the ubiquitous but misguided idea that the mind is not a form of representation of discourse concerning human intellectual and volitional powers and their exercise but rather the agent of thought and subject of experience (Essay 1). This constitutes the framework for the second bastion of error.

(ii)   The subject who *has* a mind also *knows* what passes in his mind. The subject can directly apprehend his own mind but cannot directly apprehend other minds. He has immediate, infallible, and indubitable knowledge of what passes in his own mind. To be sure, if the very idea of a mind is rejected as a dualist residue that needs extirpating and the attributes of the mind are ascribed to the brain, then the brain's knowledge of what passes within it is immediate but the brain's access to other brains and their contents is obviously problematic. How can one brain know what is going on in another brain save by means of a theory?

(iii)   It is generally assumed that the question of *how* we know what is passing in our minds can be raised. If it can be raised, it surely can readily be answered. For it seems that the subject of thought and experience (the mind, the self, the I) must have privileged access to the inner. The form which this access took was variously conceived: 'I know how things are with me *by consciousness*' was one (Cartesian) refrain. We are self-conscious beings and everything that occurs within the realm of consciousness is known directly or immediately. A slightly different story was told by Locke: the contents of the mind are perceptions or ideas and I know of the occurrence and nature of my perceptions by perceiving them. Perception of perceptions (denominated 'apperception' by Leibniz (1646–1716)) was conceived to be 'inner sense': just like outer sense save that its objects were conceived to be the contents of consciousness or the contents of the mind. Later this faculty of inner perception was characterized by William James (1842–1910) as 'introspection', which, he explained, is a matter of looking into one's mind and seeing what is there.

(iv)   Accompanying the misconceptions about the mind and about subjective knowledge of the mind are equally egregious misunderstandings of what is to be deemed *behaviour*. If the mind is the agent of thought and experience and if we can neither see the minds of others nor see into them, then what we observe of others is merely *bare bodily movement*. We have to infer what is going on in other minds from our observations of bare behaviour. The mental is hidden *behind* behaviour. It is not in public view but must be inferred.

(v)   This already commits one to a particular picture: the inner/outer picture of the mind and its behavioural output. That picture operates ever more powerfully if the mind is jettisoned in favour of the brain or the so-called mind/brain.

It is these doctrines that we must demolish if we are to free ourselves from ramifying conceptual incoherence and see ourselves and others aright. Only then shall we be able to see what the genuine problems of understanding others are and the extent to which mutual misunderstanding and ignorance as well as constitutional indeterminacy are part of the human condition.

3.   It is striking that over the many centuries in which these questions have been discussed it did not occur to anyone other than Wittgenstein (1889–1951) that the place to root for the dissolution of the philosophical problem of other minds is in our preconceptions concerning knowledge of our own minds. Knowledge of other minds appears problematic only when contrasted with a particular picture of self-knowledge. Once that misconceived picture is eradicated, the problem concerning the knowledge of the psychological attributes of other human beings becomes tractable.

It is, to be sure, correct that normally a mature language-user can say whether he is in pain, what he is perceiving, what he thinks and what he remembers, what he likes or dislikes, whether he is feeling happy or sad, what he wants to have or to get, and what he intends to do. What is not true is that a human being's ability to tell us such things rests on the deliverances of consciousness, the perception of his own ideas or perceptions, inner sense or apperception, self-consciousness, or introspection. These are so many red herrings drawn across the conceptual tracks. It was a confusion to suppose that I can see whatever passes in my mind *and that is why I can say* how things are with me. So what grounds are there for my being able to say what I experience, feel, think, or desire if I do not perceive, apperceive, or introspect what passes in my mind and the contents of my consciousness? None! In all the pivotal kinds of case, *one's utterance is groundless*. This, at first blush, seems shocking. A groundless assertion is surely unwarranted! In the joint absence of evidence and of a cognitive faculty (of 'inner sense', 'apperception', or 'introspection') a groundless assertion would surely be wholly arbitrary. Not so.

Some of my utterances are such that truthfulness guarantees truth, for example, that I am in pain, that I thought I heard a noise, that I believe that NN will arrive before 7:00 p.m., that I would like a gin and tonic. These utterances *have no grounds whatsoever*. How is that possible? How can one rightly say that one has a headache, sees (or seems to see) something, that one is thinking, or that one intends to do such-and-such *without any evidential grounds* and *without the exercise of any cognitive faculty*? Is this not sheer dogmatism? No! These utterances are typically *expressions* or *manifestations* of sensation and perception, of thought and belief, of likes and dislikes, of desires and intentions.

This subclass of psychological utterances, as Wittgenstein showed, is essentially Janus-faced. One can be said to possess these concepts only if one has mastered the behavioural grounds for applying them to others and can apply them groundlessly to oneself. A condition for the possibility of groundless self-ascription is mastery of evidential other-ascription. The grounds for applying them to others are not empirical discoveries but *constitutive criteria*. Pain behaviour is not inductive evidence for someone's being in pain, it is *logically* good evidence. Learning the grounds for ascription of pain to others is part of what is involved in learning what the word 'pain' means. An avowal of pain no more needs evidence than does a groan of pain. The utterance, 'I want such-and-such' is not a report based on introspection, any more than trying to get something is based on introspection. But 'He wants such-and -such' is a report based on observation of what he does and says. 'I'm going to go shopping' is an expression of intention that heralds an action and licences the reliance of the addressee, 'He is going to go shopping' is a prediction. 'I dreamt such-and-such' is a dream-utterance expressed on waking, 'He dreamt such-and-such' is a report based on what he said. I may have grounds for taking what I see or hear, smell or taste, to be such-and-such, but I don't have grounds for asserting that I see whatever I take myself to see. To be sure, the senses are fallible sources of knowledge – I may be mistaken for subjective or objective reasons, but I cannot mistake my seeing for my hearing. I don't have grounds for saying that I see or hear something. By contrast, asserting of another that he sees something rests on the evidential grounds of his discriminatory behaviour as he wends his way through his environment in the light (but holds out his hands to feel anything in his way, bumps into things, and falls over things in the darkness). In all these, and many other cases too, mastery of the first and third person uses are two sides of one and the same coin. They cannot be prized apart. One cannot be said to have mastered the concept unless one has mastered both the groundless first-person use and the grounded third-person use.

The asymmetry between first- and third-person uses of many psychological verbs is noteworthy. 'I don't know what he thinks' is a confession of ignorance. But "I don't know what I think' is an admission of lack of reflection. In the former case, I need to find out. In the latter case, I don't need to reflect on myself, but rather to reflect on the evidence for and against the thesis in question. Similarly, 'I don't know what he wants' is a confession of ignorance, whereas 'I don't know what I want' is an expression of indecision. What I need to do is not examine myself to find out what I want but to examine the alternatives and opt for the most favourable. 'I don't know what he is going to do' discloses my lack of knowledge. But 'I don't know what I am going to do' exhibits my irresolution.

4.   A prominent feature of received reflections on a human being's ability to say how things are subjectively with him was that one knows the contents of one's consciousness infallibly and indubitably. That is because one has what was deemed to be 'privileged access' to one's own mind but not to the minds of others. So one's own subjective judgements are completely certain, whereas one's judgements about other minds can never reach that degree of certainty. They can at best reach 'moral certainty', 'inductive conjecture', or 'probability'.

This is misconceived. It is a distortion of the logical grammar of psychological expressions. First, it is mistaken to suppose that I have *access* to my mind, let alone privileged access. My mind is not a domain, but talk of the mind is a form of representation. I don't *have access* to a form of representation. Rather, I master a mode of speech and thought. I need access to the college library, namely a library card that gives me entry. I have access to a certain club in as much as my membership entitles me to enter it. I may be given access to the president if he grants me an interview. But I don't 'have access' to my mind. Nor do I have access to the contents of my consciousness. It is true that I may be conscious of my rising anger or of my overwhelming grief, but not by privileged access. Rather, by my rising anger's intruding itself on my awareness or by my grief overwhelming me with tears. Moreover, others may be conscious of my rising anger, even when I am not, if their attention is caught and held by the behavioural manifestations of my anger; and my grief may be visible to all.

Second, as we have already suggested, the idea that I know what is in my mind or what are the contents of my consciousness with certainty – a certainty absent from my judgements concerning the minds of others – is an egregious error. It is true that there is a subset of psychological expressions which are immune to doubt in the first-person case. I cannot doubt whether I have a pain, an itch, or a tickle. I cannot doubt that it seems to me just as if I were perceiving such-and-such nor can I doubt whether I am thinking that *p* or am thinking that *q*. But in all these cases, it is not that I *do not* doubt, but rather that I *cannot* doubt. These first-person utterances are *immune* to doubt – doubt is *logically excluded*. That is to say, we attach no sense to the affixing of the phrases 'I doubt whether' or 'I doubt that'. But by the same token, certainty too is excluded. Since doubt is already excluded by grammar, there is nothing for certainty to exclude, no work for it to do. If someone were to say 'I am certain that I have a splitting headache', we would not understand what he was trying to say. So it is misconceived to suppose that the first-person cases provide standards of certainty that other ascriptions cannot meet. We *can be* completely certain of how things are with others, and we sometimes are. (But, of course, others are not brains in skulls.)

5.   A deep misconception about behaviour bedevils the whole debate about ascription of psychological attributes to others. Human behaviour is not 'bare bodily movement' any more than human vision consists of nothing other than patches of colour, shape, and motion. We see people smiling and scowling, talking and laughing, weeping with grief or joy. We see our fellow human beings waving and beckoning, doing their shopping and walking home, digging in the garden and picking flowers. Although they may sometimes not reveal their thoughts and feelings, they often do. Their emotions and attitudes are commonly *manifest* in their behaviour, their mien, and their facial expressions. Joy is not *hidden behind* joyful behaviour, grief is not *concealed behind* the tears streaming down a person's cheeks, anger is not *suppressed* but revealed by the angry voice and the enraged face. These patterns of human behaviour are the forms that human occurrent emotions take – not externalities, but the very thing itself. When someone sincerely tells us what he thinks, then his thought is patent, not latent. When a person honestly declares his plans and intentions, we are not left in the dark. The inner/outer picture of the mind needs to be eradicated.

6.   Scepticism about other minds is a tangle of knotted threads, most of which we have unravelled. We do, sometimes, know what other people (not other minds or other brains) think and feel, like and dislike, want and intend. But sometimes we do not. Other people are predictable in the small, but sometimes radically unpredictable in the large. Norma Helmer, in Ibsen's *The Doll's House*, unpredictably leaves her husband and children. Hedda Gabler, in the same playwright's eponymous drama, shockingly and unexpectedly commits suicide.

Philosophical and cognitive scientific conceptual entanglements concerning other minds have served to mask from our eyes the reality of the human condition in respect of knowledge and understanding of other people.

We are rarely transparent to each other. At best we are translucent. Sometimes we are opaque. Human opacity has many roots. Sometimes it is simple ignorance. Often, people do not tell others what they are thinking. Often, they keep their plans to themselves. Commonly they do not wear their hearts on their sleeves. Sometimes our beliefs about others are false because other people dissimulate, and we succumb to the confidence trickster, the lying politician, or the deceitful seducer. Often human opacity is rooted in subjective indeterminacy. The thoughts, beliefs, and emotions of others (like our own) are commonly inchoate: it is not as if other people themselves are always clear what they think, believe, or feel. Our difficulty in understanding another may mirror their difficulty in understanding and explaining themselves. That may be exacerbated by self-deception, at which we are all past masters.

Sometimes we cannot understand others despite the fact that they are doing their best to explain themselves to us. What counts as someone's reason for thinking or believing, for feeling or acting, may not be intelligible *as a reason* to another. 'Why did he strip naked and jump into a prickly cactus bush?' – 'Because it seemed like a good idea at the time.' is a sadder joke than it initially seems to be. Practical reason is underdetermined by the facts and human opacity is a part of the human condition.

PART II

Epistemology

6

Knowledge

"When a man's knowledge is not in order, the more of it he has, the greater will be his confusion."

Herbert Spencer

1.   We value knowledge. We find it natural to compare knowledge with light and ignorance with darkness. Those who act in ignorance are benighted – they know not what they do. We value knowledge, or at any rate ought to value it, because of the value of truth and understanding. For only if we can attain knowledge can we conform our lives, our thoughts, our passions, and our actions to how things are, and not merely to how things seem to us to be. Only if we know how things are can we hope to achieve understanding of why things are as they are and to make sense of the world we live in and of ourselves within it. Only if we possess knowledge can we be reliable sources of information for our children and for our fellow human beings, most of whose information depends upon authority and upon dependable testimony in as much as we are 'eyes and ears unto each other'. Each generation is a custodian of the fund of knowledge achieved by the past endeavours of mankind which it is obligated to transmit to future generations. Knowledge of other human beings, difficult though it is, is a prerequisite for mutual understanding. Self-knowledge is a prerequisite for self-understanding. Knowledge of good and evil is what

Solving, Resolving, and Dissolving Philosophical Problems: Essays in Connective, Contrastive and Contextual Analysis, First Edition. P. M. S. Hacker.
© 2025 John Wiley & Sons Ltd. Published 2025 by John Wiley & Sons Ltd.

God, in the Garden of Eden, wished to deny us lest we become 'as one of us [the gods] to know good and evil'. It is knowledge without which we are not fully human and knowledge the loss of which implies our descent into fanaticism and inhumanity, with the consequent the loss of our souls (see Essay 14).

2.   The concept of knowledge (*episteme*) prominent in ancient Greek philosophy was very different from the common-or-garden conception of knowledge that is familiar to us all in contemporary culture. It was distorted by an obsession with geometry, which was one of the crowning glories of Greek intellectual achievement. This fostered the misleading association of the objects of knowledge with the certainty, generality, and necessity the Greeks ascribed to geometry. So sense perception could not qualify as *episteme*.

A comparable Platonic conception of knowledge was revived in the early modern era by Descartes. He too advanced a sublimed conception of knowledge, which he called *scientia* and linked it with certainty and indubitability. Cognition, he held, is of true thoughts. The mark of truth, he averred, is clarity and distinctness of apprehension. The mark of clarity and distinctness is indubitability. A remote heir to this account, shifting from objective certainty of things to subjective certainty of people, was advanced by A. J. Ayer (1910–89) in the mid-twentieth century. Ayer argued that A knows that p if and only if it is true that p, A is sure that p, and A has the right to be sure. Hobbes (1588–1679), a contemporary of Descartes, also advanced an account of knowledge, which he called *science*. Knowledge, he contended, was truth of a proposition that is evident. Observational knowledge ('experience of fact') is evident to the senses, science is knowledge of the truth of a proposition that is supported by 'concluding evidence'. Here is an ancestor of the modern ideas that knowledge is *justified true belief*, and that *what* we know are truths. So, knowledge became conceived (by Bertrand Russell (1872–1970)) to be a *propositional attitude* – a relation between the knower and a true proposition. Locke, half a century after Descartes, held knowledge to be 'the perception of the connection and agreement, or disagreement and repugnancy, of any of our ideas'. This was the remote ancestor of the coherence epistemology embraced in the mid-twentieth century by one of the leading figures of American philosophy, W. V. O. Quine (1908–2000).

So, the seeds of contemporary analyses of knowledge that things are thus-and-so were planted in the early modern period. Eighteenth- and nineteenth-century reflections on the nature of knowledge added relatively little. From these early modern seeds grow the roots of modern epistemological confusions.

3.   As always, our point of departure has to be linguistic usage. How is the verb 'to know' and its cognates used? What are their combinatorial possibilities? What are their roles in utterances?

One may not only know *that* things are so ('He knows that it is late'), one may also know things to be so ('He knows it is late'). One may know people and places, know whether things are so and know when, where, who or what. One may know how to do something, know to do something ('he knows to lock up before he leaves') and know better than to do something ('he knows better than to leave the lights on'). One may know Latin or Greek well or a little, know 'The Waste Land' by heart but not well or a little, know the multiplication-tables, know physics or chemistry. This suggests that great care needs to be taken over generalizations concerning the concept of knowledge, since what may be true for one grammatical form may be excluded for another. It is moot whether knowing that things are so implies believing that things are so (see Essay 7). But it is obvious that knowing Latin does not imply believing Latin, since there is no such thing as believing Latin any more than there is any such thing as believing Paris or London. Similarly, knowing Jill is being acquainted with Jill, but knowing the time does not imply being acquainted with the time but being able to answer the question 'What time is it?'.

4.   The categorial status of knowledge requires investigation. What one knows, what information one possesses, is obviously not a mental state, process, activity, or act. But it is moot whether the knowing of it is a mental state or not. If knowing something to be so is a clear and distinct apprehension of the truth of a thought, then it may appear to be a mental state that is self-certifying and self-presenting to the thinker, as Descartes supposed. If knowing something to be so is perceiving the connection and agreement, or disagreement and repugnancy, of our ideas, then too it may appear to be a mental state, since according to Locke, we perceive our perceptions. These conceptions are far removed from ours, even though they have modern echoes. Nevertheless, we continue to cleave to the idea that knowing something to be so is a mental state. Some philosophers may suppose that knowing something to be so *must* be a mental state since knowledge, on analysis, includes believing things to be so and believing is held to be a mental state.

However, knowledge is not a mental state (nor, as we shall see in Essay 7, is belief). Nor is knowledge any other kind of state. One is *in* a given mental state, *in* a state of anxiety or good cheer, but there is no such thing as being *in* a state of knowledge or of knowing. Knowledge is acquired and once acquired is possessed, but one cannot acquire or possess a mental state. Mental states, like all other states, are actualities. Knowledge is more akin to a potentiality than to an actuality. If someone possesses information that things are so then there is an indeterminate range of things he can do: he can act, reason, or feel for the reason that things are so; he can inform others that things are so and correct others who deny that things are so; he can reflect on the information that things are so and construct plans for himself or for others on the basis of this information; he can retain the information and call it to mind when necessary, or he can store the information in writing or on a computer; and so on.

One might object that one can be in a blissful state of ignorance and if one can be in a blissful state of ignorance then surely one can be in a blissful or hard-won state of knowledge. Our account shows why that is mistaken. An ability is a potentiality, but *lack of an ability is not*. If one is distraught, one may be in a state of complete confusion, unable to make rational decisions. If one has lost the power to move, one is in a state of paralysis. The manifold forms of aphasia are states. Indecision is a state (an inability to decide), but when one makes up one's mind one is not making a transition from a state of indecision to a state of decision, since there is no such thing as a state of decision. So, that powers and abilities are potentialities and not states is perfectly compatible with the lack of a power or an inability being a state. That is why ignorance is a state, whereas knowledge is not.

5.   One cannot dispute the contention that knowledge is essentially linked to truth. 'To know' is a factive verb. If A knows that p, then it is true that p. 'A knows that p, but it is false that p' is a contradiction. Propositions, assertions, declarations, statements, and other sayables are true or false. It does not follow that when A knows that p, what he knows is a proposition.

We must distinguish between

(i)   knowing that things are so;

(ii) knowing the proposition that things are so – as when one knows what someone said (i.e. that he said such-and-such), or when one knows the third proposition in Euclid's *Elements*, or Newton's inverse square law. Note that one may know propositions without actually understanding them or knowing whether they are true.

(iii) (a) knowing that the proposition that things are so is true, that is, knowing the proposition that things are so to be true
       (b) knowing the proposition that things are so to be false
       (c) knowing whether the proposition that things are so is true or false, that is, being able to answer the question 'Is it true that *p*?'

Knowing that things are so is knowing how things stand. It is, figuratively speaking, directed *at reality*, not *at reports about reality*. It is commonly referred to by contemporary philosophers as 'propositional knowledge' and conceived to be knowledge of propositions. But propositional knowledge is knowledge *expressed by propositions*, not knowledge *of* propositions. What a person knows when he knows that *p* is not a proposition, but how things are.

Knowledge is sometimes said to 'aim at the truth'. This is misleading. Knowledge does not *aim* at anything, but human beings commonly want to know how things are. When they know how things are, they can express their knowledge by means of true propositions.

If one thinks that *what* is known when one knows that *p* is a proposition, it is but a short step to a further (Russellian) confusion, namely: to conceive of such knowledge as being a *propositional attitude*. But to know the proposition that things are so does not signify an attitude to a proposition any more than to know the Treaty of Amiens signifies an attitude towards a treaty or 'to know London' signifies an attitude towards London. To know the proposition that things are so is not to stand in a relation towards a proposition or towards an object called 'that things are so'. One may know, be acquainted with or be familiar with, a proposition without knowing whether it is true or indeed without understanding it. One may know many false propositions and one may or may not know that they are false.

To be sure, there are attitudes towards such sayables as propositions, claims, rumours, stories, announcements, declarations, or statements. One may *endorse* the proposition or averral that things are so, one may *ridicule* or *dismiss* the rumour that things are so, one may be *amused* by the story that things are so, and one may *approve* of the declaration or statement that things are so. But one cannot endorse, ridicule, dismiss, be amused by, or approve *that things are so*. So *knowing that things are so* is *not* an attitude towards a proposition.

6.   From the mid-twentieth century the idea that knowledge that things are so was analysable into justified true belief became popular among philosophers. A knows that *p* was held to be definable by the conjunction of 'A believes that *p*', 'It is true that *p*', and 'A is justified in believing that *p*'. A notorious objection to this analysis was formulated in 1963 by Edmund Gettier in a three-page article in which he argued that one might be justified, for example, in believing that it is 8:20 a.m., since one looked at the clock, which is normally reliable, the clock showed 8:20, and it was 8:20. But in fact the clock had stopped at 8:20 the previous night. So, Gettier argued, one's belief was true and justified, but since it was purely accidental, one could not be said to know the time. This led to hundreds of papers over the next seventy years that tried to add a condition to the tripartite analysis that would immunise it from a Gettier construction. Various conditions were essayed: for example, that one's belief was not accidental; that it was arrived at by a reliable process; that it was caused by the fact known; and so on. Few noted that the Gettier argument depended upon the idea that one may be justified in holding a false belief, or, more specifically, justified in holding a belief that would have been false but for an accident. But one may deny that assumption. For one could with at least as much warrant say that one's belief (that it was 8:20) appeared to be justified but actually was not (since the clock had stopped).

The deeper objection to the tripartite analysis was more straightforward. It is a checkmate in contrastive analysis, in accord with the principle: always examine the negation of any problematic claim. The negation of 'A knows that *p*' is not a tripartite disjunction of negations. If someone does not know that *p*, that does not imply that either it is false that *p* or that he does not believe that *p* or that he is not justified in believing that *p*. 'Jack does not know that today is my birthday', in typical contexts, implies that he lacks the information, *not* that either it is not my birthday or that Jack lacks a justification for believing that today is my birthday, or Jack does not believe that today is my birthday. (Indeed, 'Jack doesn't believe that Jill is forty today' would normally be taken to imply that Jack had been given the information but would not credit it.) In general, 'A does not know *that* things are so' defeasibly presupposes that things are so. Similarly, 'A does not know *whether* things are so' is normally rightly taken to imply that he is ignorant of the answer the question 'Are things so?'.

The relation of knowledge to justification has commonly been inflated. There are indefinitely many things we know to be so, even though we can give no justification for our belief. Most of what we know, we know on the authority of experts, teachers, books, and other sources of information from whom or which we learnt that things are so, although we no longer remember the sources (e.g. that the battle of Zama was fought in 202 BC; that whales are mammals; the inverse square law; that the capital of Japan is Tokyo; that smoking causes cancer). Some of what we have been taught may turn out to be false. So, in such cases, we thought we knew, but were mistaken. That is why credulity (being too quick to believe) is an epistemic vice and a modicum of scepticism and incredulity is an intellectual virtue.

Much of our knowledge is obtained by the use of our senses, unwarrantedly downgraded in the dominant epistemological tradition going back to the Greek conception of *episteme*. Our perceptual faculties *are* sources of knowledge, but *they are fallible*. To answer the question 'How do you know?' by saying 'I saw it' is not to give a *justification* for one's assertion that things are so, but to specify the source of one's knowledge. Perceptual knowledge is *evident to the senses*, not evidence from the senses, although someone who possesses perceptual knowledge may give evidence in a law court. Perceptual knowledge can often be validated by having another look, by improving observation conditions, by getting others to confirm or disconfirm one's observations. By the same token it is often defeasible, and what we thought we observed to be so may turn out only to have deceptively appeared to be so. Perceptual knowledge is fallible. But fallibility is part of the human condition.

7. There is a long tradition of associating knowledge with certainty. On some accounts, what is known must be objectively certain and indubitable. On others, the knower must be certain or sure, and have a right to be sure. Both are mistaken. Knowledge and certainty are independent.

It is mistaken to suppose, as Descartes did, that if we cannot *logically* doubt something to be so, then it follows for certain that it is so. It makes no sense to doubt whether one is in pain, whether one seems to perceive something, or indeed whether one doubts something. But it does not follow that one therefore knows with certainty that one is in pain, seems to perceive, or doubts. On the contrary, since the exclusion of doubt is logical, certainty is likewise excluded. For in these cases, there is no work for certainty to do, nothing for it to exclude, since the negation of what was perceived to be so is *already excluded* by logical grammar.

That one cannot in fact doubt something to be so is not a mark of indubitability, but only of one's subjective certainty or faith. For most of human history, people did not and could not bring themselves to doubt the existence of their god or gods. They were completely certain that God exists (or, more likely, that *their* god exists). But that does not imply that they knew for certain that God exists or that the existence of God was indubitable.

It is perfectly possible for someone to know something and to be unsure, indeed to doubt, whether he does. The examination candidate may be very unsure of himself and of his answers, but if he gets the answers right, then that shows that he knows the right answers. I may think I know the dates of the English monarchs but be unsure. If I rattle off the dates correctly, that shows that I do know.

Nevertheless, there is a modest truth lurking in the background. If one harbours doubts whether things are so, then one should not *claim to know* that they are so. *Absence of doubt*, which is not the same as presence of certainty, is a normative (rule-determined) condition for *claiming to know* something to be so. But it is not a condition of knowing something to be so. To assert something to be so, *a fortiori* to claim to know something to be so, is, in many contexts, to give one's word to another. It is to indicate to them that they can rely on what one says. To *say* 'Things are so, but I doubt whether they are' or 'I know things are so, but I'm not sure' is a solecism. It is akin to 'Take my word for it, but I wouldn't'.

8.   It is time to question the widespread assumption that the concept of knowledge, or even just the concept of propositional knowledge, can be explained by specification of a set of necessary and sufficient conditions for knowing something to be so. Rather, we should look to contextual, connective, and contrastive analysis to disabuse us of this illusion. Indeed, the analysis of knowledge is a paradigm case of the indispensability of contextual analysis. The pivotal question here is not: What is the essence of knowledge? but rather: Why do we need this expression? What would we lack if we had no such word? What needs does it fulfil in human thought and discourse?

We are, as previously noted, eyes and ears to each other. Information that one person lacks may be available to others. We may ask for information in many different ways: by means of sentence-questions ('Is it the case that …?') or by Wh-questions ('Where is …?', 'Who is …?', 'What is …?', etc.). Such answers to such questions do not require the verb 'to know', but only a declarative sentence the utterance of which answers the questions and imparts the information. It is when one *cannot* supply the requisite information that one needs the verb 'to know', together with the sign of negation, namely: 'I don't know'. Similarly, in the same interrogative contexts, there is need for qualifiers on assertions that things are so, namely: 'As far as I know, …' or 'To the best of my knowledge, …'. Like some uses of 'I think' or 'I believe', these qualifiers serve to indicate that the grounds for one's assertion of how things are, are less than optimal, not beyond dispute, and not completely reliable.

A quite different need is to question a person's word or to challenge his credentials for asserting things to be so, or to enquire how he came by the information that he possesses (perhaps one already knows what he asserts to be so, but it is meant to be secret or confidential). Hence the utility of 'How do you know?' as well as 'Why do you believe that?'. Inadequacy in reply in turn gives rise to the riposte, 'So you don't actually know!' or 'You should never have been told'.

A human society is a knowledge community. Needing information, or wishing to satisfy our curiosity, we must often find out whom to ask. Hence the utility of 'Do you know whether …?' or 'Does he know what (when, where, who, etc.)?' or more generally 'Who knows whether …?'. Here the role of 'know' is *to find out who can tell us*. Sometimes we may already possess the information in question, but we want to find out *whether someone else needs to be told*. So we ask, 'Does she know that …?' or 'Do you know that …?', which question presupposes that *we* know that things are so. In similar contexts of information transmission, we may start telling another something and he may interrupt us by saying 'I already know', that is, there is no need to tell me.

A quite different use, as we have already seen, is to express uncertainty as to whether one has got things right. Hence 'I think I know' and 'I believe I know', which are often tantamount to 'If I am right, then I know, but I may not be'. A further use is not to impart information, but to indicate that one has taken the information into account, as when one says, 'I know that things are so, but nevertheless I am going to do such-and-such.' Yet another first-person use is to forestall or repress doubt, as when one rummages in a drawer saying, 'I know I put it here!'

A paramount need for 'know' and its negation is in explaining, justifying, or excusing one's own behaviour and reactions as well as predicting and understanding the reasoning, reactions, responses, actions, and omissions of others. For possession of information implies that it can be taken into account in reasoning in pursuit of given goals, whereas ignorance may foreclose actions and responses, as well as explain and excuse omissions.

9. We can draw general conclusions from our survey. First, in accounting for the use of the verb 'to know' and its cognates, primacy should be given to the notion of possession of information, to being able to say or to tell how things are. Information is given in the form of declarative sentences stating how things are. To possess information is to be able to say how things are, to be able to inform others how things are, and to reason from how things are. It is to have the facts at one's disposal in thought and talk – what one can reason from and no longer needs to reason to.

Second, the primary rationale for the concept of knowledge turns on the fact that information is shareable and commonly shared, that a large part of the information we possess – the stock of knowledge that we have – is derived from others. Hence the paramount point and purpose of the verb 'to know' and its cognates lies in the quest for information and sources of information.

Third, given the multiplicity of roles of this cognitive verb and the variety of contexts in which it is called on to fulfil one or other of its functions, it is evident that what is presupposed by its use and what is demanded of its user will vary from context to context, speaker to speaker, and questioner to respondent. Hence the indispensability of contextual analysis. The evidential demands of courts of law, on the one hand, and of the scientific community, on the other, are very different from the demands on answers to requests for information concerning common cultural knowledge, on the one hand, and for passing on practical information and gossip in daily life, on the other. Furthermore, the requirements that have to be met for someone to be said to know something vary according to the information already possessed and known to be possessed by speaker and hearer. 'He already knows' will commonly forestall the need to tell him in numerous Gettier types of case – how he knows is simply irrelevant. (The fact that the clock in the hall stopped at 8:20 last night may simply be irrelevant, if, for example, he has a train to catch. Then it is perfectly correct to say, 'He already knows that it is getting on for 8:30 – you needn't tell him.')

Fourth, given human capacity-rationality (our ability to reason and to act for reasons), what another knows is pivotal for predicting, explaining, understanding, and justifying his action. This too supplies a shifting scale for the warranted application of the concept of knowledge. For often the only relevant factor for correct prediction and explanation is that the person under consideration has the right answer – not whether he has the right justification.

The idea that we might be able to give an analytic definition specifying necessary and sufficient conditions for someone to know something to be so is clearly chimerical – a residue from a bygone quest for *scientia*. What can be done is to give a context-sensitive analysis. This we have now done.

10.   Thus far, we have concentrated on knowing things to be so and knowing that things are so. Knowing what, when, where, and who (sometimes referred to as Wh-knowledge) are simply other forms of knowing things to be so. To know what happened is to know that such-and-such happened; to know when the next train is due is to know that it is due at such-and-such a time; to know where the keys are is to know that they are in such-and-such a place; to know who is in the garden is to know that so-and-so is in the garden. To know the colour, height, or weight of something is a variant on Wh-knowledge, since to know the colour of the sofa is to know what colour it is, just as to know the weight of the sofa is to know how heavy it is. However, it would be remiss not to examine the forms of practical knowledge that are central to our lives.

Among the various grammatical forms the verb 'to know' can assume is *knowing how to V*. Some cases of knowing how to do something are, in effect, just further forms of knowing that things are so. To know how to spell 'Edinburgh' is to know that it is spelled 'E-d-i-n-b-u-r-g-h'. To know how the late Queen was to be addressed was to know that she was to be addressed as 'Ma'am'. By contrast, to know how to ride a bicycle or a horse, how to swim or hang-glide, how to make shoes or jewellery, how to win battles or elections are not different forms of knowing that things are so.

It was Gilbert Ryle (1900–76), in *The Concept of Mind* (1949), who drew attention to the irreducibly practical nature of innumerable forms of knowing how to do things. Knowing-how, he held, is an autonomous form of knowledge – there is more to intelligence than intellect. Some philosophers, especially at Oxford, disagreed. It was argued that to know how to do something is to know the manner in which to perform a task and the means and method by which to succeed. It is to know that it is done *so* – which may be described or *demonstrated*. It was also claimed that to know how to V is to know of some way *w* of

V-ing, that *this way* is a way to V. Demonstration, it was again argued, is the key to reducing knowing-how to knowing-that. So practical knowledge is not a special kind of knowledge, but only knowledge of a special kind of thing. This dispute requires adjudication.

We must first disentangle the concepts of *being able to, having an ability to*, and *knowing how to*. One may be able to do something on an occasion (e.g. hit a bull's-eye), even though one lacks the ability – it was mere beginner's luck and cannot be repeated regularly. One may have the ability to do various things even though one cannot be said to know how to do them – for example, to blink, breathe, move one's limbs, to see distant things (if one has good eyesight), to hear faint sounds (if one has good hearing), to fall asleep at will. No know-how is involved in such cases. One may lose such abilities through accident or age, but one cannot *forget* how to do such things. By and large, one can be said to *know how* to V only where there are means and methods of V-ing, which one may learn by practice. Where learning the means and methods amounts to mastering a technique, the ability is a skill. Mastery of a technique commonly involves knowledge of maxims, principles, and precepts, but it is not reducible to such knowledge. To know the rules and principles of a practice is not equivalent to knowing how to engage in the practice.

It is misguided to conflate knowing how something is done with knowing how to do it. That one is able to point at a swimmer in the pool does not imply that one knows how to swim as may be patent when one falls in. Not only is demonstration (ostension) not sufficient for exemplifying knowing how to V, in innumerable cases no ostension is possible. To know how to win battles is not knowledge that can be *explained* demonstratively nor is it knowledge possession of which is proved by pointing at another's successful exemplification of such military prowess. One may study the principles of strategy in books, but it does not follow that one will know how to win battles. One may know the theory of a practice without knowing how to put the theory into practice. Knowing-how is not in general reducible to knowing-that. Both are indispensable for all forms of human life.

7

Belief

1.   The web of belief is ramified, connecting a multitude of nodes. One may indeed reason from what one knows to be so, but often we are in practice not so fortunate as to possess knowledge and we must base our reasoning and planning on what we believe. Similarly, whether we reason from what we know or from what we believe, the conclusions we come to may fall short of knowledge. They may be, and, in practical matters often are, no more than reasonable belief. It is reasonable to withhold belief from something we know to lack adequate support. So the concept of belief is interwoven with the notions of rationality, reasonableness, and grounds of judgement. Equally, the concept of belief is entwined with the concept of knowledge, as we saw in Essay 6. We argued there that knowledge that things are so is not to be analysed as 'belief plus something', but it is evident that in many cases, when knowledge claims fail, belief is 'knowledge minus something', being the default epistemic position. As we saw, one may know, but not believe that one does, and one may believe one knows, but be wrong. One may not know what to believe, which is a form of indecision, and one may not know what another believes, which is a form of ignorance.

Belief is primarily 'directed' at reality, at how things are, and only secondarily at how they are or might be said to be, viz. at the truth of

Solving, Resolving, and Dissolving Philosophical Problems: Essays in Connective, Contrastive and Contextual Analysis, First Edition. P. M. S. Hacker.

propositions and other sayables. One's belief is correct if things are as one believes them to be, incorrect if they are not. Being correct (right) or incorrect (wrong) are the primary 'values 'of believing something, as being true or false are the primary 'values' of sayables. But, to be sure, beliefs too may be true or false. Truth and falsehood are not *truth-values*, they are *truth-possibilities*. Truth and falsehood are not objects of any kind, they are not values of functions for arguments, and they are not the meanings (*Bedeutungen*) of sentences (as Gottlob Frege (1848–1925) supposed them to be).

2. To find our bearings before we commence, some logico-grammatical analysis is needed. Like many other psychological verbs (e.g. 'thinks', 'assumes', 'hopes', 'fears', 'suspects', 'expects') that take nominal clauses ('that things are so') as their grammatical objects, so too 'believes' yields a Janus-faced nominal, namely: 'belief' (logically comparable to 'thought', 'assumption', 'hope', 'fear', 'suspicion', 'expectation'). These nominals make it possible to refer concisely to the belief that A and B have in common when they both believe that *p*, to the thought they both share when they both think that *p*, and to the assumption they both make when they both assume that *p*, and so forth. It also enables us to speak of possible beliefs even though no one has them, of suspicions that might have been raised but weren't, and of assumptions that might have been made had anyone thought of them. The grammatical convenience is bought at the price of a systematic ambiguity which has caught many a philosopher on its prongs. Whenever A's belief is in focus it is necessary to establish whether the subject is *A's believing* (which may be wise or foolish, reasonable or unreasonable, rational or irrational, typical, fervent, passionate, whole-hearted – since it may be wise or foolish, reasonable or unreasonable *to believe* that p) or whether it is *what A believes* (which may be true or false, possible or probable – since it may be true or false, possible or probable *that p*). Note that the qualifying adverb 'truly' in 'A believes truly that p' is misleading (unlike the adverbs 'fervently' and 'passionately'), since what is true is not the believing but what is believed, whereas when one believes fervently or passionately, what is fervent or passionate is the believing. This differentiation between the two faces of belief is essential if one is to avoid falling into the trap of arguing that the concept of belief is, as was supposed by an eminent twentieth-century philosopher Donald Davidson (1917–2003), 'the concept of the state of an organism which can be true or false, correct or incorrect'. But this is doubly wrong. First, what can be true or false is what

can be advanced, asserted, stated, claimed, supposed, or conjectured, that is to say: nothing mental or neural, in particular not a mental state or state of an organism but rather *what is believed*. Secondly, as we shall see, *believing something to be so* is not a mental state.

Belief is *essentially individuated* by its content, that is: by its nominalization-accusative ('that *p*'), which answers the question, 'What do you believe?'. It is *externally individuated* by circumstances of believing, for example, the belief acquired on such-and-such an occasion or imparted by so-and-so. It is *internally related* to what makes it true – namely: things being as they are believed to be. Contrary to widespread metaphysical doctrine derived from Wittgenstein's *Tractatus Logico-Philosophicus*, this internal relation is not a word/world relation between belief and a so-called 'truth-maker'. There is no such thing as a 'truth-maker'; in particular, facts are not truth-makers. For facts are not items 'in the world' (and the world does not consist of facts, rather true descriptions of the world are statements of fact). Facts are not *items* of any kind, and they have no spatio-temporal location. The Battle of Hastings was fought in 1066 in Hastings, but the fact that it was fought in 1066 in Hastings is neither in 1066 nor in Hastings. Nor is it anywhere else. Rather, the Battle of Hastings was *in fact, as a matter of fact, actually*, fought in Hastings in 1066. Facts are simply *what is given* – what may be argued from and need not be argued to (and that includes such facts as the wickedness of torturing children). It is correct to say that the belief that *p* is made true by the fact that *p*, but all that means is that the phrase 'the belief that *p*' and the phrase 'the belief that is made true by the fact that *p*' are two different ways of referring to one and the same belief. That is the way with all metaphysics – it dissolves in the acid of grammar.

3. It is tempting to agree with the distinguished twentieth-century philosopher Bernard Williams (1929–2003) that belief is directed at the truth: 'to believe that *p* is to believe that it is true that *p*'. Since it is *sayables*, including propositions, that are true or false, the objects of belief would then seem to be propositions. The temptation should be resisted. What one believes when one believes that things are so is precisely *that things are so*. What one believes when one believes something to be true is a proposition, statement, assertion, declaration, allegation, or announcement to the effect that things are so. These can be believed *or disbelieved*. One can disbelieve, misunderstand, or mistrust the statement, declaration, or allegation that things

are so, but one cannot disbelieve, misunderstand, or mistrust *that things are so.*

A further consideration often invoked to support the idea that what one believes when one believes that *p* is a proposition is the claim that belief is a propositional attitude (Russell, Frank Ramsey (1903–30). But that is mistaken. For, as we have seen in Essay 6, genuine propositional attitude verbs, such as 'approve', 'endorse', 'dismiss', take nouns signifying sayables, such as statements, declarations, announcements, rumours, as their grammatical objects. They do not take noun clauses of the form 'that *p*' as their grammatical object – one cannot approve, endorse, or dismiss *that things are so*. But one believes *that things are so.* So belief is not a propositional attitude.

A clinching argument against the supposition that what one believes when one believes that things are so is a proposition is that what A believes to be so may be what B hopes to be so, what C fears is so, and what D supposes will be so, but one cannot hope, fear, or suppose the proposition that *p*. The Wh-pronoun 'what' in this context is an interrogative pronoun, not a relative one.

Belief is first and foremost directed at what is so, and only secondarily at what is said to be so – that is to say, at propositions, assertions, statements, declarations. To be sure, one's beliefs are *expressed* by propositions, assertions, statements, and similar sayables. It does not follow that what we believe when we believe that things are so *is* a proposition.

Of course, in expressing one's belief, one may be saying something true. But that is no reason for thinking that what we believe when we believe that *p* is a proposition or other true or false sayable. For to say of an expression of belief that it is true is simply to affirm it ('Things are so' – 'True'/ 'True enough' / 'Indeed they are'). It does not follow from the truth-ascription that what one believes when one believes that things are so is a proposition.

4.　To obtain a distinct idea of belief we must engage in connective, contrastive, and contextual analysis. Believing something to be so and thinking something to be so run along parallel tracks for a short while. Both verbs can be used in the first person to qualify the strength of an assertion when one's supporting grounds are less than adequate. Like 'As far as I know' and 'To the best of my knowledge', 'I believe that things are so' and 'I think that things are so' are commonly used to indicate to one's addressee that one cannot give one's word that things are so. They signify that the nominal-accusative that follows falls short of the knowledge that would be expressed by the simple assertion 'Things are thus-and-so'. Both 'think' and 'believe' have a role in expressions of moral commitment (e.g. 'I believe that justice should override utility') in aesthetic judgements on essentially contested matters, and in commenting on things that are matters of taste ('I think the dessert was better than the main course'). Hence their prominent role in predictions, in judgements about what policy should be adopted, and in giving advice. There is another usage in which the two concepts diverge markedly. In certain contexts, 'I believe' converges on 'I gather' and is used to indicate second-hand information – as in 'I believe your roses are beautiful this year'. By contrast, having looked at your rose beds, I may say 'I think your roses are spectacular' – which is an expression of opinion based on personal observation rather than hearsay. This usage of 'I think' is far removed from the qualifying role described above: one could not here add 'but I may be wrong' ('I think you are very good looking, but I may be mistaken' would not go down very well.) In general, the concepts of believing and of thinking diverge radically: one can think, but not believe, quickly or slowly; one can ask what someone is thinking, but not what he is believing; one may be sunk in thought, but not in belief; one may be interrupted in the middle of thinking, but not in the middle of believing; one can believe people and their assertions, but one cannot think people and their assertions.

The nexus of belief, certainty, and doubt is noteworthy. Since we often have, or should have, reasons for believing what we believe, our supporting reasons may make us certain that things are as we believe them to be. One may believe with certainty, or one may believe without being certain. But one cannot believe things to be so and simultaneously doubt whether they are so, that is, be *uncertain* whether they are. 'He believes that the next train is at 12:30, but he doubts (is uncertain) whether it is' is awry. That one is *not certain* does not imply that one is *uncertain*. If one is uncertain whether things are so, then one doubts whether they are, and if one doubts whether things are so one cannot also believe that they are. As we have seen in Essay 6, knowledge here differs from belief: one can know something despite being uncertain, as is evident from the nervous examinee who may doubt whether he has got things right, just as one may doubt whether one knows the dates of the English monarchs. But if the correct answer is forthcoming, one can be said to know despite one's uncertainty. As we showed, it is the sincere *claim* to know that is incompatible with uncertainty, for one should not aver things to be so if one harbours doubts.

It is common for philosophers, psychologists, economists, and theologians to speak of degrees of belief, ranging from the total certainty of unshakeable conviction to the thinnest of suspicions. Economists associate degrees of belief with degrees of probability (and hence with betting quotients), and theologians link degrees of belief (faith) with degrees of feeling. This is mistaken. To believe that something is possible, probable, or certain is not to enjoy different degrees of belief. To believe that it is possible that things are so is not to *believe weakly* that they are so, nor is it to have *a lesser degree of belief* than if one believes it probable that things are so. If I believe that it is certain that *e* will occur and you believe that *e* is only probable, it does not follow that I have more belief than you. One may feel sure, certain, or convinced that things are so, but one cannot *feel belief* that they are. After a long discussion I may feel more convinced that things are so, but I will not feel *more belief*. Degrees of conviction are not degrees of belief. To be sure, a belief may be strong and firm, or tentative, wavering, and half-hearted. These are not degrees of belief, but degrees of tenacity with which one cleaves to a belief. A belief may be entrenched, but an entrenched belief is not greater than an unentrenched one, only less readily surrendered.

5.   It is tempting to suppose that to believe is a mental act. Both Descartes in the seventeenth century and Thomas Reid in the eighteenth held this categorial view. Accordingly, it is a voluntary act of affirmation or denial, and we are at liberty to give or withhold our assent in judgement. Believing, they thought, is something for which we can and should be held responsible.

There are indeed affinities between believing a person and his story, on the one hand, and doing something, on the other.

(i)   We can ask someone to believe a person and his story just as we can ask someone to do something. We can urge someone to believe something, and we can warn another not to believe someone. While we cannot ask someone to want, mean, or intend something, since wanting, meaning, and intending are not actions, we can and do say such things as 'Believe me!' or 'Please believe my story!', just as we may order someone 'Don't believe him, he is an inveterate liar!' or 'Don't trust a word she says!'.

(ii)   We speak of it being easy or difficult to believe someone and their story ('I can well believe it' or 'I find it difficult to believe that'), just as we speak of it being easy or difficult to do something.

(iii) It seems that believing can be voluntary or involuntary, for we say such things as 'I refuse to believe him', 'I couldn't help believing her', and 'I am unwilling to believe that!'.

(iv) We give reasons for believing, for refusing to believe, and for being unable to believe someone or something, just as we give reasons for doing, for refraining from doing, and for being unable to do something.

(v) We hold people responsible for (some of) their beliefs, as we hold them responsible for their deeds: 'It's all your fault', we may say, 'You should never have believed him', or 'You should know better than to believe such tosh!'.

Nonetheless, believing someone or something is *not* a mental act. This can easily be shown by one form of contextual analysis, namely: logico-grammatical discourse analysis.

(i') 'Believe me!' and 'Believe this!' look like orders or requests to *do* something, but they are not. For one cannot reply, 'Not now, but I'll do it tomorrow morning'. Nor can the speaker follow up his entreaty by saying 'Well, have you done it?', but only 'Well, do you?'.

(ii') One cannot plan to believe something or intend to believe someone before lunch. One cannot excuse one's failure to believe something by saying that one forgot to do so. One cannot believe something accidentally, inadvertently, or on purpose; and although one's belief may be mistaken, one cannot believe something by mistake. One may wish one could believe someone or something, but one cannot excuse one's failure by saying that one tried one's best.

(iii') 'How can you (or 'How could you') believe that?' *looks like* a request for an explanation of how one does or did something, it is not. For the possible answers do not specify ways and means of believing or ways of bringing it off. Rather, we give reasons for believing that make what we believe plausible, or we explain that we did not know something that makes what we believe implausible.

(iv') 'I find it hard to believe that' does not mean that it is too difficult for me to do, nor can one reply like the Red Queen, 'You need more practice'. It means that the reasons against the proposal are weighty and that I cannot explain them away.

Responsibility for our beliefs needs more extensive scrutiny.

6.   We do hold people responsible for their beliefs, and we sometimes praise or blame them accordingly. We are, sometimes, ashamed of believing something that on reflection we should not have accepted, credited, endorsed, or subscribed to. How can this be? To clarify this, we need to reflect on what exactly is meant by 'being responsible for believing', on the contexts in which we hold people responsible for their beliefs, and on the kinds of belief for which we hold someone responsible.

The core of the family of notions of responsibility is, as etymology suggests, the idea of *being answerable*. In avowing or averring a belief, one lays oneself open to the question, 'Why do you believe that?'. This is a demand for reasons. Not all our beliefs are supported by reasons. Many such beliefs are none the worse for that. Some, discussed by Wittgenstein in his *On Certainty*, are such that there could be no supporting reasons, for example, our belief that the earth has existed for a long time (any supporting reason will presuppose what it is meant to support). Others are such that we have long forgotten their authoritative source (e.g. that the Battle of Hastings was fought in 1066, or that e = mc^2). Many rest on the exercise of fallible cognitive faculties, namely our perceptual senses, and are normally none the worse for that. For all that, no one can intelligibly avow a belief that he admits is *contrary* to reason. 'I believe that Aliens are out to get me, but I know it isn't true' makes no sense. One can be saddled with self-acknowledged irrational desires, but one cannot be saddled with self-confessed irrational beliefs, since to recognize that everything speaks against it is already to cease to believe it. One is then left with a haunting, obsessive thought, a delusion or fantasy, but not a belief.

Responsibility for one's beliefs is a corollary of the rational powers of a language-user, of the ability to reason, to give reasons, and to act for reasons, to demand reasons, and to understand behaviour done for reasons. One is subject to criticism if the reasons one offers for one's belief fail to support it, if one insists on the adequacy of one's belief despite knowing and understanding the overwhelming reasons to the contrary. Harbouring such beliefs makes one less than rational or reasonable – which we all often are. It does not yet make one culpable, blameworthy, or wicked. One is answerable for one's beliefs when failure to believe what one should have believed or failure to disbelieve what one should have disbelieved has deleterious consequences in one's attitudes, in one's actions and omissions. For here lie the roots of bigotry, prejudice, and dogmatism. The bigot ascribes features allegedly true of some members of a class to all members of the class. The prejudiced are unwilling to consider or reconsider countervailing evidence to their beliefs and opinions. The dogmatist harbours ill-grounded beliefs and is impervious to counter-argument. Here one is open to criticism for accepting, crediting, and endorsing something without adequate reflection, without demanding evidence or without critically examining the evidence on offer. One is culpable for allowing one's biases to dominate one's reasoning, for permitting one's material interests to sway one's judgement on matters that demand disinterest, for being precipitate in judgement, for not asking probing questions and demanding good supporting reasons.

Being responsible for one's beliefs is perfectly compatible with one's believing not being an act and with its not being either voluntary or involuntary, as acts may be. It is an essential part of human rationality and autonomy. Other animals may be said to think and believe in a very limited sense accessible to non-language users, but they are not held responsible for what they think or believe.

7.   The overwhelming majority of late twentieth-century and contemporary philosophers and psychologists assert that believing is a mental state or state of mind. This is a view held by such distinguished philosophers as H. H. Price (1899–1984), Bernard Williams, Donald Davidson, John Searle (b. 1932), and Joseph Raz (1939–2022). It is not supported by argument but taken for granted. It is clearly misguided to suppose that a mental state and state of mind are equivalent. States of mind converge on frames of mind, mental states do not. There are ten marks of mental states. One can be *in* them, but one cannot *possess* them. They obtain during periods of waking. They are states of consciousness, that is, they cease with loss of consciousness (we don't continue to feel cheerful when we fall asleep). They are interruptible by distraction of attention (as when our state of intense concentration is interrupted by a telephone call). They can be resumed after interruption (as when we resume concentrating on the task at hand). They may have more or less determinate beginnings and termini (one may have been rendered acutely anxious by the dire report on the one o'clock news, which may be abated upon hearing that one's family is safe). They admit of degrees of intensity. They may wax and wane. They have distinctive forms of facial expression, mien,

and tone of voice. A noun signifying a mental state commonly has an adjectival form which goes with the verb 'feel' ('feels frightened', 'is feeling cheerful', 'has been feeling anxious').

It is patent that there is no such thing as a state of believing or mental state of belief, any more than there is such a thing a mental state of knowing (see Essay 6). One cannot answer the question 'What sort of state is Jill in today?' by replying, 'She is in a state of believing that Jack is coming'. One may be feeling depressed, cheerful, or joyful, but one cannot feel belief-ful. Of course, one may feel that things are so, that is, have a presentiment. But to have a presentiment that things are so is not to believe that things are so, rather: that things are so is what one is *inclined to believe* without determinate grounds. To be sure, one may come to believe something at a given time (e.g. when told that things are so) and cease to believe when one finds out the truth of the matter. But being told that things are so does not put one into a state of believing, rather: it indexes the acquisition of a specific belief. Believing something to be so is not a state of consciousness – one does not cease to believe whatever one believes when one falls asleep in the way in which one ceases to feel despondent or cheerful when one falls asleep. One's beliefs can no more be interrupted by distraction of attention and later resumed than can one's knowledge. It may be hard to believe something, but that does not mean that it is hard to get oneself into a certain state of mind (as it is hard to feel cheerful in the face of adversity) – it means that it is difficult to explain away the countervailing evidence.

To be sure, this is perfectly compatible with disbelief, like incredulity, sometimes being a state. In this respect, disbelief is analogous to ignorance (see Essay 6). For the *absence* of something, namely belief, may be a state of a human being even though believing something to be so is not a state.

8. As a last categorial resort, behaviourist-minded philosophers may suggest that believing something to be so is *a disposition to behave*. But they will doubtless note that the belief that things are so (e.g. that it is going to rain) may be the grounds for a variety of acts (e.g. not going out, going out with an umbrella, putting on a raincoat, bring in the washing, not taking the washing out, cancelling a garden party). So they may aver that belief is *a multitrack disposition*.

But this is mistaken. An inanimate disposition is a tendency or proneness. But apart from dispositions of health, a human disposition is a character trait. Believing something to be so, unlike gullibility and credulity, is not a character trait. So it is not a disposition in that sense. So, is the concept of believing something to be so a multitrack *tendency concept*? That too is mistaken. Tendencies and pronenesses are individuated by what they are tendencies or pronenesses *to do*. Beliefs are essentially individuated by their content. Dispositions (that are not character traits) and tendencies are frequency concepts, but believing that things are so signifies no behavioural frequency. Different people may share the same belief, but it does not follow that they have common behavioural tendencies. What they do depends upon their respective personalities, their situations, goals, and purposes. We often explain a person's behaviour by reference to his belief, but that is to give its rationale, which is altogether unlike citing a habit or behavioural tendency. One may believe something for a few moments (e.g. until one realizes that what was said was a joke), but one cannot have a tendency or proneness for a few moments. 'I believe that things are so, but they are not' is a kind of contradiction, but 'I tend to behave as if things are so, but they aren't' is no contradiction at all. Finally, if A believes that things are so, then he is either right or wrong, but while a behavioural tendency may be beneficial or detrimental, it cannot be right or wrong, correct or incorrect.

9.   Finally, we are now in a position to confront the question of the relation between knowledge and belief that was left hanging in the previous essay. We sometimes say, 'I don't believe it, I know it!' Is this like 'It isn't large, its huge'? that is, 'I not only believe it, I know it', or is it like 'I don't remember it, he told me'? that is, 'I don't believe it, but I know it'?

It is evident from our investigations that the two concepts belong to two very different conceptual networks (or 'semantic fields'). Knowledge is linked to observing, finding out, and discovering; with the upshot of reflecting; with becoming and being aware that things are so, and with realizing, noticing, being conscious of, and recognizing how things are (forms of cognitive receptivity). It is bound up with learning how things are, with proof and evidence. To learn how things are is to acquire information. To know how things are is to possess information. If one knows how things are one can correctly answer questions concerning how things are, transmit the information that things are so, reason from things being so, and act for the reason that things are so. Knowledge is linked with remembering, since knowledge retained is information previously possessed and not forgotten.

Believing that things are so, by contrast, is embedded in a very different circle of concepts, none of which exclude things not being so. Whereas to believe something to be so is to be either right or wrong, to know something to be so is to be right. Believing things to be so has kinship with thinking, opining, and judging, with gathering things to be so, with trusting another and relying on his word, with subscribing and endorsing the claim that things are so, with taking a stand on how things are. We ask, 'Why do you believe?' but not in the same sense, 'Why do you know?' We ask, 'How do you know?' but not 'How do you believe?' One can try to acquire knowledge of whether things are so, but one cannot try to acquire belief that things are so. 'I believe' is an expression of belief, but 'I know' is not an expression of knowledge, for sincerely saying 'I know that things are thus-and-so' does not imply that I do. One can know for certain, but one cannot believe for certain. 'I don't know whether' is a confession of ignorance, but there is no such thing as not believing whether.

So, is believing a constant accompaniment of knowing, that is, whenever A knows something to be so, does he also believe it to be so? It is true that there is no use for the sentence 'I know it is so, but I don't believe it' (unlike 'I know it is so, but I *can't* believe it'). But that may be because in many cases of knowing something to be so, the question of believing does not or cannot arise.

It is also true that if someone claims that things are so and they are not, then he believes, falsely, that things are so. So false belief seems to be knowledge minus truth. Does it not follow that knowledge is belief plus truth (and whatever other conditions are deemed fit)? No; as we have seen, this is fanciful conceptual arithmetic. (Hallucination is things sensibly, subjectively, seeming to be so, even though they are not; but perceiving things to be so is not things subjectively seeming to be so plus things being so.)

We have made it clear that the concept of believing things to be so is a multi-purpose instrument. As we have seen, it straddles (i) asserting something to be so with qualification; (ii) opining; (iii) gathering or taking things to be so; (iv) trusting another, accepting his word, and relying on it; (v) subscribing or endorsing the proposition that things are so; and (vi) taking a stand on things being so. Which use or uses of this multi-purpose instrument is involved in any given occasion depends on what is believed, what the speaker or hearer knows or assumes, and the context of utterance. There seems little prospect that in all cases of knowing things to be, one or another of these doxastic uses is involved.

There are many things one knows with respect to which the question of whether one believes them cannot arise. I look out of the window, turn around and say, 'It is a sunny day'. Obviously, this is something I know – I just looked out of the window and there was not a cloud to be seen in the blue sky. Do I believe what I just said? What a bizarre question! My utterance was not a qualified assertion, but an unqualified assertion expressing a knowledge claim. I was not voicing an opinion. It is not something I have gathered from others – I can see that it is a sunny day. I am not taking a stand on anything, just making a casual remark. Of course, it would be misguided, indeed unintelligible, for me to say that I don't believe what I just said. For that would suggest that I *disbelieve* my own statement, and I certainly don't disbelieve it, I know it to be true. Were someone to ask, 'Do you believe that?', I should not know what he meant. Were someone to say of me in these circumstances, 'He believes it is a sunny day?', he would not be understood. There are innumerable contexts in which adding a belief-operator would be mistaken – not false, but unintelligible.

Of course, we do sometimes say "I don't *believe* it, I know it to be so'; but on other occasions, 'I don't *just* believe it, I *know* it to be so'. How can this be? Denial of belief in the first utterance is tantamount to denying that what follows is the expression of *opinion* or unconfirmed *supposition*. The second, by contrast, signifies that I am not only *taking a stand* on things being so, but I am doing so advisedly – I *know* that things are so. The different utterances focus on different facets of belief. Similarly, if I rightly assert things to be so (make a knowledge claim) and am asked 'Do you believe that?', that would normally be a request for me to *underwrite* what I said, to which I should, of course, reply 'Yes'. From case to case and context to context, when we raise the question of whether someone believes what he said, we need to know whether his utterance that things are so is an expression of opinion, a qualified assertion that cannot be relied on, an endorsement, the taking of a principled stand, and so on.

It follows that the question 'Does knowledge imply belief?' is a bad question. The answer is neither 'yes' nor 'no' – for both are misleading. The better question is 'How is knowledge related to belief?' – and we have now investigated that question thoroughly by connective and contrastive analysis, categorial elucidation, and contextual discourse analysis.

8

Memory

> "Memory, of all the powers of the mind is the most delicate and frail."
> Ben Jonson

1.   Without an articulate memory, we should be like other animals. We should have an awareness of what is present to our perceptual faculties; we should possess recognitional abilities; command a limited range of knowledge of how to do various things, and an array of inarticulate expectations or anticipations consequent on past experience. Non-human animals possess intelligence of varying degrees and forms characteristic of their species and its environmental adaptation, but they have no concept of the past. That is why a herd of zebra, one of whom is taken down by a lioness, will be found grazing placidly fifteen minutes later (as soon as the adrenalin has dissipated) in full view of the lions who are still gorging themselves. They do not remember, there is no such thing as their remembering, that one of the herd was killed a short time ago (let alone fifteen minutes ago). For what, no matter whether inner or outer, could *count* as a zebra's remembering this? Lacking articulate memory, mere animals, in this sense, do not live in time. If, as Wittgenstein averred in the *Tractatus*, we take eternity to mean not infinite temporal duration but timelessness, then eternal life belongs to those who live in the present. In that sense, non-language-using animals, unlike us, enjoy eternal life.

Solving, Resolving, and Dissolving Philosophical Problems: Essays in Connective, Contrastive and Contextual Analysis, First Edition. P. M. S. Hacker.
© 2025 John Wiley & Sons Ltd. Published 2025 by John Wiley & Sons Ltd.

An articulate memory is the prerogative of language-users. Other animals, to be sure, use signs but in their natural environment they do not master the use of symbols – meaningful words employed in the performance of acts of speech and discourse. Human beings learn *what is past* as well as *what the past is* by learning to answer past-tensed questions ('Did you do that?', 'Who did it?', 'When did it happen?'), to use past-tensed sentences in relating what they have been doing and what they have or have not done ('Look at what I have done!'; 'I didn't do it'), to relate what others have done ('He did it'), and to respond to questions not only with 'I don't know' but also with 'I don't remember'. It is precisely because we are language users that we have been able to free ourselves from the limitations of animal transmission of knowledge by mere emulation and evolution by natural selection. For we pass on, from one generation to another, a huge fund of common knowledge and expertise.

Amnesiacs apart, we have a powerful mnemonic sense of our own identity, of our past experiences, of our childhood, our parents and siblings, of our determining social associations, acquaintances and friendships, of shared experiences, of our likes and dislikes, of our customs and habits. It is because of possession of an articulate memory that we have the joys and griefs of recollection and of shared reminiscence. Our memories are the repository of our culture and cultural traditions, and constitutive of the institutional memory of social organizations.

Without mnemonic powers we should not be moral agents, answerable for our deeds, and taking responsibility for our acts and omissions. Could we not recollect what we have done, we should not feel guilt and remorse for our misdeeds, satisfaction at having done our duty in the face of adversity or take pride in our achievements.

Given the centrality of memory to human nature, moral agency, and personal responsibility, it is small wonder that philosophers have spent much time investigating the nature of this cognitive faculty. Its conceptual character, however, is formidably difficult to survey and its characteristic nature is surprisingly elusive. As we shall see, false theories and incorrect conjectures litter the pathways down which philosophers, psychologists, and cognitive neuroscientists have ventured in their quest for an overview of memory.

2.   Throughout the history of European thought, it has proved surprisingly difficult to pin down exactly what memory is. Aristotle declared that the object of memory is the past. Cicero, rightly

distinguishing between the faculty of memory and its exercise, held that memory is the faculty by which the mind recalls the past. Both are misleading – although all knowledge of the past is memory, not all memory is knowledge of the past. To remember the Pythagorean theorem, the laws of gravity, the time of next week's party, how to fly an aeroplane, is not knowledge of the past. So too, although it is important to distinguish the faculty of memory from its exercise in recollection, it is mistaken to suppose that it is the mind that remembers. It is the human being that remembers.

Thinkers in the early modern era did not fare better. Locke averred that memory is the power to revive ideas the mind has once had, coupled with the apprehension that it has had those very ideas before. Leibniz agreed: memory is the recurrence of a prior perception in the absence of the object perceived, while knowing that one has had that perception before. Hume claimed that ideas of memory are fainter reproductions of antecedent impressions, the mark of pastness being their relative vivacity by comparison with ideas of the imagination. William James argued that memory proper is knowledge of an event or fact of which we have not been thinking, with consciousness that we have thought or experienced it before. Russell followed suit, holding that when we remember, the knowing is now, while what is known is past. It is evident that philosophers were in the grip of the thought that memory essentially involves the *recurrence* of a perception, idea, or experience, *coupled with the awareness that one has had it previously*. The fundamental problem for the philosophy of memory seemed to be: *what is the mark of pastness that attends ideas of memory?* We shall explore this mesmerizing notion in this essay.

Scientists, who turned to the subject of memory, discovered a mass of experimental data of great value. But when it came to the characterization of memory, they added little more than confusion. They proposed a distinction between two kinds of memory: short-term memory and long-term memory, since different parts of the brain are implicated in each. But these are not *kinds* of memory at all, any more than short and long pieces of string are different kinds of string. They are degrees of temporal retention of knowledge acquired. This distinction is indeed of pivotal importance. Neuroscientists distinguish between declarative and non-declarative memory. The former, they declare, is what is ordinarily meant by the term 'memory': it is 'propositional' and is involved in modelling the external world and storing representations about facts and episodes. The latter, non-declarative memory, they write, is concerned with retention of motor skills (such as driving a car) and is also exhibited in classical conditioning and sensitization, that is, strengthening of a reflex response. However, research on reflex reactions of sea slugs (for which a Nobel prize on memory was awarded) is not on memory at all, for changes in reflex reaction speed do not manifest retention of knowledge of any kind or of an acquired skill (know-how). To test changes in a person's blinking in response to puffs of air blown into his eyes is not a test of his mnemonic powers. Declarative memory, that is, remembering that such-and-such is the case, is not involved in 'modelling the external world', since remembering that Hastings was fought in 1066, that $25^2 = 625$ or that my dental appointment is for next Wednesday models nothing. Most importantly, this distinction fails to discriminate between forms of memory that presuppose mastery of a language and those that do not. But it is that which is pivotal for all that makes us human.

3.   These unfortunate mischaracterizations of what memory is and of what it is to remember were accompanied by a plethora of generalizations. Some contemporary philosophers hold that philosophy is nothing but theories, that generalizations made by philosophers are not in principle different from generalizations in the natural sciences – both are answers to questions. To be sure, if someone wishes to use the term 'theory' to encompass all answers to questions, they may do so. But then they will have to introduce a new term to distinguish between a simple answer to a simple question, such as 'What is your name?', a detective's conjecture as to 'who dunnit?', and scientific theories such as the theory of gravity, of general relativity, of evolution, or of electricity. There is nothing to be gained from this innovation other than the blurring of boundaries and the loss of distinctions.

Philosophers and scientists alike have made numerous questionable generalizations about memory throughout the ages. It has been claimed that to remember is to have learnt and not forgotten. To be sure, that does not look like anything as august as a theory but is merely a stab in the dark in the quest for an illuminating characterization. Little reflection is needed to see that while it fits many uses of 'remember', it does not fit all. I remember my childhood, but I never learnt it. I remember my grandparents, but I did not learn them or their features and behaviour. Another claim (theory?) has been that to remember is to retain information previously acquired. This too fits many cases, but not all. To remember how greatly I enjoyed seeing Callas sing in *Tosca* is not to retain information acquired but to recollect an experience. A third claim (theory?) is that to remember is to know now something one knew previously and to know it now *because* one knew it previously. But this too, while it fits some cases, does not fit all. To remember one's joys and griefs, to remember one's youth, to remember that one had a headache yesterday, are not cases of knowing now something one knew previously. Moreover, as we shall see, the 'because' here is not a causal 'because'.

The theory-mongering does not stop there. The faculty of memory is held to be a store of knowledge. Nobel prize winning neuroscientists have allegedly demonstrated that memories are stored at synaptic connections. But while one may store what one remembers in a notebook, on a card index, or type it into one's computer, there is no such thing as storing a memory at a synaptic connection. Many forms of memory involve retention of information, but to retain information is not to store anything – it is *to be able to do* a diffuse range of things: to answer questions correctly, to correct others' errors, to act on the information one possesses, and so forth. One can store memories only if they are expressed in some medium and there is no medium for the expression of information that can be stored at synaptic connections.

A further 'theory': it is widely held that the brain is the organ of memory and that memories are stored in the brain. But while it is true that one would remember nothing but for the normal functioning of certain parts of one's brain, one does not remember anything by using them as one walks by using one's legs (the organs of locomotion), looks by using one's eyes (the organs of vision), and listens by using one's ears (the organs of hearing). In *that* sense, there is no organ for remembering. So where are one's memories if they are not in one's brain? Why should they be anywhere? *Roughly* speaking, *what* one remembers is information previously acquired. As was shown in Essay 7, to possess information is *to be able* to do a diffuse variety of things – it is, like all knowledge, more akin to potentiality than to actuality, and abilities and potentialities *have no location* – the horse-power of the car is not to be found under the bonnet. You can ask where I remembered such-and-such. The answer will specify where I was when I recollected it. But the question 'Where do you retain your memories?' is as meaningless as 'Where do you retain your ability to drive a car (to hit a bull's-eye; to solve crossword puzzles)?

The lesson from this brief survey is simple. A historical overview is of great importance. We can glean great insights from past thinkers. Modifying a famous remark of Paul Valery's, we might say that a mistake is a light; a great mistake is a sun. We can also learn from the mistakes of past philosophers, and even more from digging down to

disclose the roots of their errors in their unchallenged presuppositions. But when we come to engage in our own conceptual elucidation,
we should wipe the board clean. We should start from scratch. What
is scratch? It is connective and contrastive analysis of the use of the
words 'remember', 'memory' and their cognates. That provides the
raw material from which we can extract a conceptual overview.

4. The objects of memory are, unsurprisingly, as varied as the objects
of knowledge. They are disclosed by grammar. One may remember N,
where 'N' is a proper name or definite description (people, places,
things, colours, smells, tastes). One may remember e, where 'e' is an
event- or act-designation (events, actions and reactions of others), as one
may remember the F-ness of N or of A's V-ing (the modes of things and
characteristics of actions or events). One may remember that p (how
things were, are, will be, are omni-temporally or atemporally). One may
remember the proposition, story or rumour that p (something said or
sayable). One may remember that the proposition that p is true/ is false
(the truth or falsity of a sayable). One may remember what one learnt or
learnt by heart (facts, verses, melodies, tables, lists), as one may remember languages and how to speak them. One may remember V-ing or
being V-ed (what one did, experienced or underwent). One may remember the answers to Wh-questions and one may remember how to V
(previously acquired skills and know-how). And one may remember to
V (acts, actions, activities, and omissions called for). This should disabuse us of the supposition that memory is essentially 'of the past'. Why
did so many philosophers take for granted that memory is essentially of
the past? Because they failed to distinguish *when they acquired* whatever specific memory they possess from *what they remember*. *All
memory is acquired* in *the past, but not all memory is* of *the past.*

5. We must distinguish between memory qua remembering and
memory qua what is remembered, parallel to distinguishing between
knowing and what is known. 'My memory is getting weaker these
days' stands in contrast to 'My memory is that he came on a Thursday'.
   Similarly, we must distinguish between

  (i) the faculty of memory
 (ii) the retention of acquired knowledge and the ability to call to
       mind past experiences
(iii) the actualization of these abilities when remembering and
       recollecting

The faculty is a second-order cognitive power: the ability to retain information acquired, to call to mind one's past actions and experiences, to acquire recognitional skills and to retain learnt skills. The faculty is exercised whenever one comes to know something and does not forget it, learns something and retains it, experiences something and can later recollect it. The present tense frequentative 'NN remembers who / why / where / what / when / whether / how / …' is often used to signify such mnemonic abilities. Thus used, 'remembers', like 'knows', lacks duration. Just as one cannot ask 'When do you know how to play tennis?', so too one cannot ask, 'When do you remember how to play tennis?', for abilities and possession of abilities are not occurrences.

Mnemonic abilities are *actualized* whenever one calls something to mind, reflects on one's past experience, engages in reasoning from what one has learnt, recognizes something previously encountered, or engages in skilled activities once learnt. The past-tense non-frequentative 'I remembered …' is often used to signify such actualization. Mnemonic abilities are *manifest* in one's statements about one's past experiences and activities, in one's expression of previously acquired knowledge, in acting on the basis of what one recollects, and in the exercise of previously learnt skills. 'Recall', 'recollect', and the progressive form 'is remembering' are apt for current actualization, as are 'recount' and 'reminisce' for its verbal manifestation. Here one *can* ask when someone remembered, or how long it took him to remember.

6. Although one can try to remember, as one can try to believe someone or something, remembering is not an act or activity. One can no more deliberately, intentionally, or voluntarily recollect something or remember to do or how to do something than one can deliberately, intentionally, or voluntarily know something. To call something to mind, like bearing something in mind, is not an act that consists in doing anything. What actually happens when one remembers something may be nothing more than acting on information previously acquired or on an instruction previously received, for example, one hurries to the bus stop because it is nearly 6:30, or one buys a loaf of bread at the grocer's. Forgetting to do something is to omit the performance of an act, but it is not to forget to perform an act of remembering. Remembering to turn off the lights may consist of no more than knowing that one has to turn off the lights and turning them off. No 'act of remembering' need take place. Answering '1314' in answer to the question 'When was the Battle of Crecy?' is a manifestation of remembering, but in a different context, saying '1314' may be giving the

result of a calculation (e.g. 'Add 104 to 1210') or answering the question 'What is your room number?'. Remembering where one left one's keys may take the form of getting them out of the drawer; of phoning one's wife to tell her where they are; or of making a note in one's diary. What counts as a manifestation of memory is context-dependent and may take many different forms.

If remembering something is not an act, is it an experience? It has seemed to many thinkers that remembering something must be an experience annexed to a recurrent idea or thought, an experience that marks out the idea or thought as a memory. But memory is not an experience. When one says 'I remember seeing Jill' one is reporting a past experience not a present one. 'He left in haste because he remembered his dental appointment' explains what he did, not by reference to a current experience he had, but by reference to something he knew and suddenly realized. Of course, suddenly remembering may be accompanied by various experiences, such as of sudden alarm or anxiety, but these are not the remembering. Moreover, they no more 'flow from an act of remembering' than they flow from an act of knowing – and as we have seen, there is no such thing as an act of knowing.

7.   One's faculty of memory may be good or poor. Loss of personal memory is amnesia. A poor memory is a proneness to forget things, to forget how to do things, and to forget to do things. It is a proneness to remember only vaguely, just as poor eyesight is not a matter of 'seeing things' that are not there, but of not seeing or not seeing clearly things that are there. The exercise of one's memory in recollection of past experiences may be more or less vivid, detailed and accurate. Contrary to what Hume supposed, a vivid memory is not akin to a vivid painting in bright colours, which is to be contrasted with ideas of the imagination which are fainter pastels. Being vivid, detailed, and accurate are not features of the mental imagery that may (or may not) accompany recollecting or reminiscing, rather, they are features of the account one can give of the experience recollected. To remember vividly, as Marcel Proust did, is to be able to give a vivid, that is, lively, account of a past experience, to give an accurate and detailed description of what happened. Such are the virtues of a good memory.

However, one may also misremember or remember something incorrectly, as one may misperceive or perceive incorrectly. Mnemonic verbs are factive. If A remembers that such-and-such is the case or recollects such-and-such an experience, then such-and-such *is* the case and A did indeed experience such-and-such. One cannot remember what is not so. For memory is, among other things, a form of knowledge. It is a cognitive faculty. But, as in the case of knowledge, the factivity is cancellable. One may not be sure, just as one may not be sure one knows something. Remembering correctly, like knowing, is compatible with not being sure. But the statement that one remembers is illegitimate if one is not sure. When we are unsure of ourselves, we qualify the mnemonic claim by 'As I remember' or 'As far as I can recollect', 'I think that' and so on. This is parallel to 'As far as I know' and 'To the best of my knowledge'. It indicates to the hearer or questioner that one's word is not altogether reliable.

Misremembering is a form of mnemonic failure. One may be good at remembering, but one cannot be good at misremembering or forgetting any more than one can be good at misperceiving. Just as misperception must not be too wayward, so too misremembering must not be too wayward. Thinking that I met you at a conference in Paris in 2002 is a case of misremembering if I actually met you at a conference in Paris in 2004 or met you at a conference in Berlin in 2002. But if it wasn't you, and if I have never been to Paris, and I have never attended a conference in my life, then this is not a case of misremembering, but of a mnemonic hallucination. George IV's sincere avowals of his participating in the charge of the Greys at Waterloo was a mnemonic hallucination.

Memory is a form of knowledge and up to a point has a similar representational form. Like knowledge, memories are acquired, possessed, retained, shared, or kept to oneself. Like knowledge, memories may be detailed and precise or fragmentary and incomplete. However, there are also differences. Memory is a faculty, but there is no faculty of knowledge. There are exercises in remembering, but no exercises in knowing, only in learning. One can have profound knowledge, but not profound memories. One may know a subject thoroughly, but one cannot remember a subject thoroughly. One may misremember, but one cannot misknow, just as one may remember incorrectly but not know something incorrectly.

8.   We mentioned previously the fact that recurrent generations of philosophers held that to remember is to have an idea, perception, experience, or thought that one had had previously coupled with knowledge or awareness that one had had it before. It was thought to be essentially a re-experiencing. Hence the pivotal question in the analysis of memory seemed to be: How does one know of the current mnemonic experience that one has had it before? After all, one cannot

compare for verisimilitude the present experience that one is having with the past experience that it recapitulates. Nor is one's current memory akin to a picture or photograph of a long-lost scene or event, for merely to have a mental image before one's mind

(i)   does not tell one what the image is an image of;
(ii) it is not to remember at all, but presupposes memory in order for one to know what the picture is a picture of;
(iii) it would not be to remember the past occurrence at all, but to have in mind an *ersatz* stand-in for the long-lost scene or event. But when we recollect a past event, it is the event itself we remember, not a substitute.

So, it seemed that there must be some *mark* of memory that *certified* that one's current experience *is* a memory experience and not imagination. The mnemonic experience must carry a certifying marker. Hume, labouring under the common illusion that all memory is of the past, suggested that the order of the currently recollected ideas must preserve the correct order of the recollected events, but he noted that this would still not be a pastness certificate and would not inform one that the ideas before one's mind were *of* the past. Notoriously, Hume suggested the mark of pastness is the intermediate degree of vivacity of memory ideas. A memory idea is not as vivacious as the original impression which it recapitulates but is more vivid than a mere idea of the imagination – as if the original impression is in technicolour, its recollection in pastels, and a similar imagination in watercolours. Thomas Reid rightly made fun of Hume's account: hit your head hard against the wall – that will give you an impression; hit your head less hard against the wall – that will give you an idea of memory; now just tap your head against the wall – and behold, you will have an idea of imagination.

Despite Reid's remonstrations, the quest for a memory certificate went on. More than a century later, in 1890, William James was arguing that mnemonic ideas must be accompanied by a *feeling of pastness* and a *belief* that things were as one's mnemonic image represents them as being. Bertrand Russell, as late as 1921, argued that memory demands an image coupled with a feeling of belief that *this* has happened before. The time determination, he insisted, is wholly due to the belief feeling. How one can identify 'feelings of pastness' as feelings of pastness. Moreover, how does one connect them with the past remembered *independently of memory*?

So, generation after generation of highly intelligent thinkers were held in the grip of a vice from which they were unable to escape. What they needed to do was to jettison conceptual baggage. To remember something is no more *to have an experience* than is to know something, although remembering on an occasion may be accompanied by various experiences, such as the sadness or joy we feel when we recollect long-lost times. (Similarly, suddenly realizing that one knows the answer to the question in a quiz-game may be accompanied by feelings of delight and relief, but the knowing is not an experience.) The idea that the mental image must be certified as being of the past sets us off on the wrong trail before we have even had time to take our bearings. But the memory image, if there is one, *is an image of what is remembered*, not a *reminder* of it. A memory image may be correct or incorrect, just as one's memory assertions. Reminders, by contrast, cannot be correct or incorrect, only more or less effective. What is needed, above all, is to start afresh. And the point from which to start is the thought that memory is a human faculty for the retention of knowledge and information acquired in the past and for the recounting of past experiences – their content and character.

Once this is borne in mind, it becomes obvious that traditional puzzles about distinguishing memory from imagination dissolve. There is no such thing as confusing remembering something correctly with imagining something. For to imagine something is to think up a possibility, whereas to remember something is to possess knowledge, and one can't confuse knowing something with thinking up a possibility. Of course, one cannot distinguish, in one's own case, between remembering and misremembering. But misremembering ('merely imagining it', as we misleadingly say) is not a successful exercise of the faculty of imagination, but a defective exercise of the faculty of memory. *These* cannot be confused any more than one can confuse trying to open the door with trying to compose a tune.

9.   It would be amiss to conclude our overview without mentioning a further episode in the dialectic – the logic of illusion – of memory. Plato invoked the image of the mark of a stamp on wax as a metaphor for memory. Aristotle, unfortunately, transformed the metaphor into a proto-theory, suggesting that the explanation of why very young children have poor memories, adults reasonable memories, and the elderly failing memories. His explanation was that the physical organ causally implicated in remembering was too wet in the young and too dry in the old for the experience to register, that is, to leave an

impression. Only when it is neither too wet nor too dry (as we would say today, only when adequate synaptic transmission is possible) can experiences register *and leave a trace*. Trace theory sank from sight in the fourth century AD, with the advent of the ventricular doctrine that all cognitive and cogitative operations occur in the fluid that lies within the ventricles of the brain. It was revived only in the seventeenth century by the great pioneer of brain science Thomas Willis (1621–75). By the end of the nineteenth century, as is evident from William James, it had become the accepted view. A neural memory trace is the cortical storage of memory. This, in greatly more sophisticated and complex form, is current neuroscientific doctrine.

A quick sketch will make the conceptual form of the theory clear. Like almost all analyses of memory, the basic supposition is that *what are remembered are past experiences*. Experiences, it is held, *leave brain traces*. They are *long-lasting circuits*. This is a purely physiological phenomenon. The brain traces are held to be *representations* of the experience. They are stored memories and are available for *recall*. Recall occurs when *a current experience activates the memory trace*. This happens by means of a *perceived reminder* that *fits* part of the imprinted memory-circuit. This activates the whole circuit. Successful recall consists in *having current mnemonic experiences* that are *faint reproductions* of the previous experience. *Recognition* consists in the *coinciding* of a neural trace of a current perception with a memory trace. This produces a *recognitional experience*.

This tale marries the worst confusions of a long and misguided tradition with the sophistication of modern neuroscience. Let us briefly apply what we have already learnt from our conceptual survey. Modern trace theory presupposes that the object of memory is past experience. This, we have seen, is mistaken. Nevertheless, let us grant restriction of the neuroscientific account to remembering past experiences. Even thus restricted the account is sorely defective. First, to remember doing, undergoing, experiencing something is to remember *one's* doing, undergoing, or experiencing. But the only thing that could possibly leave a brain trace would be the perceptual input, that is, *what was perceived*, and not the perceiving of it. So all that I would be able to remember would be *what* I perceived, not *my perceiving of it*.

The account confuses storage with retention. Memory, we have seen, is retention of knowledge previously acquired and the ability to recollect past experiences. To be sure, storage implies retention, but retention does not imply storage. Memory is retention of abilities precisely to the extent that knowledge is an ability, but there is no such thing as storing an ability. Of course, one can store information – by writing it down and storing the inscription, recording it and storing the record, entering it on a computer and preserving the hard drive, taking a photograph and keeping it in an album. Being thus stored, the information is *available* to one. But, of course, all these operations *presuppose memory* and cannot explain it, since one must remember to read the inscription, how to retrieve the information stored, what the photograph is a photograph of.

It should be obvious that there is no such thing as storing information in the brain in the form of strengthened synapses or neural circuits. For such a hypothesized store of information is not *available* for retrieval by the human being remembering. One cannot read or hear neural traces. Moreover, a store of information *contains* information, but does not *possess* any. But a human being who remembers something possesses information but does not contain information. For to remember information that things were or are thus-and-so is to *know* that they were or are.

Trace theory presents neural traces as *representations* of what is remembered. But whatever a neural trace may be, it is not a semantic or iconic representation of what is remembered. It is at best a causal effect in the form of a long-lasting circuit. This hypothesized causal effect *must* allegedly be the cause of the memory experience of recollection – otherwise the past experience remembered would not be causally connected with its mnemonic reproduction. It would be a mysterious 'action at a (temporal) distance'. This is dire confusion. For what one experienced is not the cause of one's remembering, it is its *object*. *What* one remembers is not a *surrogate* of a past experience, but the past experience itself, not a surrogate of antecedently acquired knowledge, but the very knowledge acquired. The relationship is logical, not causal. Trace theory conceives of a memory experience as the terminus of a causal chain – an idea, impression, thought, or image, which, it seems, must be causally linked with its origin. But that is misconceived. For remembering is not a current *experience*, but a current *knowing* – and knowing is not an experience.

The trace theorist may remonstrate: surely there are causes of remembering! And, indeed, there are. They are known as *reminders*. Reminders make one remember, cause one to remember. But *what one remembers* is not a reminder – it is the thing itself. Causes of remembering are needed *when one does not remember*, not when one does. The brain is not a store of memories and whatever experiential traces there may be, they can be no more than causal conditions of mnemonic abilities.

9

Imagination

<blockquote>

"C'est l'imagination qui gouverne le genre humaine."

Napoleon

</blockquote>

1.   In this essay on the imagination and in the next essay, which is on thinking, we shall be examining widely ramifying concepts. They are concepts that connect a multitude of different manifestations of human life, forming a complex network of ideas that would never have been connected by design. They have multiple centres of variation, each one of which demands meticulous scrutiny. Although we have all mastered the complex use of such kinds of expression, we are singularly ill-equipped to describe it. For mastery of the use of a word does not require mastery of the description of its use. Faced with questions about the nature of imagination or of thinking, we almost uniformly go wrong, intuitively seizing upon a particular paradigm and misguidedly generalizing it. The connection between imagining and having a mental image is prone to guide us down the wrong path before we have begun, just as focusing on The Thinker (*Le Penseur*) forces upon us a false picture of what thinking is. The methods of connective and contrastive analysis that we are deploying throughout this book will be put to the test by such ramifying concepts as thinking and imagining and by the phenomena of thought and imagination. They will not be found wanting.

Solving, Resolving, and Dissolving Philosophical Problems: Essays in Connective, Contrastive and Contextual Analysis, First Edition. P. M. S. Hacker.
© 2025 John Wiley & Sons Ltd. Published 2025 by John Wiley & Sons Ltd.

2.   Mankind is blessed and cursed with the powers of the imagination. It is by the use of our imagination that we can daydream of heavenly bliss and have waking nightmares of the terrors of hell.

> The lunatic, the lover, and the poet
> Are of imagination all compact …
> Such tricks hath strong imagination (*A Midsummer's Night Dream*)

It is a mainstay of our moral sensibility and of our compassion. The grief we commonly cause to those we love is often through failure to imagine the impact of what we do or say. The harm we inflict upon others is often a manifestation of inability or unwillingness to imagine their condition. Imagination is a primary source of creativity in the arts and sciences, as it is of wit and humour. For bisociation, the apprehension of the unexpected association of a situation or idea in two distinct and normally incompatible frames of reference, needs imagination that is manifest in jokes (e.g. a blasphemous cartoon of Joseph and Mary in the manger saying, 'We wanted a girl', which bisociates the sacred and profane) no less than in science (the bisociation of hydrodynamics and electricity theory) or art (the Baroque conceit of an elbow of the subject of a portrait emerging from the painted, engraved, or etched frame (bisociating what is depicted and extra-pictorial space). Einstein (1879–1955), writing about science, observed that imagination is more important than knowledge, but he should have borne in mind Joubert's (1754–1824) wise observation: 'He who has imagination without learning has wings without feet.'

We characterize the imagination as a faculty. Unlike our perceptual faculties, the imagination is not a cognitive faculty, although, as just noted, it is a cognition-facilitating one. Rather, it is a *cogitative faculty*. One cannot acquire knowledge by the exercise of the imagination in the manner in which we can achieve knowledge by the use of our senses and powers of reasoning. This is built into the concept of the imagination, since the verb 'to imagine' is not a *factive verb*: 'A imagined that things are so' does not imply that things are so, even though they may be. One can imagine things that do not exist as well as things that do. One can imagine what is not the case as well as what is, just as one may imagine doing things that one goes on to do as well as doing things that one would not dream of doing.

Imagination is interwoven with thought, in as much as one of its primary exercises consists of thinking up fresh, original, amusing, exciting *possibilities*. It is interwoven with perception, in as much as it takes imagination to perceive figures in cloud formations or in Rorschach spots, to perceive aspects in double-aspect drawings, to see similarities of pattern or of human faces, as well as to hear variations on a theme in a musical composition. It is linked to fabrication and to making things up, not merely in storytelling and in playing charades, but in deceiving and pretending. It is linked to the notion of *mental image* and the power to conjure up mental images, which may be visual or auditory. This link is an unfortunate historical accident, manifesting back-seepage of philosophical confusion into ordinary language. As we shall see, our thought would be less beset by pitfalls were this link severed.

Imagination being a faculty, we speak of people as having a rich or poor, powerful or weak, fertile or arid imagination. Hence their *imaginings* may be vivid, lively, original and creative; or vague, feeble, wild and implausible, and even ridiculous. A person is said to be *imaginative* if his creations, plans, and projects exhibit admirable originality, and if his stories, make-believes, and game-playings are lively, interesting, and vivacious. A person is *unimaginative* if he does not come up with anything out of the ordinary when something unusual and lively or amusing is wanted. A mark of mediocrity is lack of imagination. The things we do or create are imaginative or unimaginative to the extent that they display or lack imagination. The *imaginable* is problematically linked to the *conceivable*, and the conceivable to the possible. What is *imaginary* stands in contrast to what is actual, although not everything we imagine is imaginary, since what we hopefully or fearfully imagine may actually be the case. However, everything that is imaginary is imagined. These cognates of 'imagine' will be analysed in what follows.

3. Before proceeding further, it is meet to sketch the wide range of grammatical complements of the English verb 'to imagine'. Where other languages differ, the concept thereby expressed may differ to some degree. The verb 'to imagine' may be followed by a sentence or by a nominalized sentence (a 'that-clause') or gerundive nominalization ('the birth/death/success/ of NN'). It may take Wh-nominalizations as its grammatical object: one can imagine who, why, where, or when (but not whether). One can imagine how to do something, or how something was or will be done. One can imagine NN or an X, no matter whether they exist or not (Father Christmas, a unicorn). One can imagine oneself or someone else as a so-and-so, or as V-ing. One can imagine being, doing, becoming, or undergoing this, that, or the

other. These brief grammatical reminders provide us with poles of description and should be borne in mind to ensure that we don't dine on too limited a range of examples.

4.   One form imagination takes is thinking of possibilities and thinking up novelties. Within this category, we can distinguish between the *cogitative imagination* and the *creative imagination*, while recognizing that these are not exclusive. The cogitative imagination is manifest in lateral thinking, in which unusual and unexpected ways of problem-solving are advanced. More generally, it is at work in all imaginative non-algorithmic problem-solving. Rather differently, it is exhibited in sympathy and compassion, when we imagine the joys and sufferings of others. This is sometimes characterized as 'putting oneself in another's shoes'. One exercises one's imagination in thinking what another must be feeling in a given situation or predicament. Note, in passing, that 'Imagine you were Napoleon at Waterloo' means no more than 'Imagine you were confronted by the problems faced by Napoleon at Waterloo' or perhaps 'Imagine you were exhausted and in pain, as Napoleon was a Waterloo, and that you were confronted by the problems with which he was confronted'. For one cannot intelligibly imagine oneself to be someone other than who one is, any more than one can intelligibly imagine oneself to be a stone or a sofa.

The creative imagination, as already noted, is manifest in thinking up novel, unexpected, and original possibilities in the arts and sciences, as well as in jokes and wit – both in their production and in their comprehension. It is also exhibited in *fantasy*: in thinking up fairy tales, fantasy fiction (e.g. Tolkien, Ursula le Guin) and science fiction (Jules Verne, H. G. Wells, Isaac Asimov). The expression 'fantasy' is used to signify our faculty for imagining the impossible (e.g. time-travel) and wildly improbable, exhibited in fantasy fiction, in pictorial representations illustrating such fiction (paintings of God creating the universe, or of the Olympian gods engaging in their antics) and in corresponding cinema, as well as in fantasy epics and poetry (e.g. 'Beowulf', 'Morte d'Arthur'). The creators of such successful fantasies are rightly characterized as imaginative.

The creative imagination is exhibited not only in thinking up novel possibilities, but also in thinking up comic and bizarre *impossibilities*, new and bizarre forms of verbal or pictorial nonsense. This is manifest supremely in Lewis Carroll's *Through the Looking-Glass*, which is a book of philosophical jokes, in Carroll's and Edward Lear's brilliant nonsense poems, as well as in the scintillating surrealist nonsense of Spike Milligan's Goon Show. Masterpieces of pictorial impossibilities are Magritte's witty surreal paintings and Escher's etchings of ever-circling staircases or never-ending water-flows. To be sure, this casts doubt on the traditional link between conceivability and logical possibility, which we shall investigate further in this essay.

Nevertheless, to imagine is not the same as to think. To think that Britain fared better within the European Union than outside it is not to imagine that it fared better. To think that global warming is out of control is not to imagine that it is. To speak with thought is not necessarily to speak with imagination, and a thoughtful speech may or may not be an imaginative one. To think before one speaks is not the same as imagining something before one speaks, and to imagine that one is speaking is not to think that one is. To do something thoughtlessly is not to do something unimaginatively. To do something without thinking is to act spontaneously or automatically or negligently, which are not the same as acting without imagination, which is to act in a routine or habitual manner without investigating alternative possibilities.

5. A different form imagination takes, a different grammatical dimension the verb 'to imagine' and its cognates occupy, is the *fabricative imagination*. It is not surprising that the imagination should be linked to falsehood and deception. The link between thinking up novel and original possibilities and fabrication is formed by the notions of *make-believe* and *making things up*. Make-believe is an activity, a distinctive language-game, of children and adults alike. The child who pretends that he is flying an aeroplane by running around the garden with arms outspread and making engine-like noises, and the adults who play charades at a party are exercising their imaginations. The child who gives her dolls a tea party is making things up, pretending that there is tea in the toy teacup and pretending that the dolls drink. Making things up converges on pretence, on the one hand, and fabrication, on the other. These links, together with the connection between the imagined and the imaginary (whatever is imaginary is imagined, but not vice versa), also illuminate the nexus between imagining and falsehood that will now be examined.

Imagining is linked to make-believe and to making things up. Both are essentially connected to what is not so, to what is not actually the case. The imaginary is what is unreal – castles in the air and flights of fancy. The creative imagination is the spring from which the fictitious flows. This suffices to make clear the connection between imagining and falsehood, and between imagining and misperceiving. 'You are only imagining things', we say to the child who thinks that there is a tiger under his bed, 'don't be afraid; come and look.' If someone thinks he perceives a man in the bushes, we may respond, 'You are just imagining it; there is no one there; it is just a shadow of the tree.' Similarly, when someone misremembers, we may address him with such words as 'It did not happen like that at all, you are just imagining it.' Clearly, when someone suffers from mnemonic delusions, as did George IV, who in his later years thought that he had fought at the battle of Waterloo, we should say of him that he was just imagining things. It is important to note that when a person is given to misperception or misremembering, or is the victim of mnemonic delusions, we would not say that he is exercising his powers of imagination, let alone that he has a rich imagination. Such propensities to false beliefs are not conceived to be an *exercise of the faculty of imagination*. The reason for this is that the faculty of imagination, unlike the faculties of perception and memory, is not concerned with or constrained by literal truth and falsehood. There are no 'misimaginings' as there are misrememberings and misperceivings.

Make-believe and play-acting converge on pretending. They also converge on fabricating and hence are connected with deceiving. The confidence trickster, the malingerer, and the spy pretend to be something they are not. In playing their deceitful role, they may use their imagination in spinning their web of lies.

There are conceptual connections between pretence and imagination. Both are logically linked to what is unreal or not actually the case. Neither pretending to do something nor imagining doing something involves actually doing it. Neither pretending to be an X nor imagining that one is an X imply that one is an X. The limits of imagining and the limits of pretending partly coincide. I cannot pretend to be Peter M. S. Hacker any more than I can imagine being Peter M. S. Hacker, just as I cannot pretend to be a fellow of St John's College, Oxford any more than I can imagine that I am. For one cannot, logically, imagine or pretend to be what one knows one is and/or what others know one is and one knows that they do.

Nonetheless, pretence and imagination differ profoundly. Pretence is linked to performance; imagination is linked to thought. The ability to pretend is an ability to *act* as if such-and-such were the case. The ability to imagine is (among other things) the ability to conceive or think up possibilities. Actually pretending is a performance – it is doing something. By contrast, actually imagining is thinking, not doing. The difficulties in pretending are difficulties in performing; the difficulties in imagining are difficulties in conceiving. To ask someone to pretend is to ask him to perform – the request is a prelude to behaviour. To ask someone to imagine is to ask him to think – a prelude to thought, not to action. To ask someone why he pretended to be a so-and-so or to do such-and-such is to ask for his reasons, purposes, or motives for acting as he did; but to ask someone why he imagined such-and-such is to ask him what led him to imagine whatever he imagined. Confidence tricksters, malingerers, and spies pretend; artists, writers, hypochondriacs, and neurotics imagine. The skills involved are quite different. Good storytellers are good at imagining but may be quite unable to pretend convincingly. To be good at pretending is to have mastered the arts of make-believe and acting, and to possess the skill to deceive others into thinking that things are other than they actually are. To be good at imagining is to possess the skill of thinking up new possibilities, of conceiving things in novel and original ways, of perceiving unobvious patterns, of discerning similarities and differences not commonly noticed. Pretending may be courageous, deceitful, dishonest, convincing, or hollow and easy to see through. Imagining can be none of these, but it may be vivid, original, and lively. 'Don't pretend that …' is commonly an order not to deceive others; 'Don't imagine that …' is often an order not to deceive oneself.

6.   A further form imagination takes is the *perceptual imagination*. For the faculties of perception and of imagination criss-cross at crucial junctions and their intersections play a pivotal role in our experience. It takes imagination to see resemblances between faces, to perceive that Jack has his mother's smile and his father's eyes. Similarly, when one studies art history, one needs imagination to apprehend what unifies a painting style and what differentiates distinct painting styles, such as Bolognese baroque paintings (e.g. the Carracci, Guido Reni, Guercino) and the Caravaggisti baroque in the late sixteenth and seventeenth century, the School of Rembrandt as opposed to the fijnstyle followers of Gerrit Dou, Impressionist paintings in the nineteenth century by contrast with post-Impressionists. So too, it needs auditory imagination to perceive a piece of music as variations upon a theme (the 'Goldberg Variations') or to hear an auditory representation of nature in programmatic music, as in the opening bars of Strauss's *Also Sprach Zarathustra*, which represent a

dramatic sunrise, or the rain and thunderstorm in Beethoven's *Pastoral* symphony. Slightly differently, it needs visual imagination to see a 'quotation' in a painting, such as Michelangelo's *Isaiah* in Reynolds's *Mrs Siddons as the Tragic Muse*, just as it needs auditory imagination to hear one composer's variation on a theme by another (e.g. Brahms's *Variations on a Theme by Paganini* or Rachmaninov's *Rhapsody on a Theme by Paganini*). Similarly, it needs visual imagination to see double-aspect figures in drawings (such as Jastrow's duck-rabbit) or to see figures in a Rorschach spot or in cloud formations.

In these and doubtless in many other ways too, the perceptual imagination is pivotal in our culture and for the enrichment of our lives. It is a crucial contributor to good taste and aesthetic judgement. Moreover, it is no less in play in quotidian arrangements of flowers in a vase or in the choice and juxtaposition of cushions on a sofa or of rugs on the floor, in the choice of decorative colours on the walls of a room and the matching of curtains to the wallpaper or colours. Without a perceptual imagination human life would be immeasurably impoverished.

7.   Aristotle introduced the idea of the faculty of *phantasia* (imagination) as being an intermediate between perception and thought, rightly noting that it is connected with but differs from both perception and discursive thought. He invoked the notion of *phantasmata* to characterize the *appearances* which he held we are presented with in perceptual illusions (when things appear to be other than they actually are), in after-images, delusions and hallucinations, in recollection, in dreams, in hypnogogic and hypnopompic images, as well as when we desire, hope, or fear, and in the pleasures of memory and expectation. This notion was, it seems, introduced in the endeavour to mould a concept to meet a need in his attempt to articulate the essential features of the *psuchē* (the psyche: the distinctive powers of mankind) and to elucidate the materials of thought. It is arguable that this endeavour failed, that such a general conception of *appearances* was ill-advised, assimilating what is logically too disparate to be subsumed under a single category. But this will not be argued here. What is important from our point of view is that Aristotle conceived of *phantasmata* as 'a kind of weak perception' or 'perception without matter'. In this respect, he sowed the seeds of confusion that are still flowering more than two thousand years later.

The concept of imagination was prominent in early modern philosophy. Hobbes more or less copied Aristotle. He conceived of sensory and perceptual experience as the reception of appearances which he characterized as 'images' or 'phantasms' and described them, as Aristotle had done, as 'decaying sense' or 'weakened sense'. Descartes held that to imagine is to have an image or sensory *idea* before the 'eyes of the mind', which he contrasted with the non-sensory ideas of the intellect. The 'New Way of Ideas', pivotal for Locke's investigations of human understanding, its forms and limits, dominated European thought, especially among the empiricists, for the next century and a half, to the colossal detriment of philosophy and psychology. They held ideas to be the raw materials of thought, conceived of thinking as the concatenation of ideas, and of the limits of thought as the limits of the combinatorial possibilities of ideas. Hume held that in imagination we are confronted by ideas that are faint copies (again, decayed or weakened sense) of antecedent impressions received in experience, fainter even than ideas of memory – for which, as we have seen (Essay 8 on memory), he was parodied by Reid. Imagination was held to be a kaleidoscopic faculty that had the power to conjoin or separate ideas independently of judgement. The limits of imagination were conceived to be the limits of the combinatorial possibilities of mental images.

Kant (1724–1804) freed philosophy from the incubus of ideas, shifting philosophical discourse from idea (*Vorstellung*) to concept (*Begriff*). He in effect demolished the house that Descartes and Locke had built, shifting the focus of philosophical investigation from the actuality of ideas to the potentiality of concepts as contributory to possible judgements. However, he remained trapped in the rubble. For he conceived of perception as the reception of *appearances* (*Anschauungen*, usually and misguidedly translated as *intuitions*), and held that imaginations are 'appearances without the presence of an object'. But that was a retrograde step. For, as we have already seen, we can imagine things that have no appearance, such as a new constitution for our country or all (many, some or no) A-s being B-s; and we can imagine subjective appearances that have nothing to do with the imagination, such as hallucinations of rats during *delirium tremens*. There is no *essential* link between the faculty of imagination and the mental-image-making faculty. There may be a contingent heuristic link that is exhibited in some people with a powerful creative imagination, but not in others. One would not think less of the imaginative powers of Titian or Rubens, of Shakespeare or Tolstoy if one were to learn that they explicitly avowed that they lacked the ability to conjure up visual mental images. The faculty of imagination is not the same faculty as the faculty of mental-image-making. The latter, which I shall call *eidetic power* is no less associated with memory than it is contingently associated with imagination. However, the connections are complex and the concept of a mental image is the source of interminable conceptual confusions. So the logical grammar of mental images stands in need of connective and contrastive analysis.

8.   The links between our eidetic powers and imagination, on the one hand, and memory, on the other have deep etymological roots. *Phantasia* is linked to *phantasmata*, *imaginare* with *imago*, *imagination* with *image*. Idioms of natural language exhibit the linkage: we *picture things to ourselves*; we *conjure up images in our imagination*, we *vividly picture* our past experiences and our beloved dead family and friends when we call them to mind in loving memory.

> I heard your voice calling
> While darkness all around
> Was silently falling:
> There was no other sound.
>
> Would you come back to me, my darling,
> So dear to me over the years,
> Along with outstretched hands
> And smiles, not tears?
>
> I know you can't come back again;
> From nowhere none returns,
> No, I am left with the pain
> Of a heart that yearns.
>
> Edward Greenwood

We connect the notion of an image with that of a *representation* in as much as we speak of an accurate portrait of someone as 'a *spitting image*', and of sculptures as '*graven images*'. It is but a small step, and a great error, to think of mental images as 'internal representations'. It is an error because the extension of the notion of representation beyond its natural limits that confine it primarily to public human artefacts made for perceptual scrutiny and comparison leads to profound confusions in the mental sciences and in cognitive neuroscience. Furthermore, there is a lexical association between images and perception. We speak of 'visualizing' things in our imagination and of 'seeing things in the mind's eye' and of hearing a melody 'in our imagination' as well as of a tune 'running through our head'.

These are traps laid for us by our language. Others we dig for ourselves in our misguided empiricist and neuroscientific reflections on the nature and limits of experience, thought, memory, and imagination. Philosophers, especially but not only empiricists, have supposed perception to involve the receipt of sense impressions, memories to be the retention of copies of sense-impressions in the form of vivid ideas, thinking as the combining and separating of ideas preparatory for judgement, and of imagination as the unconstrained combination of faint ideas that are perceived by 'inner sense'.

9.   To be sure, there is a conceptual link between visual perception and visual mental images, as there is between auditory perception and auditory images (hearing things in the imagination). For the same vocabulary is used to describe both what we perceive and what we imagine when we imagine perceptibilia. Moreover, it makes sense to ascribe imagining perceptual qualities such as colour, sounds, or smells only to those who *can* perceive such qualities (the blind from birth cannot intelligibly be said to have mental images of colour).

However, describing or reporting what one perceives is *categorially* different from describing or reporting what one imagines. Of a perceptual report one can typically ask: Are you sure? Did you look again? Might you have made a mistake? Did you double-check? Did you make sure? Could you have got closer? Did you try in better light? But no such question is appropriate in the case of images of the imagination. A visual image that one may see *in* one's mind's eye (not *with* one's mind's eye) is not a picture; moreover, it is not visible – it is *had*, not *seen*. One cannot, logically cannot, watch or look at the visual images that may come before one's mind when one imagines visibilia. There are no imaginability conditions analogous to visibility conditions for the exercise of one's powers of sight, no 'More light, please!'. There is no asking someone else to have a look too.

The phenomena of perceiving are categorially distinct from the phenomena of imagining. Perceiving requires the use of one's organs of perception. Limiting ourselves to vision, seeing may involve watching, observing, looking for, looking at, looking under, as well as glancing, gazing, and staring. It may need endeavour – for one may try to see better by screwing up one's eyes, moving closer, turning on the light, taking the object under scrutiny into the light. Seeing objects in one's environment is bound up with behaviour as one navigates one's way through one's surroundings – one steps over puddles, steps around obstacles, avoids bumping into things. It is linked to reactions and responses to what one perceives: to surprise, delight, disgust, fear, hesitation, curiosity – none of which apply to one's exercises of one's visual imagination. One may feel trepidation if one imagines one's children in danger, one may weep if one vividly imagines them suffering, but one's responses are not responses to what one sees, since one cannot see one's visual images. Nor is it a response to the images one has – it is a response to what one imagines and, of course, what one imagines is not the image one has but what it is an image of.

Not only are the phenomena of perceiving and of imagining categorially dissimilar, the concepts are equally so. What one can see, one can also notice or overlook, become and be conscious of; but one cannot see, notice or overlook the images before one's mind's eye. One can be dazzled by what one sees as one can be deafened by what one hears, but to imagine something dazzling does not dazzle one and to imagine a deafening explosion is not deafening. For a choreographer to imagine the *pas de deux* that he choreographed being faster than the ballet-dancers danced it in rehearsal does not mean that they danced faster in his imagination. The order 'Look!' is altogether unlike the order 'Imagine!'. The first is obeyed by doing something, the upshot of which is seeing or noticing. The second, if it is in the form 'Imagine that ...', is a prelude to a hypothesis – akin to 'Suppose that ...', which awaits further elaboration. If it is in the form of 'Imagine the faces of your children (parents, comrades)', it is still categorially unlike 'Look!'. 'I can't see ...' is an admission of failure to detect or discern; 'I can't imagine ...' is more akin to 'I can't believe ...' (see Essay 7) or to 'It's unthinkable' (i.e. it clashes with everything I know or believe on the subject).

10.   What one imagines when one conjures up an image before one's mind's eye or when an image comes before one's mind's eye is not an image, but what the image is an image of. To paint what one imagines or to paint something imaginary is not to copy a mental image. How could it be, since one cannot *see* one's mental images? They are had, not seen. What we picture to ourselves is not a picture, unless we are calling to mind what we saw in the picture gallery or are ruminating on what to paint on the canvas before us. We can picture or imagine some things vividly or clearly and distinctly,

others only vaguely, unclearly, and indistinctly. This phenomenon, or *this form of characterization*, was the source of egregious confusions in the writings of philosophers, especially the empiricists, and among empirical psychologists. Hume notoriously held that images of the imagination were less vivid than images of memory. Francis Galton (1822–1911), who pioneered psychological questionnaires, asked his respondents to report on whether the picture before their mind's eye was as bright as the scene they were imagining, whether the objects in it were as well-defined as when they actually saw them, whether the colours they imagined were distinct and natural. Hume and Galton viewed the lesser vivacity of mental images as opposed to sense impressions as an empirical datum ('well, colour photos just do fade!'). If that were so, then someone with a very vivid imagination might mistake his mental images for after-images or hallucinations, and someone might find that his vivid mental image might interfere with his vision in the way an after-image does. But that is absurd, since images of the imagination are not in the same logical space as sense impressions, after-images, and hallucinations. One could no more confuse the images of one's imagination with after-images or hallucinations than one could confuse the weight of one's obligations with the weight of one's shopping basket. One's mental images, unlike one's hallucinations, cannot literally be more vivid than one's visual impressions any more than a negative attitude can be more negative that a negative number.

How is one to dispel the hex of this incubus? Only by examining the use of 'vivid' and by using our intellectual imagination. Colours are vivid if they are bright; light is vivid if things stand out sharply in it (a landscape in the raking light of sunset under a clear sky); feelings are vivid if they are strongly felt; coloured things are vivid if their colour is brilliant and they stand out in their context. A description, report, or history is vivid if it presents its tale in a lively, clear, detailed, and striking manner. This provides the key that we need. Mental images cannot be vivid, vivacious, and lively in the sense in which what they are images of may be. Contrary to Galton, they cannot intelligibly be compared with visual impressions for vivacity at all. Rather, whether one imagines something vividly turns largely on one's ability to describe or represent (in acting, painting, or music) what one imagines and how one imagines it. The criterion for the vividness of one's imagination is the sharpness of the detail in which one can describe what one imagines, present it, or express it. It is on the whole easier to give a detailed description of what one sees than to describe the images before one's mind's eye or to think up and describe possibilities in detail. That is one reason why we are inclined to say that mental images are less vivacious than sense-impressions.

11.	It has often been supposed that there is an essential link between imaginability, conceivability, and logical possibility. It seems plausible to suppose that whatever is logically impossible is inconceivable. For, as has been recurrently noted in these essays, to say that something is logically impossible is not to say that a possibility is impossible, but rather to say that a form of words is excluded from use (e.g. 'a square circle', 'being red and green all over').

We have already noted that the eidetic powers do not coincide with the powers of imagination. There is much that we can imagine that we cannot picture to ourselves (e.g. a new constitution, a number greater than a million, a just society). Similarly, the powers of fantasy and the creative imagination far outstrip what is logically possible: the great works of religion, mythology, fairy tales, fantasy literature, drama, opera, sculpture, and painting are not constrained by what is logically possible. They capture our fancy, are awesome, wondrous and powerful, entertaining, witty and amusing, ingenious, clever, and imaginative. They give expression to the joys and horrors of human life, to the hopes and aspirations, the fears and suffering of mankind; and they do so by transgressing the boundaries of logical possibility and the limits of intelligibility.

Of course, as we have emphasized, a logical impossibility is not a possibility that is impossible. A logically impossible object (such as a disembodied mind or a transparent white window) is not an object the existence of which is excluded by logic. Rather, a form of words that appears to signify a possible object does not really do so. Logically impossible events or actions, such as travelling backwards (or forwards) in time, turning into a frog while retaining one's identity, metempsychosis, are not species of events or actions. Rather they are forms of words that superficially seem to describe possibilities but do not actually do so. They are, strictly speaking, nonsense – not rubbish, but forms of words that make no sense.

This may seem implausible. After all, if they are nonsense, if they make no sense, then how can we understand them? For surely we do understand Greek myths, fairy tales, fantasy fiction, and we take great pleasure in them. Tread carefully – the matter is delicate and subtle. There is nonsense and nonsense. Not all nonsense takes the form of 'gobbledegook', just as Escher's wonderful etchings of impossible objects are not akin to scribbles. Saul Steinberg's drawing of a hand drawing itself amuses us, even though it is pictorially, perspectivally, incoherent. In both cases, the rules of perspectival representation are transgressed.

In general, we are entertained and charmed by imaginative transgressions of the bounds of sense in art and fiction, mesmerized by it in the flights of metaphysics, and awed by it in religion. What should by now be clear is that the imaginable is not a criterion for what is logically possible, and that imaginability is not a sufficient condition of possibility.

How do things stand with regard to conceivability? The following propositions seem reasonable:

(i)   anything that is logically possible is conceivable.
(ii)   what is logically impossible is inconceivable—cannot *coherently* be conceived.
(iii) anything that makes sense is conceivable.
(iv)   what makes no sense is inconceivable.

Conceivability displays four forms of relativity. First, something may *seem* to be conceivable although it is not. We may await a demonstration that it is inconceivable. The idea of trisecting an arbitrary angle with a compass and rule in Euclidean plane-geometry seemed for almost two thousand years to be conceivable, but it needed an impossibility proof to show that it is not, that is, that there is no such thing.

Secondly, conceivability operates *within the available logical space of what makes sense*, which is determined by our conceptual scheme that changes over time. In ancient Greece, it was inconceivable to subtract 5 from 3 (one can't have less than nothing) and it remained so until the introduction of negative numbers and their interpretation in application. Similarly, it operates *within the realm of known facts of nature* at any given time. We know many facts that were not merely unknown to the Greeks, but were inconceivable, such as the existence of black holes, of superconductivity, of nuclear fusion or fission. The intelligibility of such notions depends upon knowledge of laws of nature involving theoretical concepts unavailable to the ancient world, such as mass, gravity, electricity, conductivity, electrical resistance.

Thirdly, conceivability is constrained by what is already known. There is, therefore, a perfectly good sense in which we may say that the existence of giants or winged angels is not *really* conceivable, since giants would not be able to move or even stand and angels would require a sternum protruding three feet beyond their shoulders. To conceive of such creatures, we would have to imagine the abrogation of the laws of nature – and that makes no sense. We can imagine angels and imagine them flying. But we cannot conceive of them consistently with known laws of nature.

Fourthly, we often relativize conceivability (and imaginability), as well as inconceivability (and unimaginability) to a person. Someone may find something inconceivable that another may well conceive. The German civilian population found it inconceivable that their army had been defeated in 1918, the soldiers at the front found it perfectly conceivable, since they knew it had happened. Hence the myth of the 'stab in the back'.

10

Thinking

"Getting hold of the difficulty deep down is what is so hard. Because if it is grasped near the surface, it simply remains the difficulty it was. It has to be pulled out by the roots; and that involves our beginning to think about these things in a new way. The change is as decisive as, for example, that from the alchemical to the chemical way of thinking. The new way of thinking is what is so hard to determine."

Wittgenstein

1. The concepts of thought and thinking are, like those of imagination and imagining, ramified, connecting profoundly different phenomena of human life and experience and linking a wide variety of subordinate concepts. It does not need much wit to note that thinking links reasoning, reflecting, musing, imagining, remembering (e.g. thinking about the beloved dead), acting with thought, meaning something or someone, thinking things to be thus-and-so, taking a cogitative stand. These are the varieties of thought. Each is a distinct centre of variation.

Reasoning is a mark of mankind: we have the capacity to reason from premises to a conclusion that is supported by the premises. We are able to draw inferences, that is: to *apprehend* that a set of premises *warrant* the conclusion. Inferring, unlike calculating, is not a process but a form of apprehension of relations between

Solving, Resolving, and Dissolving Philosophical Problems: Essays in Connective, Contrastive and Contextual Analysis, First Edition. P. M. S. Hacker.
© 2025 John Wiley & Sons Ltd. Published 2025 by John Wiley & Sons Ltd.

propositions. This no other animal can do. It is a prerogative of language-using, concept-exercising creatures. This distinctive capacity is often employed erroneously: our deductive reasoning may be invalid (i.e. the conclusion does not follow) or unsound (i.e. one or more premises are false); our inductive reasoning may be unsupported or ill-supported by the available evidence; our supporting arguments in a disputation may lack weight, that is, be unconvincing. That we are able to reason does not imply that we often do so. Nor does it imply that when shown our errors in reasoning we always change our mind: most commonly we cleave to a favoured conclusion in the face of error with spurious rationalizations and dogmatic or bigoted stubbornness in denial of the facts. Self-deception, alas, is also a mark of mankind.

The upshot of reasoning is arriving at a conclusion and hence judging: taking a cogitative stand. This in turn is linked to a further centre of variation in the conceptual analysis of thought, namely: *thinking things to be so*. Here are clustered *believing* things to be so (in many contexts there is scant difference between thinking and believing); *opining* or *assessing* things to be so; *estimating* that things are so; *assuming, supposing*, and *taking for granted* that things are so. Each of these differs from the others, but all are forms of thinking. Nevertheless, there are important differences between believing things to be so and thinking things to be so. One may believe something with complete certainty, but one cannot think something with complete certainty, just as one may passionately believe something but not passionately think something. One may cleave to one's beliefs, but not to one's thoughts. One may think, but not believe, well or ill of someone; one may believe, but not think, in someone or some cause. These are not mere idiom, for there is a rhyme and reason to each difference, and each logico-grammatical difference demarcates a *conceptual* distinction.

A different centre of variation is clustered around *reflecting*. This does subsume cogitative activities. Unlike inferring or drawing a conclusion, *thinking about* something is process-like: it takes time, goes on in time, can be interrupted and later resumed. One cannot answer the question 'What are you doing?' by saying, "I was inferring that the First World War was not inevitable', but one can answer, 'I was reflecting on whether the First World War was inevitable'. A cousin of thinking about is *deliberating*, which may precede coming to a conclusion about what to think or may antecede action. Reflecting may take the form of *thinking through* a theoretical problem or of *considering* what is to be said for and against a certain conclusion. But reflecting may take the more relaxed form of *ruminating*.

Ruminating in turn provides a link with another centre of variation, namely *musing*. This may be *daydreaming*: thinking how wonderful it would be if ...; or it may be *idle thinking* that is not harnessed to a purpose. Musing may be voluntary and intentional, but unlike reasoning and reflecting, not methodical or systematic. Ruminating is in turn linked to imagining: as we saw in the last chapter, a primary form imagining takes is *thinking up* possibilities; another common usage is 'just imagining things', that is, *thinking falsely*. A further link formed by ruminating is thinking about the past, often in fond recollection of past experiences, like Wordsworth remembering the daffodils he saw while walking in the Lake District:

> For oft, when on my couch I lie
> In vacant or in pensive mood,
> They flash upon that inward eye
> Which is the bliss of solitude;
> And then my heart with pleasure fills,
> And dances with the daffodils.

Rodin's statue of The Thinker (*Le Penseur*) is an emblematic representation of reasoning, reflecting, and ruminating. Here we most commonly contrast thought with action and speak of being 'sunk in thought'. Diametrically opposed to being sunk in thought is the thinking that is bound up with action, both positive and negative (i.e. omitting, refraining, and abstaining). For one may not only think of doing something or think how to do something, but one may *do something with or without thought*. Acting with thought may take very different forms. *Acting attentively* is concentrating upon what one is doing, as opposed to acting negligently and acting thoughtlessly. Someone who is acting attentively acts with awareness of possibilities that may arise and of mishaps that may occur, bears them in mind and is prepared to encounter them. *Acting intelligently* is engaging in an activity not merely with thought and attention, but with ingenuity, cleverness, and cunning, applying one's intelligence swiftly to changing circumstances – as does the chess-master, the outstanding tennis player, and the skilful debater in the cut and thrust of disputation. A further, central, form of doing something with thought is speaking. We should often think, deliberate, before speaking. But to speak without thinking does not necessarily mean speaking without antecedent deliberation.

Nor does it mean speaking without an accompanying activity of thinking. It means speaking without taking into account factors that should have been borne in mind and which, had one heeded them, would have led one to speak differently or not at all. To speak thoughtlessly may mean to speak insensitively, tactlessly, inconsiderately. To speak without thinking may mean to speak absent-mindedly, while thinking about something else. But it may mean to speak impulsively or imprudently.

Here we have a *rough* map of the terrain – an outline of the logical geography of the concept of thinking. It should be unsurprising that philosophers, psychologists, and cognitive neuroscientists, lacking such a map, should lose their way. Without a map, one is all too prone to seize upon one variant of thinking and treat it as a prototype, failing to realize that thinking is polymorphous.

2. To traverse such a variegated conceptual landscape as this without a map is almost bound to lead to mishaps, as one goes down pathways that lead nowhere, attempts to cross bogs rather than to circumvent them, and tries to scale rockfaces without pitons and rope. But the endeavour was rendered prodigiously more difficult by an array of preconceptions, misconceptions, and methodological confusions. These are worth mentioning, since they are still with us. Like garden weeds, they can be eradicated only for a season and are bound to recur, perhaps in mutated form, in a generation's time.

The question 'What is thinking?' puzzles all thinking people. The puzzlement does not stem from unfamiliarity with thinking: after all we spend much of the day thinking in one form or another. Nor does it arise out of unfamiliarity with the use of the verb 'to think' and its cognates, or with the large variety of subordinate cogitative verbs that we have just surveyed. For these are part of the verbal equipment of competent speakers. So whence the puzzlement?

One root lies in confused methodology. We are prone to suppose that if we want to find out what thinking is, all we need to do is observe ourselves while we are thinking. Like William James, we advocate introspecting and observing what goes on within us when and while we think. James confused the ability we all have to *say* what we think with the ability to *see* – by introspection – what we think. Like most philosophers throughout the ages, he mistakenly thought that the answer to the question 'How do you know what you think?' demands an observational answer as does the question, 'How do you know there is a cat in the garden?' But 'I don't know what I think about such-and-such', as we saw in Essay 6 – does not mean that one has not 'introspected', but that one needs to examine the evidence and come to a conclusion.

To be sure, if we follow James's advice and reflect on what is passing through our minds, what we find is disappointing even in the most favoured process-like thinkings. We find jumbles of disconnected words, occasional mental images flashing through our mind, fragments of an internal monologue. It was an egregious confusion of stream-of-consciousness writers (e.g. James Joyce, Virginia Woolf) to suppose that a true description of thinking consists in garbled semi-grammatical sentences. But to find out what someone thinks on a given question, what we want is his cogent statement of what he thinks, not a description of what crossed his mind while he was thinking on the matter. We can know perfectly well what Kant thought about the Enlightenment, not because we have a verbal snapshot of what crossed his mind, but because we can read his essay 'What is Enlightenment?'.

Of course, in many of the varieties of thinking that we have surveyed, such as meaning someone or something in an utterance, expressing one's opinion or judgement, or speaking thoughtfully, *nothing at all need be crossing one's mind*. This may leave us baffled. In our bewilderment we may have recourse to science: will an fMRI (functional magnetic resonance image) scan not show us what thinking really is? But that is absurd, for all an fMRI scan shows is minute increases in oxygenation in select parts of the brain of someone engaged in some cogitative exercise. But whatever thinking that, thinking of, thinking through, thinking up, thinking how, when, who, or what may be, they are not: emitting BOLD (blood-oxygen-level-dependency) signals. Moreover, to watch the pictures on the screen of an fMRI scanner is not to see thought for the first time in its true form (as one renowned cognitive neuroscientist proclaimed), since it is not to see thought at all. Such artificial, computer-generated, images show neither thinking nor what is thought, but at best a representation of oxygenation processes in parts of the brain when the patient is exemplifying one or another of a limited range of varieties of thinking.

We are mesmerized by the idea that thinking is something that goes on in our head. Is the coat of arms of thinking not Rodin's *Le Penseur*? Do we not wonder what is going on in his head? Do we not tell someone to use his head, that is, to think? Do we not speak of thoughts flashing through our mind, lurking at the back of our mind, of having a thought in mind? Surely, thinking takes place in the head – to be sure, not in the brain, but in the mind. Is thinking not the discourse of the soul with itself (Plato)? But if so, is thought inner speech? Well, do we not say, 'My French is getting so good I even talk to myself in French'? But surely, thought antecedes speech. What differentiates the parrot's squawk 'It's time for tea' from a human utterance is that the latter is accompanied by, informed by, the thought that it is time for tea. But that does not mean that the thought that animates the uttered words is just more words uttered in the mind, for then those words would need animation too. But if thought is not essentially composed of words, what is the medium of thought? Is it ideas? And what precisely are ideas? Are they mental images? Is it concepts? Or is it mental representations 'in the language of thought'? Dozens of misguided pictures crisscross here, each convincing us for a moment, until it is overtaken by another.

Matters are rendered worse by our susceptibility to mystification. It is easy to make thought and thinking appear quite magical. The *intentionality of thought* can seem a mystery. Is it not amazing that when we say, 'It is Jack's birthday tomorrow', we can be thinking of, *meaning*, Jack in New York and not the thousands of other Jacks. Our thought seems to traverse the ocean in a split second and pinpoint just Jack and no other – like a super-ballistic missile. Even more amazingly, we can think of people who are no longer alive. 'Caesar was murdered in 44 BC', we say, thinking of Julius Caesar, and our thought reaches back into the past and pinpoints precisely Julius Caesar, and not Cassius or Brutus standing by his bloody corpse. How can that be? Even more amazingly, we can think of Santa Claus or Adam and Eve, who never even existed. How is that possible? Note what appears to be the miraculous *speed of thought*: a mathematician may see the solution to a complex problem in a flash, even though it takes him half an hour and a large blackboard to write it down. How extraordinary that he could do it so quickly in his mind! We think thoughts all the time, but when we pause to reflect, thoughts seem strange and *intangible*. What exactly is it that we think when we think a thought? Do we *grasp* it, as Frege imagined? How can we grasp something that is not even perceptible? Does it become perceptible by being clothed in the garb of a sentence? If so, how on earth do we tailor the garb to fit the thought? How do we translate thoughts into language? Are some languages better than others for this purpose? – many thinkers have thought that *their* language was *uniquely* suitable. Thoughts are not only intangible but also *elusive*. They lurk at the back of our minds just out of our reach, flit across our mind too quickly for us to grasp. Some, it is said, are deeply buried in the unconscious mind and can only be dug out with the aid of a psychoanalyst.

These misconceived pictures and mystifications threaten to overwhelm us. But we now know in principle how to handle them. It is not by proliferation of yet more theories – *that* would lead us yet further into the morass. It is by patient and methodical connective, contrastive, and contextual analysis. We already have a map of the terrain.

3.   It is very tempting to suppose that thought must have a medium. Surely, we are inclined to say, we must think *in* something. Early modern philosophers held that we think in ideas. The empiricists were prone to argue that ideas are copies of sense-impressions given in experience. These give the mind the materials of thought and determine the limits of thought. For all thought consists in combining and separating ideas: an idea or ideas thought about, and an idea or ideas thought of (predicated of) it or them. Judgement is affirming or denying one idea of another. Ideas in and of themselves are either simple or complex. The mind cannot generate simple ideas: these must be given in experience. Thinking is kaleidoscopic and communication is telementation. Words stand for ideas, sentences for combinations of ideas. An utterance produces in the mind of the hearer ideas that are qualitatively identical to those before the mind of the speaker. Accordingly, language is strictly speaking not necessary for thinking, but only for the communication of ideas.

This conception, this picture, wrought havoc with European thought for centuries. It is deeply confused. First, there are numerous concepts and kinds of concepts that could not be expressed by sense-impressions or their reproductive ideas. These include logical operators and connectives such as 'not', 'and', 'or', 'if' and quantifiers, such as 'all', 'some', 'many', 'most', 'a few', which are pivotal for reasoning (thinking) in any form. They also include categorial concepts, such as 'object', 'property', 'relation', 'colour', 'sound', and abstractions of innumerable kinds, such as truth, goodness, and beauty, as well as unpicturables such as laws of nature, the common law, human rights, a chiliagon, and so forth. Second, a mental image or picture may illustrate a thought, as a literal picture may illustrate a text. But it cannot be a substitute for a thought any more than a picture can be a substitute for the text it illustrates. One cannot read off an illustrative picture the narrative it illustrates: a picture of a knight in armour may be of Sir Lancelot (fictitious) or of Charles V (equestrian painting by Titian); it may illustrate how to sit on a horse when fully armed or how not to sit on a horse; it may illustrate the type of horse (destrier) used by an armoured knight; and so on. One cannot read off a mental image what thought it depicts. Third, a description of whatever passes before one's mind while one is thinking does not specify what one thinks nor does it describe one's thinking (which may be described as original or pedestrian, brilliant or mediocre). Saying what I think is not describing a private peep show into which only I can peer, and telling another what one is thinking is not a running commentary on what images are before one's mind. The train of one's reasoning is laid out in an explicit statement of premises and conclusion, not in a description of sequences of images, imagined diagrams, or symbols.

Furthermore, the very notion of an idea was confused. The supposition that ideas must be either simple or complex was itself mistaken, since it assumed that the notions of simple and complex are absolute, rather than context-dependent. But what counts as simple and what as complex varies from case to case and context to context and has to be laid down in advance. What is given in experience is not ideas or sense-impressions but the endless variety of perceptibilia in our environment, classifiable in indefinitely many ways. Human discourse and communication is not transmission of ideas (telementation), but engagement in linguistic activities in indefinitely diversified language-games in the stream of life. Words are not names of ideas and sentences do not signify concatenations of ideas. The limits of thought are not set by the limits of the kaleidoscopic combination of simple ideas into complexes of ideas, but by the limits of the linguistic expression of thought.

4.   Do we then think in words? Various considerations support this view. First, we do indeed talk to ourselves in our imagination. It was therefore natural to suppose, as Plato did, that thought is discourse of the soul with itself. But, in philosophy, what is natural is usually mistaken. Secondly, we are mesmerized by the phrase 'to think in'. We do say such things as 'I can speak French now, but I still can't think in French'. Thirdly, as noted, we are prone to think that the difference between a human utterance and a parrot's repetition is that in the former case thought accompanies speech – that one thinks the words before or while uttering them. Fourthly, we picture the deception of a confidence trickster as saying one thing in his heart and another out loud. Nevertheless, we must free ourselves from these philosophical

intuitions – intuitions in philosophy are usually no more than misguided hunches. In the rare cases in which they are correct, they still carry no weight until they have been shown to be correct.

Talking to oneself in the imagination is neither necessary nor sufficient for thinking. One may count sheep in order to stop oneself from thinking. One may run through one's speech in one's imagination in advance of delivering it, but that is not thinking it through afresh, it is merely assuring oneself that one knows it by heart. Conversely, doing something thoughtfully does not imply saying anything to oneself. One may come to the conclusion that *h* on the basis of evidence *e* without saying anything to oneself. All that is necessary is that thenceforth one judges that *h* and is willing to reason, act, or react in the light of it and to justify it by reference to *e*.

For someone to avow that he cannot yet think in a language he is learning does not imply that when he speaks his native tongue, he thinks in it. One does not *think in* anything, although one may talk to oneself in one's imagination in one language or another. 'I can speak in French, but I can't yet think in French' means no more than that one must first think what one wants to say and then has to struggle to find the right French words in which to say it. 'My French is getting much better, I am now even thinking in French', if it does not simply mean that I am now talking to myself in my imagination in French, means that I no longer have to think what I want to say and then pause to find the right French words.

To be sure, Polly simply parrots English phonemes without thought. The bird does not think what it squawks. But that doesn't imply that when we speak with thought, we are accompanying our words with an inner, covert, activity of speaking in our imagination. To speak with thought is to speak thoughtfully, reflectively, with understanding, taking relevant factors into consideration, having reasons for what one says, and so forth. 'To think' thus used is *adverbial*, akin not to singing to an accompaniment but to singing with expression. One can imagine people who speak only aloud, but that does not mean that when they speak thoughtfully, they say everything twice.

We picture the confidence trickster as saying one thing in his heart and another thing to his victim. But this is no more than emblematic. A confidence trickster says things he knows to be false with the intention of profitably deceiving his victim.

5. Is the medium of thought then less phenomenal than ideas and more abstract than words? Do we think in concepts, as Kant

suggested. For we think thoughts, and thoughts must surely have constituents – otherwise how could we explain the logical, inferential, relations between them? How could we explain the obvious fact that Hans, Jean, and John may all think the same thought, even though Hans speaks neither French nor English, Jean speaks neither German nor English, and John speaks neither French nor German. But they all share the same concepts, expressed by the words of their several languages. Are these not constituents of the very same thought they all think? Moreover, since languages differ in their grammatical forms and structures, one may readily suppose that some languages are better than others in reflecting the forms and structures of the concepts expressed. Aristide Briand, a French prime minister, proudly declared that French was the most logical of languages, since its word order mirrors the order of thinking that takes place in our mind. Frege held that natural languages were all defective, but that his concept script (the first-order predicate calculus with identity) faithfully reflects the logical structures of all and any thoughts.

Conceptual mythology bewitched scientists too. Theoretical linguists, psycholinguists, and cognitive neuroscientists all succumbed to the magic, the black magic, of patter about concepts. Words were held to be names of concepts (replacing the supposition that they are names of ideas), speech was conceived to be the translation of concepts into words. Some forms of aphasia were explained in terms of retention of concepts stored in a concept-module in the brain that has become detached from the word-module. Linguists, led by Noam Chomsky (b. 1928), the most influential linguist of the twentieth century, argued that the speed of language acquisition is such that it can be explained only by reference to the idea that concepts are innate and that language-learning consists in learning labels for concepts already possessed. This is a pipe dream of reason.

As we have seen in previous essays, the useful question to ask is not 'What is a concept?' but rather, what has to be true of a creature for us to say of it that it has acquired a concept. To possess a concept is to have mastered the use of a word or phrase that is said to express a concept. It is to be able to use a word or phrase correctly, in accordance with the rules for its use. It is to be able to explain what it means in a sentence one uses with understanding and to recognize as correct an explanation of its meaning in sentences one understands. It is to be able to respond intelligently to its use. Our talk of concepts enables us to abstract from local languages to commonalities shared by different languages. A concept stands to its linguistic expression in much the same way as the powers of a chess piece stand to the carved chess piece that possesses those powers. A concept is not *an* anything. Concepts are not kinds of things but abstractions from kinds of things, namely word and phrase usage. It is therefore patent that words are not names of concepts, that concepts are no more storables than are the powers of chess pieces. The idea that concepts can be stored in the brain is as absurd as the idea that the powers of chess pieces can be stored in the box into which one places the pieces. The thought of concept modules in the brain that are linked to name modules in which names of concepts are stored and that forms of aphasia can be explained by reference to the disconnection of the concept module from the name module is literally gibberish. The aphasic phenomenon is straightforward: one can remember the explanation of the meaning of a word, for example, 'the animal jockeys ride at Ascot' but cannot recollect the word it explains, viz. 'horse'.

Bearing this in mind, it is obvious that what one thinks does not have concepts as its constituents. What one thinks (a thought) is not an object of any kind. The 'what' is an *interrogative pronoun*, not a *relative one*. What one thinks is what is given in answer to the question, 'What are you thinking?' The answer to that question consists of a sentence that expresses a thought. That sentence is composed of words, some of which express concepts. But the thought it expresses is not composed of anything. What I think may be what Jack fears and what Jill expects, namely that global warming will destroy civilization. But the destruction of civilization is not composed of concepts but of catastrophes. Words are storables and the places in which they may be stored are dictionaries, but the concepts they express are not. It is erroneous to suppose that we think *in* concepts. We don't think *in* anything.

6.   So, we do not think *in* concepts, in the sense in which we speak in French or English. The analogy between speaking in a language and thinking is deceptive. If one says something, one says it *in* a language. A language is a medium of expression, communication, and representation. But concepts are not a medium and one does not think in them, even though there is precious little thought without them. In order to think anything beyond the most rudimentary, we must possess concepts, that is to say, we must have mastered the techniques of word usage in a wide variety of language games. But there is no such thing as thinking *in* the techniques of word usage.

It is becoming evident that our most fundamental error was the very idea that thought requires a medium. What is true is that representations require a medium. Any representation must have non-representational properties that characterize the medium: the colour of the pencil with which one draws a representational picture, the hardness of the metal in which one engraves a representational engraving, the texture of the paper on which an architectural blueprint is printed, the size of one's script in writing, and so forth. In short, there must be a distinction between message and medium. But *a thought is all message and no medium*. That is why it is a dire confusion to suppose that thoughts are representations.

7.   Our thoughts are *expressed* in language and commonly manifest in what we do and how we respond to circumstances and to the utterances of others. Does that imply that mastery of a language is a prerequisite for thinking in all its forms? That would be too hasty. If we restrict 'thinking' to thinking or believing that something is so, then we must grant that non-language-using animals may think things to be so – as the dog thinks its owner is at the door when it hears the familiar footsteps, thinks it is going to be taken for a walk when it hears the rattle of its leash being taken of the peg, thinks it is about to be fed when it sees its food dish being filled, thinks the cat it was chasing is up the tree it scaled, even though the cat has long since escaped. In all such cases, the animal's thinking what it thinks is expressed in its behaviour. But we rightly refrain from saying that the dog had the thought that ..., or the thought that ... crossed its mind, or that it bore the thought ... in mind. For reflecting, ruminating, drawing inferences from evidence are beyond the powers of an animal that has not mastered a language. The limits of animal thought are very restrictive – the dog may think it is about to be taken for a walk, as is evident from its excited tail-wagging and barking, but it cannot now expect to be taken for a walk tomorrow or next weekend. It may think its master is about to enter the house, but it cannot now expect its master to return home tomorrow or next week. It *makes no sense* to say of a dog that it expects to be given a bone next Christmas Day. It is not *false*, for if it were false, we should have to be able to explain what would *count* as its being true. But that we cannot do. For there is nothing in the behavioural repertoire of a non-language-using animal that could determine the temporal deixis of such thoughts.

The limits of what a creature can intelligibly be said to think are the limits of its possible behavioural expression of thinking. This is a cardinal principle. It is important not to misinterpret it. It articulates a condition of sense, not of truth. It is not a form of behaviourism, even though, like behaviourism, it acknowledges a logico-grammatical connection between thought and behaviour. But thinking is not behaving – neither 'outer', observable, behaviour, nor 'inner' unobservable behaviour (talking to oneself in the imagination; moving one's larynx). Nor is thinking a disposition to behave. There is much that we think without revealing what we think, most commonly because there is no point or no occasion to do so. We do not flaunt our reasonings, inferrings, or deducings save in public debates and classrooms, in arguments, explanations and justifications. The only way to determine what a person thinks, what he is thinking, how he thought through a problem or thought up a solution to a problem, is by reference to what he says or does. For if something is thought, it *can* be exhibited in behaviour, in words or deeds. The *can* here is logical, not circumstantial. What someone struck down by locked-in syndrome thinks is what he *would* express in utterance and deed were he not paralysed. We can understand ascriptions of thought to him, because we know what it would be or would have been for him to express such thought.

8. Unfinished business: we must strive not to succumb to mystery. There are no mysteries in philosophy, only mystifications. We are indeed impressed that someone can see the solution to a complex problem in a flash, when it takes a lengthy demonstration to articulate the solution. But we confuse the sudden *dawning of the ability* with its exercise. We conflate the Eureka experience of realizing that we *can* solve the problem with the high-speed solving of the problem. A sudden flash of inspiration is a pointer, not a product.

We are prone to suppose that thoughts are elusive. Frege thought it to be a mystery that we can *grasp* thoughts and held this greatest of mysteries to be a problem for psychology not logic. But thoughts no more *evade* our grasp than flames, and *grasping* amounts to no more than understanding. Of course, we sometimes find difficulty in articulating our thoughts, but that does not imply that our difficulty lies in clothing a pre-existing thought in words. It means that we find it difficult to formulate an opinion, come to a conclusion, or decide what to think.

We may make much of the intangibility of thoughts. But while it is true that one cannot touch thoughts as one can touch tables and chairs, that is no mystery. The antiquity of a chair or table is not tangible either, but we make no mystery of it. Thoughts are not intangible objects because they are not objects at all.

We puzzle about the location of thinking. Surely, we think in our heads – either in our mind or in our brain. But, as we have learnt (see Essay 1), the mind has no location, since talk of the mind is a form of presenting human powers and their exercise, and powers have possessors but not locations, and the exercise of powers is located wherever their possessor is when he exercises them. Where A thinks that p is wherever A is when he thinks that p. What is true is that damage to certain parts of the brain may deprive one of the power to think and artificial stimulation of certain parts of the brain may induce various cogitative phenomena. But it makes no sense to ascribe thinking to a brain. There is nothing a brain can do that would satisfy a criterion for thinking. There is no such thing as a brain ruminating, musing, drawing inferences, engaging in thoughtful debate, playing an intelligent game of tennis, concentrating on a delicate operation. We would not be able to think but for the normal functioning of our brains, but we do not think with our brains in the sense in which we walk with our legs and see with our eyes. In *that* sense, there is no organ of thought. The agent of thought is the human being who has a brain and who expresses the thought in word and deed, or would do so given appropriate circumstances.

The moral of the tale is that whenever, in philosophy, we appear to encounter a mystery in the nature of things, we may be assured that it is mystification in reasoning about those things. It needs dissolving in the acids of connective, contrastive, and contextual analysis.

11

On Dreams and Dreaming

I hear faint footsteps on the stair
Of parents, sister, brother, wife,
But I know I merely dream in hope
That dreams might bring them back to life.

They still are vivid to my mind,
With all the things we thought and did,
But touch eludes the outstretched hand
And empty air holds nothing hid.

Faint steps I said. That was not true.
I heard no sounds, however faint,
The canvas stays forever blank
However much I long to paint!

Edward Greenwood

1. Human beings have dreamt and been fascinated by their dreams since time immemorial. One concern was where do they come from or who sent them? The other was what do they mean? The answers to the first question were threefold: (i) the gods or evil spirits; (ii) from ourselves, expressing our preoccupations, wishes, longings, including, if Freudians are right, unconscious ones; (iii) from our brain. The answer to the second question was a function of the putative source.

So three kinds of answers to the question of what dreams mean were advanced, corresponding to the three supposed sources: dreams are (i) revelations and portents that reveal the future, (ii) disclosures about ourselves, and (iii) meaningless, being mere neural detritus, perhaps consequences of the brain's consolidating long-term memory during sleep. It is of interest that the third pair of options are not a modern idea. They were already advanced by Jonathan Swift in his poem 'On Dreams':

> Those dreams, that on the silent night intrude,
> And with false flitting shades our minds delude,
> Jove never sends us downwards from the skies;
> Nor can they from infernal mansions rise;
> But are all mere productions of the brain,
> And fools consult interpreters in vain.

These questions will not concern us. Dreams have been a focus of philosophical interest since the dawn of philosophy. Most forms of radical philosophical scepticism about knowledge of the perceptible world arise out of the phenomena of dreaming. For might life not be a dream? Are we not 'such stuff as dreams are made on'? How do we know that we are not dreaming now? A modern, much more baffling form of scepticism is *scepticism about dreaming itself*. Do we ever really dream, or do we merely awaken with the false impression of antecedent events experienced? Are dreams not merely mnemonic hallucinations? This form of scepticism sheds important and unexpected light on our concept of dreaming. It is these two questions that will be interrogated here.

2.   How should we begin? Casting a net in the *Oxford English Dictionary* brings a simple pattern of meanings into view. The central use of 'to dream' is straightforward: it means the same as 'to have a dream'. Dreams occur during sleep and have a content. One may dream *that* such-and-such, and one may dream *of* or *about* something. Dreams are recollected on waking. Derivative uses are analogical extensions. First, to dream is to have a vision (as in Martin Luther King's 'I have a dream') – a vision of a future desideratum to be achieved against the odds by great endeavour. It was nicely expressed by T. E. Lawrence in *The Seven Pillars of Wisdom*:

> All men dream: but not equally. Those who dream by night, in the
> dusty recesses of their minds, wake up in the day to find it was vanity,

but the dreamers of the day are dangerous men, for they may act their dream with open eyes, to make it possible.

Second, to dream of something is to long for it. Third, it is to daydream, to indulge in fantasies and hence to be occupied in reveries. Fourth, it is to believe something falsely (as one supposedly does when one dreams in the primary sense), and so to think something implausible to be the case, as in 'You are just dreaming: it could never happen – it can't be so'. Fifth, it is to judge something actual to be highly implausible, as in: 'I never dreamt that …', or 'Who would have dreamt …' Finally, and related to the previous use, 'to dream' has a negative use to avow lack of intent: 'I would not dream of doing …'.

It is obvious that 'N dreamt that' is an expression that we affix to a sentence that describes *what* N dreamt, as in 'N dreamt that – he was in New York': 'he was in New York' specifies *the content* of N's dream. Not only can it be affixed to *any* sentence with a sense, but also to many sentences *without* a sense (as is evident in *Alice in Wonderland* and *Through the Looking Glass*). For we can, and often do, dream nonsensical dreams as Alice did.

A curious grammatical question is whether the verb 'to dream' in its primary use has a first-person present tense. It seems not, since the common first-person use is 'I dreamt', uttered on waking. But that is too hasty. Obviously, a first-person present tense occurrence may be embedded in a conditional: 'If you see that *I am dreaming*, having a nightmare, please wake me up'. On the other hand, the use of 'I am dreaming' as a free-standing declarative sentence appears to have only an exclamatory role to express astonishment, as in 'I am dreaming! This can't be true!' (or, more likely, 'I must be dreaming! This can't be real!'). What about its negation 'I am not dreaming'? The only context in which it could be used is when one lies in a dark room with eyes closed, talking to oneself; someone passes by and whispers 'He's dreaming'; one might then respond, 'I am not dreaming, I am just talking to myself'. Other than such unusual contexts, it has no communicative use as an assertion, for it could not inform anyone of something they do not know. But like 'I'm dreaming' it can play an exclamatory role to express astonishment: 'I'm not dreaming: this is real'.

Does one not sometimes have to pinch oneself in order to assure oneself that one is not dreaming? Is this not evidence that one is awake? No, it is but a rhetorical conceit. For if one were really to think there is some doubt, pinching oneself could not resolve it, since one might just be dreaming that one pinches oneself and that it hurts.

3.   What is our common conception of dreams and dreaming in the primary sense of the words? How, rightly or wrongly, do we think about the topic? There is a general consensus that dreams occur during sleep – that appears unchallengeable. Similarly, we are prone to insist that to dream is to undergo experiences during sleep, which one often recollects on waking and may relate to others. Dreams commonly have causes in subliminally sensed heat or cold and subliminally heard ambient sounds and noises, which are transmuted into dream episodes. Internal physiological causes are also recognized: indigestion is prone to generate unpleasant dreams and restless sleep; genital arousal in sleep commonly accompanies erotic dreams, although whether as cause or as effect may be unclear. What one dreams, whether sensible or nonsensical, whether coherently continuous or incoherent jumble, may range from sweet dreams to nightmares. A wide range of emotions is involved in dreams, from joy to terror. Emotions dreamt affect sleep behaviour, from smiles to tossing and turning, facial expressions of fear, heavy perspiration, and utterances. Dreamt emotion also affects behaviour on waking: experience of relief, panting, post-fear symptoms such as perspiration, high pulse rate. It is also generally agreed that in so called lucid dreams one knows that one is dreaming.

4.   Systematic scepticism concerning our perceptual knowledge of the world based on the phenomenon of dreaming dates back to antiquity. It played a role in Pyrrhonic scepticism as presented by Sextus Empiricus (ca. 160–ca. 210 AD). It is most closely associated with Descartes (1596–1650), who, in his *Meditations on First Philosophy* invoked the phenomenon of dreaming in order to show that perceptual judgements are open to doubt and so cannot be the foundations of genuine knowledge. For any particular perceptual judgement, for example, that I am now sitting at my desk, might be no more than part of a dream. For all I know, I might be dreaming that I am sitting at my desk. Indeed, dreaming can be invoked to engender global scepticism with regard to experiential knowledge: *all* my experiences of the perceptible world, for all I know, might be no more than a dream. After all, I could know for certain that I am awake and perceiving whatever I perceive of my immediate environment only if there were some indefeasible mark of being awake. But there *could be* no such subjective mark, for whatever might be proposed could itself be something dreamt. It is tempting to argue that the coherence of diurnal experience is a mark of being awake. If one breaks a window it

remains broken. But since *any* description can be preceded by the dream affix 'I dreamt that ...', the sceptic will challenge one. How does one know one is not having a coherent dream in which one breaks a window and dreams that it stays broken? For *all* perceptual knowledge might be no more than a dream.

Descartes, however, was no sceptic. Indeed, he invented the method of doubt in order to refute scepticism. Once one has proved one's own existence and proved the existence of God, who is no deceiver, Descartes averred, one *can* give good reasons for thinking that one is not dreaming. For, he argued,

> dreams are never linked by memory with all other actions of life as waking experiences are. If, while I am awake, anyone were suddenly to appear to me and then disappear immediately, as happens in sleep, so that I could not see where he had come from or where he had gone to, it would not be unreasonable for me to judge that he was a ghost, or a vision created in my brain rather than a real man.... when I can connect my perceptions ... with the whole of the rest of my life without a break, then I am quite certain that when I encounter these things I am not asleep but awake. (*Meditation* 6)

This relaxed attitude is wholly dependent on the antecedent proofs of the reality of the material world, and so presupposes that scepticism about the perceptible world is unwarranted and refutable by reference to the benevolence of God.

Few today will accept Descartes's arguments for his own existence, for a criterion of truth (clarity and distinctness), and for the existence of God. The very idea of *proving* one's existence by means of an argument is not coherent. (If a student were to tell one, 'I think that there are tigers in India, therefore I exist', one would not know what he was trying to say, and one would probably advise him to take a weekend off from philosophy.) There is, alas, no general criterion of truth. And the causal and ontological arguments for the existence of God have been shown to be invalid.

What is true is that if we reject the sceptic's case (as we all do), then our attitude towards what we have dreamt is wholly disconnected from our practical attitudes towards genuine experience. There is all the difference in the world between deciding something important in the middle of a sleepless night and dreaming that one decided something important. The former carries practical weight the next day, but except for the superstitious, the latter does not since 'it was only a dream'. This does not prove the sceptic is wrong, it presupposes that he is.

This leaves us in an impasse. It seems that every attempt to answer the sceptic, who rests his case on dreaming, fails. But no sensible person believes that we don't know whether we are awake or not. What is to be done?

5.   Before proceeding further, it is necessary to clarify an inferential prohibition. From 'In my dream, I did so-and-so' it is never licit to infer that I did so-and-so. 'In my dream, I did so-and-so' is equivalent to 'I dreamt I did so-and-so'. 'I did so-and-so' is thus preceded by the dream affix, and to extract the dream-content description from the dream affix is to make an invalid inference, as is patent in 'I dreamt I was talking to Cicero', or 'I dreamt I was dead'. We shall have occasion to invoke this principle when we investigate the phenomenon of lucid dreams.

One might object: surely it is *sometimes* licit. Does it not follow from 'I dreamt that I was alive' or 'I dreamt I was breathing' or indeed from 'I dreamt I was asleep' that I was alive, breathing, or asleep? It certainly follows, but it does not follow from *what* I dreamt, it follows from the fact *that* I dreamt, since one cannot dream if one is not alive, breathing or sleeping. So one is not, in these cases, extracting anything from *within* the dream-affix (i.e. from the dream description), but merely drawing an inference from the dream-affix itself.

6.   We must probe the presuppositions underlying this Cartesian debate, presuppositions accepted both by the sceptic and by those who try to answer him. There are three unquestioned presuppositions:

(i)   The question of whether I am dreaming can arise for me.
(ii)   I might not know whether I am asleep and dreaming, or awake and having genuine experiences.
(iii)   I need evidence if I am to quell any doubts whether I am awake or asleep.

But: there are no circumstances in actual life in which the question of philosophical scepticism can literally arise. For the sceptic raises his question in a vacuum: as is evident from his behaviour – he does not *in practice* worry whether he is about to give a lecture or is only dreaming that he is about to give a lecture. Nor does he seriously doubt whether the so-called external world exists. After all, he behaves just as we all do. But if the question can never really arise in practice, *there need be no answer to it*. So the whole debate is empty.

The question 'How do you know?' has been extended beyond its logical limits and is here quite meaningless.

To be sure, there are objections. First: don't we say, 'I must be dreaming', especially when something wonderful or dreadful is unexpectedly encountered. So it does make sense to suppose that one might not know whether one is awake or asleep and dreaming. No. We already know how to repudiate this. 'I must be dreaming!' is an exclamation that means [roughly] 'This can't be true', just as 'I can't believe it!' means [roughly] 'This [actuality] goes against all the evidence'.

Second objection: there is surely the well-known phenomenon of actually knowing, while one is asleep, that one is dreaming. It was already noted by Aristotle that 'often, when one is asleep, there is something in the soul which declares that what presents itself is but a dream' (*On Dreams* 462ª5–8). This phenomenon was named 'lucid dreaming' by Frederik van Eeden in 1913 and has been much studied by psychologists. In a lucid dream, it is said by lucid dreamers, one *knows* one is dreaming and struggles to wake up. Indeed, lucid dreams occur just before one wakes up precisely because one's struggle to awaken is successful. Surely this proves that one *can* know that one is asleep and dreaming, and that normally, when having a non-lucid dream, one does not. This strikes many, including research psychologists, as completely persuasive. But it is mistaken. The principle that one can't extract the dream-content description from the dream-affix applies here too. 'In my dream, I knew I was dreaming and struggled to awaken' means no more than 'I dreamt that I knew that I was dreaming and dreamt that I struggled to awaken'. To dream that one knows something is not to know anything. To dream that one thinks this or that is not to think anything, and to solve a problem in one's dream is merely to dream one solved a problem, even if the dreamt solution is seen to be true on waking. The very term 'lucid dream' is a misnomer, and the extensive psychological research on lucid dreams rests on a misconception.

7.   Scepticism about perceptual knowledge and the existence of the 'external world' based on the phenomenon of dreaming is familiar to all students of philosophy. They do not credit it, but are typically unsure how to refute it. That, we have just argued, is not surprising, since it cannot be refuted. But it does not require refutation, although there are perfectly good reasons for rejecting it. For the philosophical questions 'Might I be asleep and only dreaming that I am discussing

scepticism with you?' and 'Might life be a dream?' can be no more than a conceit and are not to be taken seriously. They cannot really arise in practice. If a man went around breaking windows, always returning half an hour later to assure himself that the window was still broken, should we explain, 'Don't worry! He is a philosopher. He's just making sure he is awake.' If someone were to preface all his remarks in conversation with the words 'I'm not sure I am awake, but assuming I am …', would we really think that he is trapped in Pyrrhonian scepticism and try to answer him, or would we treat his remarks as 'white noise' – as a strange way of clearing his throat?

Scepticism *about* dreams, however, is not at all familiar. When people encounter it, they are typically indignant, think it obviously wrong and suppose that it must be readily refutable. But, as we shall see, it cannot be refuted, and it is *unobviously* wrong.

How do we know that dreaming occurs during sleep? After all, the phenomena of which we are speaking are strikingly simple. People wake up with the strong impression that they remember events that have just happened, but which didn't happen at all. On waking, these events seem to them to have occurred while they were asleep. They are trained from childhood to report these apparent memories with the prefix 'I dreamt that'. But a dream sceptic will argue that what people think they remember as having happened in their sleep and what they call 'dreams' are in fact no more than bogus memories that they have on awaking. In an enlightened society they would not be called dreams, but 'waking whoppers' or more academically 'hypnopompic hallucinations'.

This may seem ridiculous, even outrageous – to be rejected outright. There are three objections to this philosophical fancy. First, to dream is to have experiences, namely the experiences one dreams of having. These experiences occur in one's sleep and one recounts them on waking, since one remembers them. But that is too quick. To dream that one is experiencing something is not to experience anything. The dream sceptic will rightly insist that one never had any such experiences. It merely seems to one that one had them, when one awakens. To this the second objection may be advanced: while one is asleep dreaming, especially when one has a nightmare, one tosses and turns, flinches, mutters words in fright (e.g. 'Oh, no!). This surely proves that the person is dreaming. Not at all, the dream sceptic will respond. Before someone has the dream illusion on waking, and especially when the dream illusion is of something frightening having happened, then he will typically toss and turn, flinch, mutter words, perspire heavily. From this, observers can predict that when the sleeper awakens, he will tell dream-whoppers. This reply may call forth a third objection to dream scepticism: on waking from a nightmare, people typically display post-fear behaviour. They express relief to be awake, for their dream was terrifying, their pulse rate is high, they are perspiring heavily, they may gasp or pant for a moment or two. Does this not prove definitively that during sleep they were frightened, and that is surely an experience they underwent. Not so, the dream sceptic will reply. These are post-sleep forms of behaviour characteristic of the waking hallucination that one experienced something in one's sleep. But there can be no such things as *experiences* when one is asleep, for one can experience things, see, hear and feel things, engage in activities, only when conscious. And sleep is not a state of consciousness. Exasperated, our dream realist may advance a fourth objection: Science has proved that dreams occur during sleep. Rapid eye movement sleep (REM) was defined by Nathaniel Kleitman and Eugene Aserinsky in 1953 and linked to dreaming. It was further described by Dement and Jouvet. They thought that their empirical investigations proved that dreams occur during sleep and that a scientific mark of dreaming is REM sleep. (This has been questioned since, but let us disregard that.) Not so, the dream sceptic will again reply. REM dream research *presupposes* that dreams occur during sleep. But we could, with equal right, contend that rapid eye movements during sleep *presage* a mnemonic hallucination on waking and are grounds for predicting dream-whoppers.

This looks disturbingly like stalemate. Dream scepticism seems irrefutable. But no one is likely to accept it. What does all this show? It shows that the claim that we dream during sleep is not an empirical claim at all and is not supported by empirical evidence. It is part of our *form of representation*. It is the form in which we conceptualize and articulate what is given, namely awaking from sleep with the impression of antecedent events that did not occur. This, *we hold*, is the aftermath of dreaming. Dreaming occurs during sleep and is recounted from memory on awakening. But our discussion also shows that we could, with equal warrant, adopt an alternative form of representation in which there is no such thing as dreaming and no dream experiences during sleep but only mnemonic hallucinations on waking of things having happened. In this form of representation, there are no dream narratives, but only hypnopompic hallucinations.

It should now be clear why our dream sceptic is wrong – unobviously wrong. He has crossed two different forms of representation.

He is right to envisage a form of representation in which the phenomena in question are conceptualized as hypnopompic hallucinations. He is right that *we* conceptualize the same phenomena as dreams that occur during sleep. Where he goes wrong is when he casts doubt on whether dreams occur during sleep at all. He is wrong to characterize mnemonic hallucination as dream illusions. One form of representation has no room for dreams (any more than draughts has room for checkmate) – it is not that as a matter of fact there aren't any, it is rather that there is no such thing as a dream, a fortiori as dream illusions. In the other form of representation, namely ours, dreams occur during sleep. But that is a *conceptual convention*, not an empirical discovery.

Forms of representation are not correct or incorrect. But the cultural ubiquity of our dreaming form of representation suggests that it was found to be natural for us, that mankind felt, and still feels, comfortable with it. One may speculate why. Surely because ancient cultures, such as Sumerian, Akkadian, Assyrian, and Egyptian, found it overwhelmingly natural to think that dreams were sent by the gods or demons and that they portend future events. That thought could not fit comfortably with representing the phenomena as mnemonic hallucinations.

8.   Our favoured dream form of representation comes at a price. First, we hesitate over whether to characterize dreaming as an experience. On the one hand, we are inclined to describe nightmares as dreadful experiences undergone while asleep. We are also inclined to characterize lucid dreams as vivid experiences of realizing, while asleep, that one is dreaming. On the other hand, we link the concept of experience with that of consciousness. One can experience things only when one is awake. To be asleep is not to be conscious, and one cannot *not* be conscious and also *be conscious* of something at the same time.

It is an amazing fact that this contradiction is willingly embraced by experimental psychologists and cognitive neuroscientists, who blithely declare that one experiences things while fast asleep – namely whenever one dreams. But this is an incoherent paradox. The only resolution is to deny that anything is experienced while asleep. To dream that one is experiencing something is not to experience anything. Similarly, to dream that one knows that one is dreaming, is not to know or realize anything, and so-called lucid dreams are not cases of knowing, while one is dreaming, that one is asleep and dreaming. It is simply to dream that one knows or realizes that one is dreaming.

Secondly, we naturally think that on waking from a dream we relate what we remember of the dream we dreamt. But some of us have very poor memories. Should we not sometimes challenge a dream narrator's narrative with an 'Are you certain you are remembering correctly?' or 'Are you sure it happened like that in your dream?'? But we don't. The question of misremembering does not arise – we exclude it. There is no criterion of a dream report agreeing or failing to agree with a dream. In this area, truthfulness guarantees truth. (The dream sceptic would say that this shows that no remembering is going on at all.)

Thirdly, even though we present dreams as occurring during sleep, accept that dreaming is often interrupted by being awoken and so was occurring just before awaking, we have no way of resolving the question of the *objective duration* of a dream. Subjective dream duration is given by the dream narrative, but how long did the dreaming actually last? A sensory stimulus (a loud noise, something falling on our neck, a drop of water dripping onto our face) is commonly embedded in a lengthy dream narrative that terminates with the dream correlate of the sensory stimulus. Suppose something cold fell onto our neck. We dream that we are living at the time of the French Revolution, that we are moderate supporters of Mirabeau and the Girondin, that we offend Robespierre and St Just in the National Assembly, that when they seize power, we are imprisoned in the Conciergerie and then taken in a tumbril to the Place de la Revolution, where we are strapped to the guillotine, and that the blade of the guillotine descends – at which moment we awake. Now, the dream could not have begun before something cold fell on our neck, for this was our dream stimulus. Did we then dream this long narrative in a split second? Should we say that we dreamt very, very quickly? What is that supposed to mean? But how could the dream seem to have been so prolonged? We quietly shelve the question.

It is noteworthy that our imaginary form of representation has to pay no such price.

PART III

Axiology

12

The Place of Value in a World of Facts

[Wolfgang Koehler, professor of Gestalt psychology in Berlin in 1933, courageously wrote an article protesting against the Nazi purges from his university. "After the publication] he and his friends spent the night waiting for the fatal knock on the door, which luckily did not come. They were playing chamber music all night long. I cannot think of a better illustration of the place of value in a world of facts."
Ernst Gombrich, 'Art and Self-Transcendence', repr. in his *Ideals and Idols* (Phaidon, Oxford, 1979), p. 130.

1.   It is all too easy to stare at the starry heavens above and be impressed by the thought that there are untold billions of galaxies in an expanding visible universe that is ninety-three light years in diameter. Our world, the Earth, is a small planet orbiting a medium-size sun, only one among the hundreds of billions of stars in the Milky Way. We are small creatures living on a small planet in a vast and indifferent cosmos – how can anything we do be of any importance? How can anything that happens on Earth be of any significance? How can our lives, our loves, and our deeds be of any value?

It is also all too easy to be swept off one's feet by conceptual confusions. It is one thing to be awestruck by the beauty and vastness of the starry heavens above, it is quite another to be cowed by a meaningless cosmos. The cosmos is not indifferent to our lives and fate. Only a

Solving, Resolving, and Dissolving Philosophical Problems: Essays in Connective, Contrastive and Contextual Analysis, First Edition. P. M. S. Hacker.
© 2025 John Wiley & Sons Ltd. Published 2025 by John Wiley & Sons Ltd.

being that *can* be and show concern *can* be indifferent. But what would a universe that showed concern for us be like? We can make no sense of the idea of a concerned universe. Even astrology does not imply concern – only determinism. The universe is *neither* concerned *nor* indifferent to human lives and fate.

We are indeed small creatures, but it is not as if, were we twice the size we are, we would be twice as important. What is important in our lives – selfless love and compassion, friendship and kindness, art and science—is not rendered less important by the size of the universe in which, to the best of our knowledge, there is nothing of any importance whatsoever save on Earth.

We are mortal creatures. We live in full knowledge of our mortality. Our lives are relatively short. Most of us will be forgotten within a few decades of our death. How can anything we do or achieve be of any value? Must value not be *permanent* to be of any value? How can we avoid the refrain of the Solomonic Preacher in Jerusalem: 'Vanity of vanities, all is vanity'? A common response, including that of the Preacher, is an appeal to a transcendent source of value. One great philosopher was overwhelmingly struck by that idea and expressed it in words of sibylline beauty:

> The sense of the world must lie outside the world. In the world everything is as it is, and everything happens as it does happen: *in* it no value exists and if it did exist, it would have no value.
>
> If there is any value that does have value, it must lie outside the whole sphere of what happens and is the case. For all that happens and is the case is accidental.
>
> What makes it non-accidental cannot lie *within* the world, since if it did it would itself be accidental.
>
> It must lie outside the world.
>
> Wittgenstein, *Tractatus Logico-philosophicus* 6.41

It was at least in part these lines that inspired the most influential of twentieth-century philosophical movements, logical empiricism (also known as logical positivism), to raise the question of the place of value in a world of facts – a question that is still mooted to this day. The sphere of facts is the domain of the sciences. It is their task to observe the empirical world, to establish by observation and experiment the facts of which the world consists, and to explain those facts by reference to predictive theories that can be validated – confirmed or infirmed – in experience. The greatness of the Vienna Circle, the fountainhead of logical empiricism, lay in its powerful rationalist, scientific, challenge to the dominance of the church in education, law, and society, first and foremost in the Germanic lands. (In many respects, the Vienna Circle, in the twentieth century, inherited the anticlerical role of the Enlightenment in the eighteenth century.) The poverty of logical empiricism lay in its jejune attempts to elucidate the nature of value 'in a world of facts', and the nature of morality and moral judgement. The logical positivists fathered the meta-ethical theory of emotivism. The main proponents of emotivism were Moritz Schlick (the leading figure of the Vienna Circle) in Austria, A. J. Ayer in Britain, and Charles Stevenson in the United States. Their salient claim was precisely that there is no value in the world of facts, and that value judgements are no more than expressions of approval or disapproval (on the model of 'Good for you!' or 'Good on you!'), perhaps with a further imperatival rider in the case of so-called moral judgements that enjoin others to judge or act likewise. This was indeed the nadir of philosophical thinking on value.

The role of the present essay and of the two following essays is to demonstrate that the methods of connective, contrastive, and contextual analysis apply fruitfully to the domain of axiology (the analysis of value) and to that of morality. It will also be shown that the commonly held separation of ethical and meta-ethical reflection is for the most part untenable.

2. The first error that needs to be brushed away has already been mentioned in a previous essay. The world does not consist of facts. Rather, descriptions of (some part of) the world consist of statements of fact. Facts are not kinds of things ('entities'). They are neither in the world nor outside the world. Facts are what is, will be, or can be established to be so, what can be argued from and need not be argued to. When, in discourse, we wish to focus on how things are, we speak of facts, of what is the case, of matters of fact, of what is actually so; when we wish to focus on how things are said to be (assertions) or might be said to be (assertibles), we speak of truths.

Having signalled that dead end, we can now focus upon the fundamental principle that characterizes this segment of our conceptual scheme: *value is a phenomenon of life*. Where there is no life, there is no value. It is as much a fact concerning the world in which we live that there are items that are of value to living things, that human beings value things and possess valuable character traits (the virtues), that human beings perform valuable deeds (of generosity and kindness), and that human beings stand in valuable relations to each other (such as love and friendship), as it is a fact that there is life on Earth.

It is a philosophical illusion that there is a gap between fact and value. We do not have to jump across a logical gulf when we judge that water and fertilizer are good for the roses and that the *diplocarpon rosae* (black spot) fungus is bad for roses, or when we claim that some artefacts are good and others are poor, and that some artisans are good at their craft while other are incompetent. Nor is there a mystery about judging some people to be good or virtuous (Socrates, Marcus Aurelius, Wilberforce) and others to be wicked or evil (Hitler, Stalin, Mao, Putin), any more than there is a deep philosophical puzzle about deducing a judgement about what ought to be done from a set of judgements about what is the case – deducing an "ought" from an "is" as it used to be called. These apparent mysteries were no more than mystifications. To apprehend all this, we have to take into account the needs of living things, the preferences of sentient animals, human abilities and their exercise, human goals and projects, relationships and reciprocities, societies and their histories. All these have to be viewed within the framework of the nature of the world we live in, on the one hand, and of our nature, on the other.

3.   So, where do we start from? From grammatical, logico-linguistic data – from a brief survey of linguistic usage. 'Good' is the most general axiological concept. It can occur as an adjective, a noun, an adverb, and as an exclamation. Curiously, its adjectival comparative – 'better', and its superlative – 'best', have different etymological roots (comparable to 'bad', 'worse', 'worst'). It has a variety of adjectival opposites depending on the noun it qualifies: 'bad', 'poor', 'weak', 'worthless', 'wicked', 'evil'. It is the most general adjective of commendation, which is *one* illocutionary force that ascriptions of goodness may have: that is, one of the things we do in making such ascriptions. But there are others: some ascriptions of goodness are laudatory (e.g. 'That is a good painting'), others are approbatory (for which an appropriate status is requisite), and yet others are complimentary (e.g. 'How good your roses look'). But the different illocutionary forces with which an ascription of goodness may be uttered, sheds little light on the concept of goodness with its rich and ramifying logical character. Moreover, that illocutionary force disappears once the predication of goodness is embedded in the antecedent of a conditional (e.g. to say: 'If it is a good X, buy it' is not to commend anything), or in an interrogative (e.g. to ask: 'Is that a good painting?' is not to praise anything). Goodness is also connected to preferential choice, but not all things that are good in one sense or another are

things that one should, would or could choose to do, select or be. Even when an X can be chosen and is needed, it is not always rational to choose a good X or the best X – it may be too expensive, too fragile, or too good for one's purposes. Nor is it always irrational to refuse to become and be a good V-er: one may have no interest in V-ing. Good, unlike 'yellow', is often an attributive rather than a predicative adjective – that is to say, in a sentence of the form 'This X is an $A_{adj}B_{noun}$' one cannot infer that this X is an A and this X is a B. 'This man is a good soldier' does not imply that this man is a soldier and this man is good. (By contrast 'This piece of furniture is a red chair' implies that this piece of furniture is a chair and this piece of furniture is red, in as much as colour adjectives are predicative). But not all adjectival uses of good are attributive, for example, 'This proposal is a good plan' does imply that this proposal is good.

Something may be *good for* a being (as water is good for plants), and one may *do good to* a being (as one may benefit one's dear friend or lover). Something may be *good for* a purpose or for an artefact (as a breadknife is good for cutting bread and oil is good for an engine). Someone or some creature may be *good at* an activity (like Sherlock Holmes or a champion racehorse). Someone may *be good with* other beings (with children or dogs), with an instrument (musical or otherwise) or weapon. Things may be *good of their kind* (a good horse or rosebush) and may be *good as* a such-and-such (good as a birthday present). A human being may be *good as* a V-er (tinker, tailor, soldier, sailor) or a *good person* and *a good human being* (which are not social roles). It may be *good to do* such-and-such or *good to be* a so-and-so. It may be *good to be with* another person, or *good to be in* a place (home, in a beautiful landscape, in a wonderful city). One may *make good* or *make something good* and something may *come good*. As is patent, a colossal range of different kinds of things can be or not be good: natural objects and artefacts, animals and human beings, ways of doing things, decisions and plans, thoughts and ideas, intentions and actions, acts and activities, consequences and side effects, attributes and relations, sensations and feelings, motives and character traits. In each kind of attribution different criteria are involved and different kinds of paraphrase: something *good for a being* is beneficial for it; someone is *good at* a kind of activity if he possesses the requisite skill to do it well; someone is in *good health* if he is not suffering from an debilitating illness, injury or somatic defect; a *character trait is good* if it is a virtue; and so on. Each of these has different kinds of opposites: something not good for a being is harmful or damaging; someone not good at an activity is a poor or incompetent V-er; a creature that is not in good health is in poor or bad health, ill or frail; someone who lacks a virtue may have a vice; and so on. How can one make sense of this diversity? It is not coincidental ambiguity, since these features characterize a multitude of different languages. How can one find or put order into this complexity?

The welter of grammatical data is disturbing. Some philosophers have tried to find a unifying thread in a general definition of good, for example that all ascriptions of goodness are reducible to the notion of *serving a purpose*; or to *a fitting object of a pro-attitude*; or to *answering to certain interests*; or to *satisfying certain requirements*. These attempts are worryingly vacuous. There are logico-grammatical connections between being a good athlete and having good lungs and between both and being good to watch in action; there are connections between being a good instrument and being good (useful) for a purpose; there are connections between the good of humanity and the goodness of faring well, doing good, and being good. But they are hardly illuminated by these general definitions. Nor would anyone explain what the differences are between *being good at, being good for, being good with, being good as,* etc. by reference to such definitions.

Rejecting the proposals for a single unifying definition of 'good' may lead one to declare 'good' to be a family-resemblance concept (as Wittgenstein once did). But family-resemblance concepts characteristically allow for the addition of new classes of members over time (as photography was incorporated into the concept of art, or computer games were admitted into the concept of game). But it is not obvious that any new forms of goodness have ever been superadded to pre-existing ones over time. Moreover, family-resemblance concepts are explained by means of a series of examples together with a similarity-rider ('and other things like that'), but no one would attempt to explain what 'good' means by reference to a series of examples intended to function as a rule for the use of 'good'. In despair, one may declare (as G. E. Moore (1873–1958) did) that good is simple and indefinable, like yellow, but unlike yellow, is non-natural. But yellow is neither simple nor complex. Simple and complex are relative rather than absolute terms and we have not set standards of simplicity and complexity for colours; and 'yellow' is definable by an ostensive definition by reference to a sample. The concept of goodness is not definable by an ostensive definition and there are obviously no standard samples of goodness in general. By comparison with yellow, goodness is a highly complex and widely ramifying concept.

We are indebted to the great Finnish philosopher Georg-Henrik von Wright (1916–2003) for finding the way out of this quandary. The concept of goodness, he argued, is a *variety concept*. Among the varieties von Wright investigated are *instrumental goodness* of tools and ways of doing things, *technical goodness* of skills, the goodness of the *useful*, *medical goodness* of organs and faculties, *hedonic goodness*, the *good of a being*, and *moral goodness*. The list is not meant to be exhaustive (there is no mention of aesthetic goodness), and the varieties or forms of goodness that I shall elaborate will differ in various ways.

4. I suggested that the most fundamental principle to guide one in one's investigations into the roots of value and the place of value in the world is that *value is a phenomenon of life*. What needs to be done is to graft *an* analysis of the varieties of goodness onto the stock of this principle.

Where there is life of sufficient complexity to speak of an organism flourishing, of its being healthy or ill, diseased, or damaged, there we have value. For we can immediately speak of what is good for the organism and what is bad for it. For where there is life, there is a life cycle of birth, youth, maturation, senescence, and death. There are basic needs, the non-satisfaction of which is deleterious to the health of the creature and to its survival. Where there is sentient life of any degree of complexity there is attraction and aversion, pleasure and pain. Sentient beings of a moderate degree of complexity take pleasure in sensation, perception, activity, and achievement. They have a variety of natural and acquired powers that may be enhanced by practice and emulation. They pursue goals and may succeed or fail in their efforts, depending upon their prowess and upon fortune. They take pleasure in, are pleased at, the achievement of their goals and purposes. They may be solitary by nature or social. They reproduce sexually. Parenthood may be maternal or shared. It requires care for the offspring until the offspring can survive in their environment by themselves. Being cared for is good for, beneficial for, the young. Against this evident biological background, there is no mystery about the existence and nature of different varieties of goodness. The only mystery is that so many philosophers failed to realize such facts of life.

5.   So, the most fundamental form of value, the most fundamental variety of goodness from our perspective, is the goodness of health. What health is for a living creature is analogous to what the rule of law is for a political community. A human being cannot function optimally, as a being of the kind it is, if in ill health. The forms of medical goodness are linked to the notions of thriving and flourishing somatically and mentally, to declining and deteriorating, to being well or ill, to being damaged, injured, or maimed. Good health is a constitutive component of the welfare of a living creature. Bad, poor, or ill health detrimentally affects the life and welfare of an agent. It may disfigure, stunt growth and development. It commonly involves pain and suffering. It may prevent or impede human beings from pursuing or effectively pursuing their projects and from engaging in their characteristic activities. Good health is primarily privative in as much as it signifies the absence of disease, injury, or weakness. But it has a positive counterpart in the idea of somatic flourishing – radiating good health and vitality. Good health is enjoyed when the organs of an animal fulfil their function well, when its superfices (skin, fur, feathers) are neither diseased nor defective, and when basic needs are satisfied so that the creature can lead a normal life for an animal of its kind, free from the evils of ill-health. The idea of normalcy in this context is not merely statistical – it is also axiological, in as much as the somatic and psychological constraints of ill health, disfigurement, injury, and mental afflictions impair normal activities. The goodness of organs (heart, lungs, eyes, and ears, etc.) and of faculties (eyesight, hearing, memory, and imagination) are forms of medical goodness. Organs and faculties are characterized as good, bad, poor, or weak according to whether they perform their function well.

Neither biology nor medicine can dispense with the battery of concepts of medical goodness and its contraries. Attempts by philosophers of biology to eliminate axiology from biology in the name of value-free science are as incoherent as their attempts to remove teleology from biology. Value-free science is indeed a goal of scientists, but what it means is that they should have no axes to grind and no subservience to bureaucracies of universities, pharmaceutical companies and governments that forces them to subvert the search for truth. It does not mean that all axiological descriptions and all evaluative language should be eliminated from true science. They are as ineliminable from the sciences of life as is the concept of purpose. (Darwin's achievement was not to eliminate purpose or goal directedness from biology but to eliminate design. Evolutionary theory demonstrates the possibility of purpose independently of design. Natural selection tends to favour characteristics that benefit animals of a given species (the long neck of giraffes, the speed of cheetahs) and contribute to their welfare.)

6. We are born into communities. Our slow growth to adulthood involves language acquisition, the learning of language-games and rule-governed behaviour patterns, forms of valuation and practical reasoning. It also involves the acquisition of skills. Skills are refinements of abilities. Skills admit of axiological gradation. These are degrees of *technical goodness* which have at least four subordinate forms: the *goodness at* an art or craft, the *vocational goodness* of a professional (lawyer, doctor, nurse, teacher), *ludic goodness* (competitive sports, mountain climbing, chess, bridge), and *performance goodness* (of actors, opera singers, ballet dancers, musicians). Each subform admits of different criteria of excellence in a characteristic activity (V-ing). To become a V-er one must be able to V well – be a reasonably good V-er, be *good at* V-ing and *good as a* V-er. The opposite of a good V-er is a poor V-er: someone who can V, but not very well. A poor or bad V-er is someone who has learnt to V but has not achieved the standards of excellence required. Other things being equal, one would not choose a poor V-er if a good V-er is available for a V-ing task. A bad V-er should not be chosen since the V-ing will be substandard, may do more harm than good and may need redoing.

Human beings are born with meagre abilities. They are not born with equal second-order abilities, that is, the abilities to acquire abilities. Some will acquire better eyesight than others, some will grow to be faster and stronger than others. Some will learn faster than others. Nature is not egalitarian in distribution of natural endowments.

It is obvious that in a social group the pursuit of valued things will produce differential skills among its members. Given shortages and scarcities of desiderata, this will unavoidably generate competition. This in turn will produce inequalities of distribution. This will generate social hierarchies and inequalities of power. The central problem for human societies and for political and economic theories is how to balance the good of the individual with the good of society and how to restrain competitiveness for the sake of the welfare of the society. The good of a society, contrary to Margaret Thatcher, is not simply the sum of the good of its individual members. It is easy to see how the concept of a good or decent society is needed for rational debate, as well as the concept of the social good as distinct from the good of the individual. That debate in the West began with Socrates and the sophists, who were perceived as a threat to the traditional order.

7.   Because we are not only talkers and thinkers but also makers, there is natural need for the evaluation of our products – a variety of goodness that may be termed artefactual goodness. For evaluations of artefacts are guides to choice in their production and in their utilization. Artefactual goodness subdivides into *instrumental goodness*, which is the goodness of tools and instruments, and *non-instrumental artefactual goodness* of bridges, houses, cars, roads, harbours, ships and trains. Space must also be made for the goodness of animal artefacts, ranging from beaver's dams to birds' nests and spiders' webs. Both forms of artefactual goodness are related to the idea of purpose: artefacts are *made for a purpose, used for a purpose*, and *good for a purpose*.

Linked to both the technical goodness of skills and to artefactual goodness of products in both its forms is the *goodness of techniques* – the ways in which we use tools and instruments, correct and incorrect ways of using them and making use of them in pursuit of those ends that they are designed to facilitate. We may *use them well or badly, correctly or incorrectly* depending on our skills and our mastery of the techniques of their use. Cars, houses, and bridges are not tools but they are artefacts that we *use for the purposes for which they were made*, and we *make use* of them well or badly. They are good, better or worse to the extent that they fulfil the purposes for which they were constructed. Both kinds of artefactual goodness are bound up with yet a further subvariety of goodness, for artefacts are commonly expensive and cherished human creations and need proper care for their preservation. We patently need the category of *custodial goodness* to discriminate and evaluate the care a craftsman takes of his tools and instruments and the care owners and authorities take of the non-instrumental artefacts for which they are responsible, be they private cars, company buses, or community roads and bridges.

8.   Artefactual goodness is internally (conceptually, logically) related to yet a further variety of goodness, namely the *useful*. The goodness of the useful consists in its contribution to a purpose. One subform of the useful is *artefactual usefulness*, since artefacts are useful, *advantageous*, to possess (in the case of instruments and tools) or to use (in the case of non-instrumental artefacts). One commonly *needs* a given artefact if one is to effectively pursue a given purpose or indeed to pursue it at all. Indeed, an artefact may be useful for purposes other

than those for which it was designed. Hence we distinguish between being good *as a so-and-so* and *being good for a purpose* distinct from the purpose of so-and-so (a knife with a heavy handle may be good for hammering). A quite different subform of the useful consists of decisions, plans, and projects, the goodness of which facilitates the achievement of given goals, which may or may not be good in themselves. The opposite of the useful is the *useless*, which may signify uselessness for the purpose at hand or uselessness for any purpose, as a broken tool or hopelessly defective plan may be.

Usefulness is purpose-relative. Something may be useful *promotively* in as much as it facilitates the attainment of the goal pursued, or *protectively* in as much as it protects us from impediments that stand in the way of the attainment of our goal. Some kinds of usefulness contribute to a given end causally – as do tools, instruments, and machines; others contribute non-causally – as do plans and decisions.

9.　　The goodness of the useful must be distinguished from the goodness of the beneficial. The useful is *good for a purpose*, the beneficial is *good for a being* or *does good to a being*. Something may be useful without being beneficial or beneficial without being useful, even though the useful is commonly beneficial. It may be useful to add a further propeller to a killer drone, but that does not make it more beneficial – it merely makes the weapon more efficient. It may be beneficial to take a holiday, but it need not be useful. A good plan may be useful, but its fulfilment is beneficial only if its goal is wisely chosen.

The beneficial concerns *the good of a being* and *what is good for a being*, which may be either inanimate or animate. Oil or grease is good for an engine since it prevents rust and improves operation. Similarly, fertilizer is good for soil. But the beneficial for the inanimate is what is good *for it*, not what contributes to its good – since the inanimate have no good, that is, no welfare, flourishing or prospering that is characteristic of flora and fauna. Consequently, what is good for the inanimate is *derivatively good*, since it enables others to benefit from it, as *we* can produce more crops on fertilized soil and *we* benefit from an engine that is in good running order. The beneficial for living beings is linked to many other forms of goodness, most obviously to the health of plants, animals, and humans, but equally to technical goodness, in so far as teaching, training, and education are beneficial to human beings in that they contribute to the acquisition of skills and their cultivation – making existing skills better.

The beneficial for a living being is what protects or furthers its good: its welfare and flourishing. In the case of a human being, we may distinguish between *doing well* and *faring well*. Doing well consists in attaining the objectives one has set oneself, in prospering and achieving, for example, wealth, fame, and power. It is notoriously compatible with loneliness, unhappiness, lack of good friends, and absence of joy. Faring well is more closely associating with having a good life in which the exigencies of welfare and needs are satisfied, in which worthwhile projects are satisfactorily pursued, pleasure is taken in activities and passivities, the goods of reciprocal love and intimate friendship are enjoyed, the benefits of good reputation and the goods of liberty and maintenance of dignity are attained – these being constitutive of the good of human beings. All this is fragile, for it lies in the fickle hands of Fortuna and may be taken from one in a single fell swoop: the death of a beloved person, a catastrophic loss of health, the disasters of war.

10.   The final variety of goodness to be discussed in this essay is hedonic goodness – the goodness of pleasure, satisfaction, and gratification (moral goodness and eudaimonic goodness – the goodness of happiness, will be examined in Essays 13 and 15). Being creatures with senses, enjoying good or suffering poor health; being thinkers, doers, and makers; having abilities and exercising skills; having goals and purposes and pursuing projects; harbouring attitudes, likes and dislikes; having loves and lovers, it is inconceivable that we should not incorporate in our conceptual scheme concepts of hedonic goodness. Hedonic goodness includes the pleasant, pleasing, and pleasurable; the satisfying, gratifying, and enjoyable; the enchanting, delightful, and luxurious. Taking pleasure, delight, and joy in things; enjoying activities and finding satisfaction, gratification, and fulfilment in our lives, relationships, and projects are constitutive elements of a *good life* of a human being.

Pleasure, enjoyment and being pleased are three subcategories of hedonic goodness. They are all evaluation-involving axiological concepts. They are importantly distinct. When one enjoys something, one enjoys oneself, but when one is pleased at, by, or with something one does not please oneself. Enjoyment is a species of pleasure, but being pleased is not. Being pleased is a responsive attitude involving a favourable judgement and a preference. One may be pleased with, at, or by something because of the way it fits in with one's plans, preferences, or prejudices. But one enjoys something because of its intrinsic features. Amalgamating all this under the rubric of 'pro-attitudes' serves only to obscure important distinctions.

Among the pleasures we enjoy one may distinguish the pleasures of the senses. As Aristotle pointed out, to each of the five senses there corresponds a form of pleasure derived from its optimal exercise. The pleasures of taste and touch, together with the contrasting characteristics of being painful or repulsive to touch and disgusting to taste) are primal from the point of view of animal survival. The pleasures of sight and hearing are, for us, the most complex and capable of indefinite refinement in aesthetic appreciation. Sexual pleasure encompasses all the senses. Other forms of human pleasure are the pleasures of desire, both in respect of pursuit and of satisfaction. Related to the pleasures of desire are the pleasures of competition (the joys of winning), pleasures of the exercise of strength of will (sometimes for its own sake, as in the case of mountain climbing), and ludic pleasures. Distinct from these, although often overlapping, are the pleasures of the intellect: of learning and understanding, of thinking and reasoning, of expertise and connoisseurship. Being social creatures, social pleasures are universal among mankind, incorporating wide varieties of collective activities, ranging from dining together, enjoying dances and parties, to mass demonstrations as well as the pleasures of destruction (in the course of riots or wars of religion) and slaughter (pogroms).

Hedonic goodness is not motivationally inert. We do things for the sake of pleasure, sometimes our own and sometimes another person's. That something is pleasant or enjoyable to do is a (defeasible) reason for doing it – save among guilt-ridden puritans. To explain why one did something by saying that it was done for the sake of pleasure or enjoyment is a terminus of explanation. It makes no sense to push further by asking 'Why do you want pleasure?' or 'Why do you want to enjoy yourself?' Contrary to the utilitarians, pleasure and enjoyment are not the only reasons for action and in many contexts, not very powerful reasons for action.

It is a natural, but widespread error to suppose that pleasure and pain are either contradictories or contraries. Pleasure and pain are categorially different. Pleasure is not a sensation, whereas somatic pain is. To be sure, there are pleasant sensations and there are pleasurable sensations, but these are not pleasure sensations as painful sensations are pain sensations. One may have a pain in one's hand, but there is no such thing as having a pleasure in one's hand. One cannot ask, 'Where is the pleasure?' as one can ask, 'Where is the pain?', but only 'Is that pleasant?' (*that* being something done to one). Pain has a cause, but pleasure and enjoyment have objects. One takes pleasure *in* V-ing, derives pleasure *from* V-ing, enjoys V-ing, and is pleased that things are so. If pleasure were a sensation, it would, like sensations of pain, be externally (non-logically) related to whatever causes it. So on any given occasion on which one felt pleasure, one would have to check what it was that gave one pleasure (as one sometimes checks to see what caused one pain – a pin or an insect bite). On going to the opera, one would have to check whether it was *Così fan tutte* or the seat in which one was sitting that gave one pleasure. But that is absurd.

Pain and pleasure are not exclusive, since some pleasures are painful (as competitive sports often are) and some pains are enjoyable and desired (the scratches and bites of lovemaking). They are not exhaustive, as many activities are neither pleasurable nor painful. It is striking that English is singularly confusing in this lexical area. *Pleasure* has no opposite other than *no pleasure*, for *displeasure* is not the opposite of *pleasure* but is rather a form of anger or annoyance. One takes pleasure in things and one suffers pain, but one does not suffer displeasure. *Pain* is not an opposite of *pleasure* since some pains are pleasurable. The opposite of *painful* is not *pleasurable*, but *not painful*. The contrary of *being pleased* is *being displeased*, but it is perfectly intelligible to be displeased at taking pleasure in something (e.g. if one finds oneself taking pleasure in the excitement of a bullfight or hare-coursing).

Hedonic goodness admits of degrees – one may enjoy one activity or passivity more than another, as one may take more pleasure in one thing rather than another or be more or less pleased by something. But it is no more quantifiable than is beauty, and any attempt to get people to assign numerical values to their pleasures (or pains – as is now standard in contemporary medicine) is profoundly deceptive. It intimates that different pleasures are comparable and interchangeable without more ado (as Bentham put it 'Prejudice apart, the game of push-pin is of equal value with the arts and sciences of music and poetry'). This is not only philistine, it is incoherent. Poetry is not as good a game as pushpin, since it is not a game, and a game of pushpin is not as good a poem as 'Fern Hill', since it is not a poem. The value of a poem does not lie in how much pleasure it gives anyone or everyone. Comparability of objects of pleasure and enjoyment should not be confused with quantifiability.

11.　We have shed light on the place of value in the world and in our lives. In exploring the varieties of value, we have, for the first time in these essays, scrutinized the logic of a variety concept. Other varieties, von Wright suggested, are truth and existence. Although we may explain what it is for a sayable to be true by observing that a proposition is true if things are as it says they are, we still need to explain the varieties of truth: the truth of avowals of experience, such as 'It hurts!'(where truthfulness guarantees truth); the truth of observation statements (the fallible truths delivered by our use of our defeasible cognitive faculties); the truth of scientific theories (in all their manifold forms); the truth of mathematical theorems (and their complex relations to proof); the truth of value judgements in all their bewildering diversity; the truth of normative judgements in morality and law; and so on. Similar considerations apply to existence and the analysis of existence judgements. This will not be done in this collection of essays, but our discussion of one variety concept must serve to exemplify others.

Conspicuous in this discussion has been the absence of moral goodness. That is the subject of the next two essays.

13

Morality and the Analysis of Moral Goodness

"Of every tree of the garden thou mayest freely eat. But of the tree of the knowledge of good and evil, thou shalt not eat of it: for in the day that thou eatest thereof thou shalt surely die.… And the serpent said unto the woman, Ye shall not surely die. For God doth know that in the day ye eat thereof, then your eyes shall be opened, and ye shall be as gods, knowing good and evil. And when the woman saw that the tree was good for food, and that it was pleasant to the eyes, and a tree to be desired to make one wise, she took of the fruit thereof, and did eat, and gave also unto her husband with her, and he did eat. And the eyes of them both were opened.…

And the Lord God said, Behold, the man is become as one of us, to know good and evil." Genesis 2, 16–17; 3, 4–7; 3, 22

1.   This ancient monolatrist (pre-monotheist) legend patently echoes an archaic Semitic variant of the Greek Promethean myth. It is not a tale of the Fall of Man, as the Christian (Augustinian) tradition would have it, but, as Hegel noted, it is a 'Mythus' of the Rise of Man. Knowledge of good and evil is what distinguishes mankind from the rest of animal nature. For only mankind knows the difference between right and wrong; only mankind bears the burdens of duties and obligations; only mankind is answerable for what has been done, is responsible for acts and omissions, possesses a moral conscience, feels remorse and guilt.

Solving, Resolving, and Dissolving Philosophical Problems: Essays in Connective, Contrastive and Contextual Analysis, First Edition. P. M. S. Hacker.
© 2025 John Wiley & Sons Ltd. Published 2025 by John Wiley & Sons Ltd.

We speak of good – morally good – men and women, of morally good deeds and of the morally good reasons and intentions that inform them. We describe the morality of a society and the moral standards endorsed in past or present societies. We classify different moral systems, as we talk of different social, political, and economic systems. And we distinguish moral philosophy from other parts of practical philosophy, such as political and legal philosophy. But we are hard-pressed to answer the question, 'What is morality?'

It is common for people to raise the question of where morality *comes from* – often with the assumption that morality must have a transcendent source, that without divine authority (the authority of one's own god, to be sure) there can be no such thing as morality, but only one form or another of non-moral consequentialism. But it is parochial to suppose that there can be no such thing as a secular morality. Was Confucianism not a morality? Does contemporary humanism not advance a morality?

The first move, as usual, is not to rush in to answer the question, but to question it. Why should morality *come from* anywhere? What, in this context, does 'come from' mean? If 'come from' means 'who ordained it', why should anyone have ordained it? Why should it not be as natural to mankind as language? There are, to be sure, divers questions that may be raised. Where does morality come from may be a question concerning the evolutionary origins of morality: can sexual selection and survival of the fittest explain the emergence of such complexes of attitudes, norms (rules of conduct), and values that we characterize as a morality? Where does *our* morality, the morality of *our* twenty-first century society, come from is a quite different question – in social history. Yet another question that may take the same form is: Whence the authority of moral considerations? What gives moral considerations their special weight – for something's being morally wrong is not a trivial consideration in practical reasoning, even though it would be mistaken to characterize moral considerations as being, by definition, overriding ones (it would be foolishness, not moral rectitude, to ruin oneself for the sake of keeping a minor promise). Other questions border on the sociological: What is the social function of a morality? What is its point and purpose? Can there be a society without a morality or is a social morality a necessary constitutive element in anything we should deem to be a society? And finally, 'Where does morality come from?' may be a question concerning the justification of morality: what, if anything, validates moral values and standards of behaviour? All these are respectable questions. Not all will be addressed here. Our first concern is with the roots of moral norms and values in human nature and the nature of the world we live in. Like David Hume, we shall advance a naturalist account of social morality, denying it a transcendent source, on the one hand, and denying its derivability from reason alone (hence repudiating Kantian rationalist ethics), on the other.

2.   Any account of the nature of social morality must allow for a diversity of moralities in different times and places. But we must be careful not to sail too close to the wind of complete relativism. For *not any array of social norms and values constitutes a morality* – evil societies with no morality have arguably existed and do exist and evil social ideologies certainly have existed and do exist. What characterizes evil social ideologies is complete lack of concern for the good of human beings, their welfare, other-regarding virtues, and happiness. Some such ideologies have been concerned primarily with appeasing the gods by means of human sacrifices (Aztec norms and values). Others have been concerned primarily with advancing the dominion of an alleged race (Nazi norms and values) or creed (ISIL). But I suggest that concern with the good of human beings is an intrinsic feature of anything that can reasonably be deemed a morality.

Let us turn first to the notion of a social morality. It can be rendered intelligible by reference to the nature of the world we live in and to common human nature.

The world we live in imposes harsh weather conditions: in most parts of the world, human beings need clothing, warmth, and shelter to survive. Food is hard to come by and must be wrested from nature. Disease and injury are common. The decrepitude of those who, like Falstaff, are 'blasted with antiquity' is unavoidable.

Human beings share a profoundly defective common nature: in so far as there is a Primal Curse, it lies in our genetic make-up. Our species nature is such that we are subject to an overwhelming will to power, have intense possessive drives, are sexually driven and given to sexual jealousy, are prone to envy, anger, aggression, and vengeance. The human male is by nature aggressive, fiercely competitive, predatory, and takes pleasure in destruction and, in war, in killing. We have deeply tribal instincts (that once served an evolutionary purpose) and are intolerant of strangers, of deviant behaviour, and of deviant beliefs. We have a limited innate proneness to sympathize and a limited ability to empathize (these should not be confused or assimilated), a tendency to form friendships and group allegiances.

We are saved from being no more than repulsive killer apes by the fact that we are language users. As has already been remarked, we are not *homo sapiens* – wisdom being a rare human metal, but we are most definitely *homo loquens* – talking humans. Everything that distinguishes us from the rest of the animal kingdom is due to our mastery of a developed language. It is precisely because we are language users that we have the *capacity* for rationality, the power to reason (draw inferences from grounds) and limited sensitivity to reasons for acting, feeling, and thinking. So, to be sure, it is because we are language users and possess the capacity of rationality that we are also moral beings with knowledge of good and evil, answerable for our deeds and responsible for our actions and omissions.

It is a further sociobiological feature of human beings that their process of maturation is prolonged. Being born into a community of language users, the human child has, or rapidly acquires, an innate propensity to learn a language – a propensity characterized by strong imitative tendencies, responsiveness to ostensive training, the ability to recognize regularities, to conform to them, and to respond to them as standard-setting in a shared social practice. In the course of childhood, the young human has to master a native tongue, learn how to engage in indefinitely many language-games characteristic of the culture, learn patterns of behaviour and cooperative conduct that are indispensable for communal life and livelihood. It also implies the ineluctable valuing of truthfulness and reprehensibility of lying. For only thus can we be reliable eyes and ears to each other, bypass evolution by sexual selection and survival of the fittest in respect of sharing knowledge and transmitting information from one generation to another by word of mouth, by teaching and learning, by culture and tradition. The greater the public slippage in standards of veracity, the more corrupt the society.

Against this background of facts of nature and facts about human nature, the phenomena of morality in a human society are not in the least surprising. Our tribal character and linguistic powers, coupled with our familial existence and differentiation of skills, and our species-genetic savagery implies the ineluctable need for systematic regulation. But that would be true even if we were purely self-interested rational consequentialists. Even such beings would need a system of social norms to regulate their transactions and social intercourse. But that does not suffice for the emergence of a social morality.

What needs to be added to our tale is our emotional nature. We are subject to a wide range of emotions, well- or ill-supported by reasons.

The emotions essentially involve caring about something or someone. What we care about is what matters to us. Caring about something involves valuing it. All animals care about avoiding physical danger and about satisfying their appetites – were that not so, the species would not have survived. Animals that have to rear their young care for them and care about them – were that not so, the species would not have survived. We are social creatures that cooperate with others to mutual advantage. So we care not only about our own endeavours and projects, but also about joint projects we undertake with others. We have powers of sympathy and empathy, and we are prone to identify with social groups, ranging from small localities to regions and continents, religious or racial groups, and nation-states. Such forms of identification serve to endow members with a sense of their own identity – a conception of who they are and what they stand for. A weak sense of identity is strengthened by differentiation from minority groups (religious, racial, national) within one's society and is bolstered by cultivation of hatred of the alien. The need to hate is one of the more repulsive aspects of human nature. The endeavour to derive morality from rational self-interest, exemplified ingeniously in the writings of Hobbes (1588–1679) and de Mandeville (1670–1733), is singularly irrelevant, for while we are unquestionably prone to selfishness and disregard of the welfare of others, we are not simply self-interested beings. We are sometimes moved by sympathy and compassion. We are ideologically driven, by religion, by nationalism, by racialist doctrines, by doctrines of natural superiority and craving for aggrandisement, all of which override simple self-interest. We are capable of noble, as well as contemptible, self-sacrifice in the name of a cause.

So much for the social roots of social morality. There is no mystery and no need to have recourse to transcendent sources. Any quest for evolutionary explanations of the existence of morality among human groups is bound to be futile. For while the evolutionary value of the existence of tribal groups for the survival of species of naked apes seems indisputable, evolution operates causally. But once anything resembling a morality is in place, we have entered the domain of mastery of a language and with it the possession of capacity-rationality and hence the practices of giving reasons and demanding justifications, answerability and responsibility – all of which free us, in limited respects, from blind evolutionary forces, endow us with freedom of the will, liability to shame and guilt, susceptibility to regret and remorse. Appeal to pure practical reason alone on the Kantian model is equally misconceived, since it obscures the natural roots of the moral in caring for others and in concern for the Good of Man. But it is true that there is no morality without rationality.

3.   We may now put aside the Humean question of how the phenomenon of morality is to be rendered intelligible and turn to the analytic question of how the notion of morality is to be characterized? There are doubtless different ways. The following is but one among others. A morality – a social morality – is a part or aspect of a form of human life, of a way of living in a human community. That does not imply that an Alexander Selkirk may not exemplify moral virtues in the solitude of a desert island, namely self-regarding virtues of self-control and the fulfilment of duties to oneself. But that is obviously a secondary sense of 'morality' and a derivative kind of case. To be sure, the very idea of duties to oneself is contentious. It has its roots in Kant (and is associated with Prussian pietism). We do say that we owe it to ourselves to take care of our health ('You must take a holiday!) or not to waste our talents ('You owe it to yourself not to waste your great talents'). Failure to do what we owe to ourselves is a ground for criticism, but it is less than obvious whether the criticism is moral and whether this warrants the use of the term 'duty'.

A social morality consists of the following overlapping categories:

(i)   *Social norms (rules) and principles that specify what one must or must not do in recurrent situations.* These are duty- and obligation-imposing rules, primarily concerned with protective prohibitions and with agreements. If communal life is to be possible, there must be rule-governed control of violence (a duty not to kill, maim, or assault), of communication (an obligation not to lie), and of cooperation (an obligation to keep promises, to comply with voluntary contractual agreements, and obligations of reciprocity). Given the strength of the human sexual drive, the long period of pregnancy, and the needs of children, there must be norms of sexual behaviour, of parenthood, and of responsibility for the upbringing of children. Similarly, given the limited powers of the senescent, there must be social norms governing the care of the aged. The scope and content of these rules vary enormously from society to society and from epoch to epoch.

The domain of the deontic is normative (i.e. governed by norms), it deals with recurrent situations in personal and social life in a community. Hence, as von Wright pointed out, *the path of duty is laid out in advance.* But given the complexities of human relationships and the variability of circumstances, the dictates of duty are, for the most part, contestably defeasible although not usually defeated. Some duties may, however, be absolute and inviolable (e.g. not to torture children).

In a renowned essay 'Modern Moral Philosophy' (1958), Elizabeth Anscombe (1919–2001) advanced the view that concepts of moral obligation and duty, of the morally right and wrong, and the moral sense of 'ought' should be jettisoned by the irreligious as they are no more than residues of a theological conception of ethics as the ordinations of God and make no sense in a modern secular context. Hence, she argued, modern moral philosophy should pursue an Aristotelian virtue ethics and eschew any ethics of duty. This echoes an earlier view expressed by Wittgenstein in which he averred that 'ought' makes sense only if there is something lending support or force to it – a power that punishes and rewards. Bereft of that context, he claimed, 'ought' in itself is nonsense. This egregious view, Wittgenstein took from Arthur Schopenhauer's (1788–1860) criticisms of Kant's principle of the categorical imperative (*The World as Will and Representation*, vol. I, 523). The notions of duty and obligation are not essentially tied to the God of the Pentateuch or to any other God: the Roman senatorial and equites classes had rigorous duties and obligations without monotheist backing. They were duties of class and status. The Stoics recognized universal duties as human beings – and being a human being is not a social role. There are many flaws in Kant's principle, but this is not one of them. The auxiliary verb 'ought' (and its German equivalent *sollen*) does not require an enforcing agency as a condition of its making sense in an utterance, either in its predictive use ("The train ought to be here soon') or in its prescriptive use 'You ought to catch the 3:10 to London'). There aren't different senses of 'ought' (any more than 'possible that' and 'possible for' indicate different senses of 'possible'). In particular, there is no special moral sense of 'ought'. What is true is that 'morally ought' has a different sense from 'legally, politically, economically, strategically, etc., ought' in as much as each complex phrase signals a different reason-indicative principle of selection. What is also true is that failure to fulfil one's obligations, like failure to do one's duty or to do what one morally must, should, or ought to do is a *reason for moral criticism.*

The deontic also includes general principles of action and forbearance, such as the guiding principle of not harming others; principles of justification, excuse, and mitigation in respect of responsibility for one's action; procedural principles in interpersonal disputes (principles of reasonableness), and so forth.

Within the deontic domain that is a constitutive part of a morality, we must distinguish between what *must* be and what *ought* to be. What *must be (has to be) done* is what is necessary in a given situation – the only option available, all others being prohibited or otherwise excluded. What *ought to be done* is what is appropriate or apt in the situation in which several possibilities are available. That which ought to be the case or be done is what is right or good (and, in some cases, what is better or best in the circumstances). It is noteworthy that 'ought', 'sollen', 'devoir', 'debeo/dehibeo' are etymologically linked to the notion of what is *owing* (to the situation). A reason is always relevant to the claim that something ought to be or be done. Such a reason may be generic or occasion-specific. It may advert to features of the circumstances, of the alternative that is actually chosen, or to axiological or normative features (the good and the right).

It is noteworthy that the illocutionary force (what one does *in* saying) of 'You must V' is quite different from that of 'You ought to V', to assert the former is to insist, to assert, to demand, the latter is to commend, recommend, advise, suggest.

(ii) *Ideal norms specifying what one ought to be*. The virtues are intrinsically valuable character traits the citing of which specifies not what one *ought to do* but rather what one *ought to be*. They are exhibited in action that is intended to serve the good of human beings. The self-regarding virtues of courage, industry, temperance, patience, and fortitude may be intended to serve one's own good or may be used in the service of the good of others. The other-regarding virtues of generosity, compassion, kindness, honesty, truthfulness, trustworthiness, loyalty, are manifest in the service of the good of others. *The path of virtue and hence the exercise of the virtues is not laid out in advance* but is determined from occasion to occasion by good judgement (practical wisdom) concerning what is good and what is right (von Wright). The judgement and behaviour of the virtuous and experienced provide one with reliable guidance as to what is to be done from occasion to occasion. Human beings have to be brought up, taught, and trained in the acquisition of virtuous habits. One becomes virtuous, one acquires virtues, by doing virtuous deeds.

The relative ranking of the virtues varies from society to society and age to age proportional to social needs and ideologies. It is, however, striking that there appears to be only one new virtue that has emerged in the West since the days of Periclean Athens, namely tolerance, which we owe to Sebastian Castellio (1515–63) who argued that no one should ever be persecuted for their beliefs.

(iii)   *Values.* Anything that can reasonably be deemed to be the morality of a society will incorporate a set of abstract moral values that are invoked as prima facie justifications for action and termini of chains of justification. They are cited in specifying that *for the sake of which* one acts (Aristotle). They include such moral values as justice and fairness, generosity and kindness, and of course, the corresponding disvalues of injustice and unfairness, meanness and cruelty that are to be shunned. If it is asked why a certain act or omission, action or activity was done or is to be done, and the reply says what was done or is to be done for the sake of justice or fairness, or that failure to do it would be unjust or unfair, mean or unkind, one cannot intelligibly object: 'Why should one be just or fair?' or 'Why should one not be mean and cruel?' One can only object that, appearances to the contrary, the act does not actually exemplify the value in question, or that although it does, the requirement to act for the sake of the specified value is, in the circumstances, overridden by some countervailing value or consideration.

(iv)   *Moral conscience and social sanctions.* The complex phenomena of a social morality that informs the life of a community essentially involves a shared moral psychology without which there would be no moral community. For the shared moral standards, no matter whether they can be subjected to outside moral criticism or not, must be internalized by most members of the society. The phenomenological form which internalization of moral standards takes is *a moral conscience* and a set of *moral attitudes* towards other members of one's community, on the one hand, and a variety of forms of social sanctions, on the other. The child who matures in a stable family in a community with shared values will learn to know the difference between right and wrong behaviour in the community. Knowing the difference between right and wrong is not mere acquisition of information, like knowing the difference between baroque and rococo architecture, or between apes and monkeys, or between complex and hyper-complex numbers. Unlike the latter examples, one cannot forget the difference between right and wrong, one cannot excuse one's misdemeanours by pleading that one is out of practice, and one cannot practice doing right and wrong to keep one's hand in as one may practice one's skills. To know the difference between right and wrong is to have internalized the interpersonal attitudes and standards of conduct of one's moral community and so to be prone to feel ashamed of shortcoming, guilty for wrongdoing, and remorseful for transgression of such standards. That is what it is to have acquired a moral conscience. Acquisition of a moral conscience, in the course of growing up in a community, is a subjective matter, involving self-awareness and self-reflection, which may be exaggerated, distorted, and perverse or thoughtful and balanced. Its objective counterpart consists of the existence of shared attitudes and consequent social sanctions applied by members of a community to those who transgress the standards of behaviour. This too may be rational or prejudiced and bigoted. It may involve the manifestation of social disapproval, criticism, and severance of social relationships.

4.   Social morality is an anthropological phenomenon. Its values, norms, and ideals are constitutive of the identity of the society and impart to its members an aspect of their own sense of identity. Its lies at the foundation of the moral upbringing of children – of their learning how to behave and of their acquiring a moral conscience. In traditional societies, questioning existing social standards of conduct is unthinkable. In the West, it is to Socrates and the sophists that we owe the idea of questioning the existing moral order, of asking for justification of traditional moral rules and values, of demanding reasons why things should be done and valued as they had always been done and valued. It is to such noble minds that we owe the idea of a critical, individual morality. They are perceived as a threat to the existing moral, social, economic, and political order and to existing attitudes and prejudices. Unsurprisingly, they have often paid for their thought with their lives. Public critical reflection on social morals and mores persisted in Rome until the advent of Christianity and its institution as the official religion of the declining empire.

Medieval thinkers made a significant contribution to moral thought on such topics as conscience, free will, just war, double-effect, and the right to overthrow tyrants, but it was within the constraints of religious doctrine, deviation from which was severely, sometimes horrendously, punished. It was not until the renaissance of learning in the sixteenth century and the scientific revolution and the Thirty Years War in the seventeenth century that systematic reflection upon the social and political order slowly became the right of any member of an enlightened community. Critical morality was cultivated and encouraged by the Enlightenment, both in public debate and in private reflection and action. Its motto, as we have already noted, was *Sapere aude* (Kant): dare to know, have the courage to use your own understanding. Threatened and persecuted by autocracies, dictatorships, theocracies (both Catholic and Muslim), fascism and communism, postmodernism, populism and demoticism, and the cult of victimhood that now besets the Western world, these ideals of the Enlightenment have nevertheless survived so far in the West. But it has been and continues to be a close-run thing.

5.   I have suggested that nothing deserves the name of a morality that lacks concern for the Good of Man. The notion of the good of human beings requires elucidation, for it transcends the idea of welfare. Welfare incorporates the satisfaction of (universal) basic human needs, the satisfaction of socially relative human needs, and the satisfaction of individuals' project-relative needs. Concern for the welfare of human beings is a constitutive element of anything that can be deemed to be a morality. One of the pitfalls of some theological moralities and formal religious organizations is diminution of concern with the welfare of human beings in this world in the belief that this is compensated for by its satisfaction in the next world (in life after death). This is exacerbated once formal religious organizations (such as the papacy from Constantine onwards) are untaxed major land- and property owners.

One may pin down the idea of the Good of Man (*das Wohl*) by explicating the difference between doing well (prospering) and living well (flourishing). *Explication*, by contrast with elucidation, involves partial stipulation – snipping the ragged edges of ordinary usage (as Henry Sidgwick (1838–1900) put it). Doing well, prospering, is a class-relative notion. At the upper end of the social scale, those do well who attain power, wealth, fame, and, if they are also admirable, honour and respect. Those who are less high in the social hierarchy prosper if they 'do well for themselves' – achieve recognition of their skills and their labour, attain recompense in terms of pay, promotion, and praise. Anything that contributes to the prospering of human beings *benefits* or is *advantageous* to the recipient in their pursuit of their contingent goals. The beneficial, it will be remembered from the previous essay, is one of the varieties of goodness and the advantageous is a subform of the beneficial. Doing well is notoriously compatible both with lack of virtue and with unhappiness. One may prosper while leading a lonely life, with no deep friendships, with little pleasure and no joy (as is patent in Tolstoy's Alexei Alexandrovich Karenin or Orson Welles' Charles Foster Kane).

Living well, flourishing, consists of living a good life – fulfilling one's duties and obligations, possessing fundamental virtues of kindness, compassion, and generosity, being blessed with the good fortune of having the exigencies of welfare satisfied, as well as taking pleasure in things, enjoyment of activities, engagement in subjectively worthwhile projects, attachments of genuine friendships, the good of reciprocal love, filial and parental love, and the goods of political liberty, recognition of human dignity, and possession of self-respect.

6.   The value of dignity has ancient roots in hierarchical societies. It was linked to the notion of respect that is due to those who enjoy superior social status, those who occupy superior social roles and offices, as well as being constitutive of recognition of skills and achievements. Respect is an attitude widely demanded of children in their relations to their parents. For religious believers respect is owed to their god or gods in the form of reverence. Friendship demands reciprocal respect. *Self-respect is an essential constituent of a good human life* in as much as loss of self-respect is inimical to human felicity. It may be generated by oneself or by others. Self-generated loss of self-respect may be produced by shame and guilt, which may be warranted or unwarranted. Lack of self-respect may also result from lack of self-confidence, sometimes produced by natural shyness and sometimes by excessive self-criticism. Other-generated loss of self-respect is often produced by persistent failure in competitive activities with peer groups and also by humiliation and loss of dignity. *Formal respect* for human beings as such is an ideal that has emerged in Western societies only slowly, by fits and starts.

Formal respect is respect for any rational being with free will and responsibility, irrespective of their deeds and beliefs. The notion has remote roots in the Old Testament in the idea that Man is created in the image of God and is celebrated in Psalms 8: 'What is man, that thou art mindful of him? ... thou hast made him a little lower than the angels and has crowned him with glory and honour. Thou madest him to have dominion over the works of thy hands, thou hast put all things under his feet', a sentiment echoed in the great renaissance orations on the dignity of man (Giannozzo Manetti, Pico della Mirandola, Marsilio Ficino) and by Shakespeare in Hamlet's soliloquy 'What a piece of work is man! How noble in reason, how infinite in faculty ...'. It is suggested by the Aristotelian notion of possession of a rational *psuchē* that differentiates mankind from the rest of the animal kingdom. It is intimated in the New Testament in 1 Corinthians 3:16–17: 'Know ye not that ye are the temple of God and that the Spirit of God dwelleth in you? If any man defile the temple of God, him shall God destroy: for the temple of God is holy, which temple ye are'. But the notion of formal respect and of the formal dignity of man had little if any grip in Roman civilization, being fundamentally a slave-dependent society that treated vanquished enemies in formal triumphs with horrendous cruelty and contempt (e.g. Vercingetorix, the leader of the Gauls, who surrendered at Alesia to save his people from further slaughter and starvation, was held in prison in appalling conditions for six years, then paraded in chains in Caesar's triumph and garrotted by an executioner). It had relatively little role in Catholic Christianity, in so far as it was dominated by the ideas of original sin, dependence on God for grace and salvation, redemption only through Christ, and hence for the most part dismissive of notions of human autonomy and freedom. It had even less place in Protestant Christianity, viz. Lutherans and Calvinists, who were obsessed with predestination rather than free will, by dependency on grace rather than human autonomy, by the depravity of man rather than human perfectibility, and by the infinite gulf between God and man that is to be emphasized by self-abasement, acknowledgement of sin, and threats of hellfire. It is only with Kant, in the late eighteenth century, that the idea of the formal respect for a human being as such, irrespective of social status, and the notion of the essential dignity of man as a rational agent, irrespective of his moral standing and religious affiliation, emerge into full light and become a central theme in moral, political, and legal reflection in Western philosophy.

Even Kant did not formulate this doctrine satisfactorily. For formal respect for rational agency as such turns out to be respect for the moral law that rational agents are required to recognize. That is mistaken.

Human beings deserve formal respect, no matter how wicked they may be, in virtue of the following nine characteristics they possess:

(i)   They are free (or, as we misleadingly put it, they possess free-will) in as much as they possess two-way abilities to act or refrain from acting in given situations.

(ii)   They belong to a moral community and as members of a moral community have knowledge of good and evil, have the ability to differentiate right from wrong, a moral conscience and the ability to feel guilt, shame, and remorse.

(iii)   They possess capacity-rationality – they have the ability to reason, to apprehend the warrant which reasons give to actions, beliefs, and feelings, no matter how poorly they exercise this ability.

(iv)   They are able to deliberate in advance of action, to reflect in advance of belief formation, to form opinions and make judgements, and to revise their opinions and judgements on further consideration and in the light of new facts and changing circumstances.

(v)   They have the power to set themselves ends on the basis of their deliberations.

(vi)   They are able to make decisions on the basis of reasons and in pursuit of their ends.

(vii)   They are responsible, answerable, for their deeds and for their beliefs and opinions.

(viii)   They bear liability responsibility for their misdeeds.

(ix)   They have the ability to recognize the humanity and rational agency of others. It is in virtue of these features that human beings alone in the natural world deserve formal respect and are endowed with formal dignity, no matter how wicked or evil they are. What does this mean?

7.   All human beings are owed equal formal respect. This constitutes recognition of the rational agency of human beings, irrespective of their social status and their moral standing – their merits and iniquities. Formal respect for rational agency is internally related to what we are obliged *not to do* to human beings. It is expressed above all in the prohibition on humiliating and inflicting degradation upon human beings. For to humiliate and degrade others is to treat them as subhuman. It is to deprive them of self-respect. To do this destroys their humanity, in their own eyes no less than in the eyes of others.

Moreover, systematically to fail to grant formal respect to others is to inflict moral harm upon oneself. For in so doing, one falls below the minimal standards that qualify one for membership of the moral community of mankind. One besmirches oneself and destroys one's own soul. This thought will be explored in the next essay on the nature of wickedness and evil.

14

Badness, Wickedness, Evil and the Death of the Soul

"The belief in a supernatural source of evil is not necessary; men alone are quite capable of every wickedness."

Joseph Conrad

1. Just as 'good' is the most general adjective of commendation, laudation, or approval, so too 'bad' is the most general adjective of condemnation, criticism, or disapproval. Just as 'good' is a scalar modifier ('good', 'better', 'best'), so too 'bad' is a scalar modifier ('bad', 'worse', 'worst'). It is puzzling that the scalar modifiers have a different root than 'bad'. Curiously, 'badder' and 'baddest' are used colloquially by primary school teachers to mean naughtier and naughtiest. Just as there are varieties of goodness (Essay 13), so too there are varieties of badness. The cousins of *bad* are *weak, poor, pathetic, unsatisfactory, inadequate, harmful, worthless, defective, deficient, detrimental*. Which of these is apt, in any particular case, depends upon the variety of badness under consideration.

It is noteworthy that attributions of badness are *sometimes* privative, that ascriptions of badness sometimes signify no more than lack of good-making qualities. So, for example, a bad knife is a knife that does not cut well, a bad joke is a joke that is not funny, and one has a bad memory if one cannot remember what others can. But it is by no means always so. Food is bad if it is rotting or infected, pain is bad if it is severe, an examination script is bad if it is full of mistakes or if

Solving, Resolving, and Dissolving Philosophical Problems: Essays in Connective, Contrastive and Contextual Analysis, First Edition. P. M. S. Hacker.
© 2025 John Wiley & Sons Ltd. Published 2025 by John Wiley & Sons Ltd.

its conclusions are ill-supported, a painting is bad if it is unskilfully executed, or if it is sentimental, in bad taste, or kitsch.

Just as there are varieties of goodness, so too there are varieties of badness. *Medical badness*, like medical goodness, has as its focal point the health of a being. Someone is in bad health if he is ill, has an infection, injury, or illness. He may suffer from poor health if his condition is chronic. Conceptually linked to the badness of health of a living creature are the deficiencies of organs and faculties. An organ is bad or weak (e.g. bad eyes, a weak heart) and a sense-faculty poor (poor eyesight, poor sense of smell), when they fail to fulfil their characteristic function optimally, relative to the kind of being in question (the badness is species-relative: good eyesight in a human being would be grossly inadequate in an eagle). Deficiencies of organs and faculties deleteriously affect the agent's ability to lead a normal life for a being of its kind. Badness of health is a focal point around which are clustered the notions of a substance (stuff) being medically bad, a condition being medically bad, and an activity being medically bad for the health and fitness of a being. So, many foodstuffs are bad for one or are bad for one if consumed in excess (sugars, fats, alcohol), relative to one's needs and circumstances. Similarly, smoking is bad for one, being overweight (a condition) deleteriously affects one's health, and boxing (an activity) is liable to damage one's brain.

Corresponding to technical goodness, the goodness of skills, is *technical badness*. Like technical goodness, technical badness has at least four sub-forms: the badness at a craft (tinker, shoemaker, carpenter), vocational badness (e.g. of a lawyer, doctor, teacher), ludic badness [a much-needed new use of 'ludic'] (of sportsmen, mountain climbers, game players), and performance badness (of actors, musicians, singers). A professional or an artisan is technically bad if they are not merely poor in the exercise of their skill, but incompetent. A poor solicitor or dentist, a poor plumber or gardener, may be better than none, but a bad one should be avoided, as their work will probably be substandard, and they are liable to do more harm than good. A bad mountain climber may endanger the lives of his fellow mountaineers, and a bad actor may ruin the play or film in which he acts badly. Similar considerations apply to the derivative form of technical badness, namely: the poorness or badness of a technique. A poor technique is lamentable, but a bad one is likely to be positively harmful. So too, artefactual badness consists in the poorness, badness, inadequacy and inefficiency of instruments, tools, and machines on the one hand and of non-instrumental artefacts, such as roads, houses, bridges, airports, and harbours, on the other. Their various forms of badness make them dangerous to life and limb, inefficient in subserving the goal for which they were made.

It should by now be straightforward to articulate the other varieties of badness, such as the badness of the detrimental (as opposed to the beneficial), of the anti-hedonic (the painful, uncomfortable, unpleasant, disagreeable, unpalatable, distressing, repulsive, and the disgusting), and of the anti-eudaimonic (unhappiness, misery, grief, and sorrow). We leave the exercise to the reader (its validation can be checked against *The Moral Powers*).

To be sure, there are many other predications of badness of one kind or another that do not fit readily into the selected varieties. Currency is bad if it is debased, weak, or counterfeit; laws are bad if they are unjust, ill-drafted and so vague or ambiguous; debts are bad if they cannot be discharged; a child is bad if naughty, unruly, rude, and disobedient. And so on.

Precisely because there are varieties of badness, there are equally many different forms of bad deeds, acts that it is wrong to perform and omissions that it is wrong to make. They may be medically, economically, legally, politically wrong. They may be ill-informed, ill-advised, inefficient, undemocratic. Sometimes their consequences may be appalling (e.g. in relation to a pandemic) and moral culpability may be incurred, even though the motives for doing them may not have been malevolent. In the absence of circumstantial justification or extenuating circumstances, they are wrong, and their agents are blameworthy.

2.   With these qualifications, reminders, and elucidations, we may now turn to our main theme: moral badness. As always, our first port of call is lexical. What are the subjects of which moral badness can legitimately be predicated? *Human beings*, people, may be morally bad if they are cruel, malicious, unjust, dishonest, vindictive, or arrogant in their dealings with their fellow human beings. These are *character traits* morally bad people have, dispositions of character that are themselves morally bad, or worse – wicked or evil. They are *vices* – in the more extreme cases, *deadly vices*. Such vices are manifest in bad, wicked, or evil *deeds*, motivated by bad, wicked, or evil *motives and intentions*. Bad, wicked, and evil deeds characteristically have bad or evil *consequences*. The deadliest of vices is cruelty to human beings or to animals. Michel de Montaigne (1533–92) characterized cruelty as 'the extremist of all vices', Thomas Fuller observed that a man of

cruelty 'is God's enemy'. To the cruel man, cruelty 'is the highest kind of pleasure' (Walter Savage Landor) and it 'requires no motive outside of itself, but only requires an opportunity' (George Eliot) as is patent in master-at-arms Claggart in Melville's novella *Billy Budd*. It is bred by fear and stupidity, thoughtlessness and indifference, unlimited power and lust for revenge. Lord Acton sapiently observed: 'All power tends to corrupt. Absolute power corrupts absolutely'.

In addition to human beings, morally bad deeds are done by human institutions: international organisations, governments, non-governmental organisations and institutions, multinational corporations, banks, local government authorities, and so on. These wrongdoers will not be discussed here. It is relatively easy to see how to extend our analyses from people to institutions, although it is often difficult to allocate blame to corporate subordinates to the relevant culpable CEO.

To say that someone is a bad person or to say that something is a bad thing to do commonly has the illocutionary force of moral disapprobation, criticism or condemnation. But it is also the crudest and least informative of the triplet, 'bad', 'wicked', 'evil'. Often it is positively jejune or grossly inappropriate, as in saying that Hitler was a bad man, or that genocide is a bad practice, or that inflicting pain for fun is a bad thing to do. Wickedness and evil are deep forms of moral offense and wrongdoing. To say of something or someone that they are evil is the most severe form of moral condemnation we possess.

It is striking, and, as we shall see, significant, that 'wicked' has both comparative and superlative forms, namely: 'wickeder' and 'wickedest', comparable to 'bad', 'worse', 'worst', but 'evil' does not. It has only intensifiers, viz. 'more evil' and 'most evil'. This calls out for explanation. It is surely akin to the comparable grammatical fact that one cannot be better than best. Murdering two million innocent people is *doing* more evil than murdering one million. But someone who murders two babies or infants for fun is not twice as evil as someone who murders only one for fun. If someone has intentionally done evil, then, in the absence of justifying or extenuating circumstances, he is evil. If he does further evil, that does not make *him* more evil – it only means that he has *done* more evil. It involves a deep misunderstanding to speculate or argue over who is the most evil of the great twentieth-century dictators, Hitler, Stalin, or Mao – all one can do is debate which of them *did* most evil. But surely, if evil-doers not only do evil, but also take pleasure in the evil they do and publicly and proudly proclaim it to the world, as did the Hamas murderers on

7 October 2023 who slaughtered Israeli Jews with sadism and joy, are they not more evil than others, who do not proclaim it with pride? No; they are only more depraved, contemptible, and repulsive in their deliberate and gleeful shattering of the moral order of humanity.

3.   True to our methods, we should turn to the etymology of 'evil'. It is revealing and suggestive. The English 'evil' is derived from Old English *yfel*, Middle English *uvel*, and Old Frisian *evel*. It is related to Old High German *ubil*, which is the source of modern German's *übel*. The root meaning is 'exceeding the measure' or 'overstepping proper limits'. It is striking that although Latin (like the later romance languages) has a large toolbox of forms of badness, for example, *malus, nequam, nefas, improbus, pravus, perversus, turpe, corruptus, vitiosus*, it has no single expression that corresponds to 'evil'. Similarly, ancient Greek has no single expression that corresponds exactly to 'evil' – *kakós* signifies bad, wicked, or evil indifferently, as well as spiteful and mischievous. Like Latin, it has a rich vocabulary of opprobium, for example, *kakia, aischros, diephtharmenos, fáulos, parephtharmenos, ponēros, mochtheros*, but no single word that corresponds precisely to 'evil'. Even ancient Hebrew has to make do with *ra*, which signifies bad, wicked, and evil indifferently, although it has many other terms of opprobrium, such as *pesha, khet, avon, zadon*.

Germanic languages in general, and English in particular, are fortunate to have at hand a direct means to distinguish between the most extreme form of moral iniquity from moral badness and wickedness. *Evil* signifies what is beyond the pale. It belongs in the same toolbox as *demonic, diabolic, devilish, fiendish* – which is hardly surprising given general archaic beliefs in supernatural evil, and sits side by side with *depraved, degenerate, corrupt*, as well as *vile, foul, odious*, and *repulsive, despicable, repugnant*.

The most important clue we take away from this short etymological and comparative foray is that evil-doers, in some sense that demands explanation, set themselves irremediably beyond the pale.

4.   It has long been customary to distinguish between supernatural evil, natural evil, and human evil. The idea of supernatural evil is widespread in religions, both monotheist and duo-theist. Gods may be evil, as is Ahriman according to Zoroastrian beliefs; fallen angels may be evil, as are the Devil or Satan in Catholic beliefs; demons, the supernatural servants of Satan, are evil, as are humans who have sold their souls to the Devil. This belongs to the religious mythology of evil.

Natural evils are natural catastrophes that destroy human life, property, crops, and means of livelihood. They may be floods or droughts, earthquakes or tsunamis, volcanic eruptions and avalanches. Biological natural evils are plagues and epidemics. The evil of natural evils consists in their results, not necessarily in any conscious agency, although in the case of global warming, the natural catastrophes are caused by human beings, governments, and corporations. They are conceived to be evils because they cause the deaths, often agonized deaths, of thousands of human beings, and because they destroy the means of human livelihood. In prescientific eras, it was common to explain natural evils by reference to the gods or to God. No other explanation was available for such catastrophes. Polytheism provided ready explanations in terms of strife between gods (e.g. Zeus and Hera) or the interference of one or another god in human affairs (e.g. Apollo and Athena). Dualist religions, such as Zoroastrianism or Manichaeism, offered explanations in terms of cosmic dramas between non-omnipotent forces of good (e.g. Ahura Mazda) and forces of evil (e.g. Ahriman) in which humanity is caught up. Monotheist religions understandably had more difficulty explaining natural evils and in trying to explain the ways of God to humanity. Since a benevolent God could not be faulted, the fault must be humanity's. Guilt was imputed where no guilt was meet.

Human evil consists in the morally depraved, wicked, vicious, corrupt, and above all, cruel. Human agents may be evil (evil-doers), human deeds may be evil (evil-doing), and the upshot or results of human deeds may be evil (evil done).

There has, in recent decades, been a scientistic trend to explain evil away, in effect to deny that evil exists, to aver that human beings are not *really* evil. The scientism has its roots either in determinism (Laplacean or Marxist-historical) or in the medicalization of responsibility (psychological or psychoanalytic; behaviourist; cognitive neuro-scientific). Such forms of scientism argue that human evil is merely a surface phenomenon, since in truth science has shown that we are all victims of forces beyond our control, such forces being the economic system and poverty, the social system and social class differentiation, the political system and alienation, colonialism, the unconscious mind, the workings of the brain, and so forth. Accordingly, we are not free moral agents and are neither answerable nor responsible for what we do. In a period of glorification of victimhood, as the Anglophone world is now undergoing, this has powerful appeal. Such scientism needs robust refutation – some of it is an exaggeration of truths applicable only in special cases. The general abnegation of human responsibility is in effect the abnegation of humanity. If we are not answerable for our deeds and responsible for what we do, we are not free beings with two-way powers to act or refrain from acting in a given circumstance (liberty of indifference) and we are not able to act for reasons (liberty of spontaneity). If so, we are not rational beings at all, merely pawns on the chessboard of fortune (Omar Khayyam) or cogwheels in the machinery of causation.

It is important that we face the truth about ourselves. We *do* have capacity-rationality, however weak it may be in times of crisis. We *have* eaten of the Tree of Good and Evil – that is to say, we *do* have the capacity to do evil as well as good. We are rational beings – we *can* reason; we are moral agents; we are language users; we are not only thinkers and talkers, but, as Marx insisted against Hegel, also tool-makers; but we should not forget that the main tools our remote ancestors made were weapons, arrowheads, and war hammers.

5. Evil is the deliberate infliction of death, severe bodily harm, or extreme suffering on another innocent human being or sentient creature without adequate warrant or in excess of what is required for the attainment of a justifying or excusing goal. This is not a definition, but a characterization of paradigm cases. To be sure, such a characterization requires amplification. For there are bound to be disagreements about what counts as a warrant, as justification or excuse, and what counts as 'being in excess'. This area of disagreement constitutes the 'borderlands of evil'. It is not so much a fuzzy borderline, characteristic of vague concepts, but a broad grey area of unavoidable dispute from case to case. The disputes turn on the performance of *necessary evils*. The term is misleading, since what it signifies is, roughly speaking, doing harm in order to prevent greater harm. A surgeon who removes a patient's eye in order to prevent spread of cancer is not doing an evil. Adequate warrant for the deliberate infliction of extreme suffering may be given by medical necessity: to save a life, or to cure a patient in dire circumstances, when no analgesics are available. Killing another may be warranted by self-defence, or by saving someone from an agonizing but unavoidable death (a driver trapped in the cabin of a burning lorry). It may be excused by the necessities of a just war (World War II), by the duty of legitimate governments to preserve the state from destruction (Ukraine in 2022), or the duty of the state to protect its citizens from slaughter (Israel in 2023). What should not be open to reasonable dispute is the existence

of pure evil – cruelty, the deliberate and patently unwarranted infliction of suffering on an animal (pouring petrol over an animal and setting it alight for amusement) or on another innocent human being (a wide range of horrific examples of cruelty to children is given by Ivan in discussion with his brother Alyosha in Dostoevsky's novel *The Brothers Karamazov*).

Being evil is not a vice, any more than being virtuous is a virtue. They are not character traits. Rather, evil is the general form of deadly vices, just as virtue is the common form of the moral virtues. An important distinction can be drawn between wickedness and evil. Such a distinction is perhaps explicative: cutting the ragged edges of ordinary usage for an elucidatory purpose. Just as there are borderlands of evil in which disputation about warrants, justifications, and excuses take place, so too there is not a sharp borderline between wickedness and evil, indeed, not even a vague borderline, but a broad borderland in which casuistry finds its space.

6.   We have, in Essay 13, investigated the roots of moral goodness. Let us put it on the carpet again. Its animal roots, it was suggested, lie in feelings, in particular in our disposition to care for others, and in maternal care for offspring, which evolves into one paradigm form of love, namely motherly love, and into compassion. We do, mercifully, have a natural disposition for sympathy and empathy (not to be confused: the former is a form of feeling, the latter a form of understanding). To be sure, our natural disposition to care requires refinement and transformation by family life, moral education, social life, and reflection. Whatever innate propensity to sympathy we have is not equally distributed. It is easily crushed by adverse circumstances and brutalization. Women tend to be more compassionate than men, for obvious biological reasons. Family life varies greatly from family to family, from society to society and epoch to epoch. Moral education is equally variable, dependent upon a multiplicity of factors, and so too are the standards of public behaviour, both with regard to small morals and courtesy, and with respect to public morality and criminality. It is patent that not only does social morality vary greatly in different times and places, but the degree to which any given society lives up to its own moral standards is similarly variable. The struggle between right and wrong is part of the human condition.

What, then, are the roots of the morally bad, of the wicked and evil? They are individual, social, religious, and ideological. As we have emphasized, it is characteristic of our species, especially, but not only, of the male of the species, to be highly competitive, aggressive, single minded in pursuit of goals, to have a strong desire for wealth and possessions, and a lust for power. We have a natural tendency to selfishness and indifference to the sufferings of others that constrains and limits our natural sympathies. We have a powerful sexual drive, an inclination to sexual possessiveness, with a corresponding disposition to jealousy.

Consequently, individual motives for doing evil and the motives that characterize evil-doers are manifold, wonderfully depicted in great works of literature and drama: envy and resentment of the status, power, and wealth of another (Cassius in Shakespeare's *Julius Caesar*); jealousy of another who has taken the love that one feels is one's due (Othello); unrestrained hedonism (Wilde's Dorian Gray), boredom (Hedda Gabler, in Ibsen's eponymous play); sexual lust (Tarquin, in Roman legend); lust for power and ambition (in Shakespeare's *Richard III*); sadism and natural malevolence (Claggart in Melville's *Billy Budd*); hatred and revenge (Heathcliffe in Emily Bronte's *Wuthering Heights*); and greed for wealth. (Daniel Plainview in Upton Sinclair's novel *Oil* (1927), played by Daniel Day Lewis in the 2007 film 'There will be Blood').

The social roots of the morally bad lie in our natural tribalism, the correlate of which is xenophobia. Our need for a sense of identity, that is, for an awareness of what we stand for and to what group we belong and identify with, is greatly strengthened by finding an object to hate, either external to our own society or nation-state, or within our society or state. This is greatly exacerbated by religious and ideological systems of beliefs that encourage bigotry, prejudice, and self-righteousness.

Much evil that is done is group behaviour. Group evil-doing is an outlet for male aggression. It provides camaraderie in violence and destruction both in war and in peace, and it strengthens a weak sense of identity. When directed at weaker groups in society, it gives evil-doers a sense of superiority. Being a form of collective action, it relieves the individual of any sense of personal responsibility. If a leader is involved, loyalty to the leader unites the group and abrogates the burden of decision-making. A unifying ideology or religion, driving violent and destructive action, gives meaning to what may otherwise be dull or empty lives. Human beings, when their evil propensities are unleashed, enjoy destruction and violence as well as momentarily liberating loss of identity in mob behaviour. In warfare, it commonly offers aggressive males the temptations of booty and rape.

7.   Questions about motivation of unquestionable evil need to be raised.

Can evil be rational? If this question means: is reflection, planning, and effective instrumental reasoning involved in doing evil? – then the answer is obviously often 'Yes". There *can* be spontaneous evil, as often occurs in the course of riots and demonstrations, in which a demonstrator is swept away in the excitement of the mob and fatally injures someone. In such cases, evil is often done in a frenzy of destructiveness, in which an agent has no motive. To be sure, that does not relieve the evil-doer of responsibility. Similarly, evil is often done in an explosion of anger, in which the evil deed, perhaps killing someone with a blow, is the form in which the rage is manifest. But much evil is deliberately planned well in advance and involves rational deliberation. On the other hand, there can be no *legitimate* justification or excuse for doing evil, in as much as, other things being equal, that something is evil gives the best possible reason for not doing it.

Can doing evil be reasonable? No; being reasonable involves taking into account the legitimate concerns of other people and is linked to an appreciation of values, such as fairness and justice, as well as the demands of duty and obligation. That is precisely what doing evil precludes. To do evil is to become and be evil, and that is to be in bondage to all the baser and destructive instincts and drives of humankind.

Can evil itself be a motive for action? No, for that something is evil provides the best possible reason for not doing it. 'Because it is evil' is not an intelligible answer to the question 'Why did you do it?', since its being evil is the most extreme form of condemnation. One cannot intelligibly do something 'for the sake of evil'. Milton's Lucifer's and Verdi's Iago's, 'Evil be thou my good!', strictly speaking, makes no sense. This claim of unintelligibility, one may well say, is a version of the ancient doctrine that all fully intentional action must be done *sub specie boni*, namely: that the evil-doer must see at least *some* good in what he is doing.

It is therefore no coincidence that evil-doers find other reasons for their evil deeds. They may insist that what they are doing isn't *really* evil, that their victims are not *really human* – they are just plague germs (Enver Pasha speaking of the Turkish genocide of Armenians), bacilli of racial tuberculosis (Hitler on the Jews), parasites (Stalin on the Ukrainian kulaks during the Holodomor), a cancer in society that must be eradicated (a favoured anti-Semitic trope). Strikingly, one of the characteristic features of genocidal evil is the strenuous effort to dehumanize the victims. There is always an existential tension between holding the victims not to be human, but germs, bacilli, and cancers, and striving to humiliate them – for only human beings can be humiliated. Genocidal evil characteristically involves the gross maltreatment of the victims, the rape and murder of women before the eyes of their husbands, forcing women into sex slavery, demeaning and humiliating torture, forcing men to kill their friends. Most significantly, genocidal evil destroys the very souls of the victims by making them destroy what is most sacred to them (for example, a Nazi officer forcing an elderly rabbi to spit upon the scrolls of the Torah, and when he could spit no more, spitting into his mouth to make him continue (an episode recorded in Chaim Kaplan's Warsaw Diary, quoted by Raimond Gaita in his *Good and Evil*)).

8.   Any history of human evil makes it evident that evil-doers, in destroying the humanity of their victims, set themselves irremediably beyond the pale of humanity. For they deliberately and gleefully shatter the moral order of humanity. It is here that we can differentiate between evil and wickedness. The wicked are sometimes capable of redemption. If they come to recognize the wrong they have done, regret doing it, feel genuine remorse and try, in whatever ways possible, to make good the harm done, they *can be forgiven*. But those who have done evil have no conscience and typically show no remorse. The only senior Nazi at the Nuremberg Trials to avow remorse was Speer, who blatantly lied to escape hanging, as was demonstrated by his biographer Gitta Sereny.

Forgiveness is a problematic notion. The nature of forgiveness is unclear. The *agents of forgiveness* are human beings. People forgive others *for* their misdeeds and wrongdoings. Is forgiving *an act*? Is it voluntary or involuntary or neither? To say 'I forgive you' is a voluntary quasi-performative that commits one to abandon holding a wrongdoer to account and to cease resenting his behaviour. The offender's blameworthy deed is no less wrong as a result of forgiveness – it is the wrongdoer that is forgiven, not the wrong done. But one may forgive an offender without any speech act. So is forgiving *an event* that happens to the forgiver? No. Forgiveness for wrongdoing may take time, sometimes a long time, as the injury done heals, ceases to be an object of awareness, and no longer perturbs one. It is then neither voluntary nor involuntary. Nevertheless, one is answerable for forgiving someone when one should not have forgiven, just as one may be answerable for believing someone when one should not have believed. And one is answerable for not forgiving when one should have forgiven, as one may be answerable for not believing when one should have believed (see Essay 7). One may be under an obligation to forgive someone (for example, for the sake of the love one bore his parents), and one may be under an obligation not to forgive (if, for example, one swore an oath not to forgive, as Hannibal Barca swore to his father Hamilcar not to forgive Rome for the First Punic War). But an obligation to forgive cannot be *to* the wrongdoer, since no one has a right to be forgiven. One may beg for forgiveness, but one cannot demand it. The evil-doer does not deserve forgiveness, since the evil done puts him beyond the pale. He may not beg for forgiveness, but only for mercy.

It is not only the nature of forgiveness that needs elucidation. There are further deep questions concerning who has the right to forgive, what deeds warrant forgiveness, what are the limits of forgiveness, and what are the consequences of forgiveness. It is evident that the forgiver must have an appropriate *locus standi*. The victim may forgive, but the friend of the victim cannot. The parents of a murdered child or the children of a murdered parent may forgive the murderer in appropriate circumstances, but others cannot. Justifying or extenuating circumstances may warrant forgiveness. Beyond that, forgiveness for wrong-doing can be judged only in relation to the character and history of the wrongdoer, the available alternatives in the circumstances, the intentions and purposes of his deeds, the goals and motives he had in view. Any decision must be ideographic, rather than nomothetic, save in the case of evident evil-doing.

Self-forgiveness is as unlike forgiveness of others as self-love is unlike the love of others, or as self-deception is unlike the deception of others. To forgive oneself, one must first have lost one's self-respect, feel deeply ashamed of oneself for what one takes to be a profound wrong one has done. To forgive oneself is to cease hating oneself, to stop despising oneself, and to desist from self-contempt.

9.   Wickedness can, in certain cases and certain circumstances, be forgiven. The person who has knowingly and intentionally done a wicked deed in the absence of justifying or extenuating circumstances, may nevertheless be redeemed by his honest acceptance of responsibility, his sincere regret and remorse, and by his striving to make amends for his wrong-doing in whatever ways possible for him. Evil doers, by contrast, have set themselves apart from humanity. To deny the humanity of other human beings and to strive to destroy their

humanity, to slaughter the innocent, to inflict unbridled suffering on them as has been done by countless *genocidaires*, is not only to destroy the humanity of one's victims, it is to do evil, to do what is unforgiveable. The very idea that human beings *could* be forgiven for evil deeds is unclear. Who could possibly have the right to forgive the German genocide of the Hereros in German South-West Africa; the genocide of the Armenians, first by the Ottomans and later by the Ittihadists; who could have the right to forgive Stalin's mass slaughter of kulaks and subsequent genocidal murder of Ukrainians in the Holodomor; the Nazi genocide of the Jews; Pol Pot's genocide of his own people; the genocide committed in Rwanda, East Timor, Nigeria, and so on and so forth? One who intentionally does evil to another human being or to a group of human beings, to a tribe or a people, *have destroyed their own soul.*

10.   We need the concept of the soul, no less than we need the concept of the mind, and for similar reasons. The concept of the mind, as was argued in Essay 1, is in effect a way of presenting (by means of pseudo-entification) the rational and volitional powers of human beings and the exercise of those powers. We present the mind as the agent of thought, feeling and volition – as 'that within us which thinks and reasons' (as Reid and Mill mistakenly argued). But it isn't. It is neither a something nor a nothing (which is not to say that human beings do not have a mind). This *form of representation* is useful. It enables us readily to compare different human beings' intellectual and volitional abilities and their exercise in a compact, convenient and picturesque way. It meets a patent need in our thought and talk about ourselves.

11.   We stand in just as deep a need of a form of representation of our moral powers and our moral sensibility. We speak, rightly, of there being *darkness in the soul* of a human being – a lack of moral sensibility. We speak, correctly, of *genocidaires* as *lacking a soul* – Maurycy Allerhand, a distinguished professor of law and teacher of both the great Hersch Lauterpacht and Rafael Lemkin was, on the Nazi invasion, interned in the concentration camp at Janowska in Lvov; on seeing a Nazi officer mercilessly beating an old man, Allerhand went up to the officer and asked '*Have you no soul?*', whereupon the Nazi officer took out his revolver and shot Allerhand dead. We may remark with Martha Gellhorn, commenting on Eichmann, that we must *guard our own souls in the face of evil.*

Kurtz, in Conrad's *Heart of Darkness*, peers into his own soul as he is dying and can find nothing there but horror. We speak, perfectly intelligibly, of those who take material advantage of evil done by others (by witch-hunters in Salem or East Anglia in the seventeenth century or by *Einsatzgruppen* in the Ukraine and in Poland) by expropriating the property of the murdered, as people who have *allowed their souls to wither*. Raskolnikov is described as a 'lost soul', and Coleridge's ancient mariner is a 'damned soul'. We describe people as having a 'beautiful soul', a 'noble soul', or a 'gentle soul'. We speak of some forms of labour as 'soul destroying' – a dulling of sensibility by drudgery. Here too one's soul may be said to wither, although it would be more accurate to speak of the *withering of one's spirit*. For it is one's liveliness, responsiveness to experience, engagement with one's fellow human beings, and capacity for joy that are being crushed.

> Socrates sapiently remarked
>
> There is a part of us which is improved by healthy actions and ruined by unhealthy ones. If we spoil it by taking the advice of non-experts, will life be worth living once this part is ruined? The part I mean is the body ...
>
> What about that within us which is mutilated by wrong actions, and benefited by right ones? Is life worth living with this right part ruined? Or do we believe that this, whatever it maybe, in which right and wrong operate, is of less importance than the body? (*Crito* 47d–e)

The medical analogy is surely profound. We care a great deal about our physical integrity and our good health. Loss of a limb is a great misfortune in as much as it deprives us of our ability to function as normal human beings. Moreover, since opportunities are correlative to abilities, we may also lose many of the opportunities available to those more fortunate. Are there then not features of our non-bodily nature that can be damaged, even irremediably damaged, by abuse and misuse, namely by doing evil? With such loss of our moral powers are human possibilities for doing, becoming, and being not foreclosed? Is Plato not wise to challenge us: should we not care for our soul at least as much as we care for our physical constitution and health?

We need a secular concept of the soul no less than we need the concept of the mind. For we need a way of presenting our moral sensibility. It is noteworthy that just as we are prone to contrast the mind with the body, so too we are prone to contrast the soul with the flesh. This is not surprising, as the appetites, which we share with animals, are bound to our physical nature, needs, and cravings. The appetites may hold us in bondage if egotism, self-indulgence, and hedonism rule our lives. Alcoholism, gluttony, and concupiscence may enslave us. But these are not somatic characteristics: it is not one's body that is gluttonous, given to alcoholism, beset with the priapic afflictions of a Don Juan or the insatiable lusts of a Messalina. That is why the soul is not to be contrasted with the body, but with the flesh.

That human beings have a soul thus conceived is not an empirical statement. It is a constitutive one. It characterizes the nature of mankind, as does the statement than human beings have a mind. It can be said to be a logico-grammatical statement, since it draws our attention to what it makes sense to say. Of humans, but not of other animals, it makes sense to say that they have lost their soul, destroyed their own soul, that their soul is damaged, twisted or scarred, either by their own evil actions or by what they have been forced to do or to have undergone. Like the mind, the soul is not an 'entity' or thing of any kind. The pivotal question is not 'What is the soul?', but rather, 'What is it for a creature to possess a soul?', that is, what has to be true of a creature for it to be said to have a soul? The answer, in rough outline, is that it must be a language-using creature, it must have a mind, it must know the difference between good and evil, have a moral conscience, be susceptible to remorse and guilt for wrongdoing, and possess moral powers and moral sensibility.

15

Happiness

> "No one praises happiness as he does justice, but rather calls it blessed, as being something more divine and better."
>
> Aristotle

1.   The subject of happiness exemplifies the potential fruitfulness of etymological investigation as a source of philosophical insight. The English 'happy' and its cognates originate in the fourteenth-century word 'hap' signifying chance, or the fortune that befalls one, one's luck or lot in life. Unsurprisingly then, it takes adjectives such as 'good', 'bad'. 'evil' and 'ill' as modifiers. So those who are lucky have good hap, whereas the unfortunate have ill hap. The nexus of the concept of happiness with chance and luck characterizes many Indo-European languages. The French 'bonheur' (happiness) and 'heureux' (happy) derive from the Old French 'heur', meaning luck or chance. The German 'Gluck', to this day, is ambiguous, meaning both luck and happiness, an ambiguity mirrored in Dutch and Norwegian. Italian 'felicità', Spanish 'felicidad', and Portuguese 'felicidade' all derive from the Latin 'felix' (fortunate) and 'felicitas' (luck). The ancient Greek 'eudaimonia' signifies a lucky gift of a good ('eu-') spirit ('daimon'); 'olbos' signified divinely endowed prosperity, and 'olbios' meant prosperous, blessed, happy. Human felicity is a plaything of the gods, fragile and liable to unpredictable and sudden reversal. *Tyche* is luck and a happy human being is

Solving, Resolving, and Dissolving Philosophical Problems: Essays in Connective, Contrastive and Contextual Analysis, First Edition. P. M. S. Hacker.
© 2025 John Wiley & Sons Ltd. Published 2025 by John Wiley & Sons Ltd.

eutyches – fortunate or lucky. Strikingly, Hebrew, a Semitic rather than Indo-European language, displays no such nexus between happiness and chance. Rather the links between its eudaimonic vocabulary are with celebration and joy. 'Simcha' signifies happiness or celebration, 'osher' – lasting happiness, 'orah' means both happiness and light, 'gila' is exuberant joy, 'rina' is refreshing happiness, 'chedva' is the happiness of togetherness, 'sasson' is unexpected joy or happiness, and 'tzahala' is the happiness of dancing.

The evolution of 'happy' and 'happiness' from the medieval 'hap' is striking in as much as its surrounding nodes in the network within which it is now located developed surprisingly late. The *Oxford English Dictionary*'s first record of 'happy' as applied to a person who is *lucky, successful,* or *fortunate* is 1387. Its application to an event to signify *aptness* or *being felicitous*, as in 'happy accident' and 'happy coincidence' is more or less simultaneous (1393), swiftly followed by 'happy thought/reply/situation' (1400). 'Happy' and 'happiness' used to signify *being pleased, glad* or *satisfied* with one's condition are recorded in 1477. They are used to characterize an event or period as *contented* or *joyous*, as in 'happy occasion/childhood/times' only in 1547. *Happy memories, happy ending,* and, in stories, *lived happily ever after* followed swiftly, as did *happy birthday/Christmas/New Year*. The quite different use of the expression to signify *willingness, readiness,* or *eagerness* to do something is recorded in 1633. The extension of the word to a social group, as in 'happy ship/crew/team/home' is to be found in 1717.

This etymological foray nicely exhibits the slow development of our current eudaimonic network and contains multiple clues to be followed up in our connective analysis.

2.   In *Anna Karenina* Tolstoy sapiently remarks, 'All happy families resemble one another, but each unhappy family is unhappy in its own way'. This is no coincidence, as is made clear by contrastive analysis. 'Happy' and 'unhappy' ('happiness' and 'unhappiness') are contraries rather than contradictories, as one may be neither happy nor unhappy, and *not being unhappy* does not imply *being happy*. There are indefinitely many ways of being unhappy. One may be hapless: one's projects may fail; one's health may collapse (a sudden cancer); those one loves may die (spouse and children); one may lose one's wealth or one's job and means of livelihood; one may be weighed down with an overwhelming sense of the meaningless of life and the pointlessness of human activities. Like Solomon (or the Preacher in Jerusalem), one

may come to think that all is vanity and waste of breath. Accordingly, one's spirits may droop: one may become miserable, depressed, desolate, disconsolate. If one's projects fail, one may be unfulfilled, frustrated, discontented. One may lack all joy, be beset with boredom and vexation; one may be grief stricken, lonely, unloved. These multitudinous ways of being unhappy reflect the very large number of preconditions of happiness in life, absence of any one of which *may* be a source of unhappiness if one lacks the inner resources to withstand ill hap.

One cannot either feel happy with or be happy in one's life if one is lacking in something important to one, the lack of which deeply distresses one. For being distressed is incompatible with feeling or being happy. However, achieving or attaining something important to one may not make one happy. Each goal, once achieved may become insignificant and be replaced by yet another, as is patent in the tale of Don Juan. Or a goal, once achieved, gives one no quietus, as one's ambitions are insatiable, as is evident in the life of Alexander the Great. Or the achievement of one's goal may have involved one in great evil, which preys upon one's conscience, feeds one's paranoia, murders one's sleep, as in the case of Macbeth.

One cannot spend a happy evening at a merry party if one is feeling ill, is in pain, is distressed by some dreadful news, or if one is there against one's will. One cannot have a happy fortnight's holiday if one is beset by grief, distraught by circumstances, lonely. One cannot have a happy childhood if one is maltreated or neglected by one's parents or tormented by a sibling. One cannot have a happy marriage if one shares no interests with one's spouse or finds one's spouse repulsive (the fate of many a royal or noble marriage throughout history).

3.   It is evident from this contrastive analysis that it is necessary to distinguish between kinds of happiness by reference to temporality. While one can be pleased for a moment and take pleasure in a momentary experience, one cannot feel, let alone be, happy for a moment (unless struck dead at the onset of bliss). But one may be happy for a few hours of bliss. Here happiness is linked by means of *feeling happy* with the hedonic, with the enjoyable, carefree, blissful, and at the extreme end of the spectrum, with rapture, ecstasy, and euphoria. To be sure, this has little to do with the notion of happiness as the *summum bonum* – the Good of Man (*homo sapiens*), even though a happy life cannot be bereft of pleasure and enjoyment. Happiness of a different kind is involved in our talk of happy phases in the life of a

person, as when we speak of a happy childhood or youth, a happy marriage or career, a happy retirement and old age. Most generally, we speak of a person as having had a happy life. Here our notion of happiness makes contact with the Greek conception of *eudaimonia*. Very roughly, this constitutes an evaluation of a person's life as a whole. It incorporates both subjective and objective judgements. It involves evaluation of reciprocated loves and friendships, satisfactory fulfilment of personal projects and ends as well as an evaluation of those goals and ends, a hedonic evaluation of experiences, activities, and receptivities. A happy life need not be, or have been, happy in all its phases. One may have had an unhappy childhood or a miserable youth and yet, on the whole, have led a happy life. But a happy childhood and youth do not suffice to make for a happy life, save in the case of those who die young.

It is equally evident that we must distinguish kinds of happiness by reference to the diverse subjects that can be said to be happy. Obviously *human beings* occupy stage-centre. In so far as happiness can be said to be the *summum bonum*, it is the happiness of human beings that is in question. But, as is already patent, we speak of *happy times* in the lives of people, which may be hours, days, nights, of *happy periods* of life, and of *happy lives* as a whole. Derivatively, we speak of a *happy temperament*, insofar as a subjective contributory factor of good hap lies in character and personality traits. If someone has the good fortune to be debonair, cheerful, and optimistic by nature, they stand a very much better chance of leading a happy life than the introverted, melancholic pessimist. For one who has a happy temperament is better able than others to suit their wishes to the circumstances in which they find themselves. Such a person is less prone to be undermined by ill hap and more likely to rise successfully to its challenges. Restricting temporal duration, but remaining within the psychological domain, we also speak of being in a *happy mood*. Someone in a happy mood *feels happy*. This is Janus-faced: it may be the upshot of gratification in worthy tasks well-fulfilled; or it may be predominantly hedonic. In that sense, someone who feels happy is enjoying a happy time, finding joy in the passing hours, and taking pleasure in activity and receptivity. When feeling happy in a broadly hedonic sense, one tends to view the world through pink spectacles, relatively oblivious to the ills of the world, to the bad, the wicked, and the evil and sensitive to the good and the beautiful, to friendship and love.

As noted, we naturally extend our eudaimonic vocabulary to social groups. We say of a team, a social group, a social institution, indeed, a society as a whole, that it is a happy one. In general, a social group can be said to be a happy one if harmony prevails among its members and their interactions, if there are few animosities and no serious conflicts, if there are effective and efficient means of conflict resolution, and if there is broad consensus over morals and mores. In a happy social group, members manifest sincere mutual concern and reciprocal support.

Since happiness, in most of its forms, is a profoundly reflective and reflexive notion, it follows from our investigations thus far that strictly speaking, we cannot ascribe happiness either to babies or to animals. But we do. We speak of a happy baby, who chortles gleefully, smiles readily and cries little. We say of the cat purring while it is being stroked, the dog wagging its tail with joy at its owner's return, that they are happy. Are we wrong? No, not wrong, but ill-advised. Animals and infants can obviously be pleased at things and can take pleasure in things, but what they cannot do is evaluate their reactions and experiences, let alone periods or phases of their lives and judge them to be happy. That is a prerogative of language users, who, having mastered a developed language with devices of temporal reference, generality, and patterns of inference, are able to reflect on their past, present, and future condition, to compare it to alternative possibilities, to judge its various forms of goodness, can evaluate themselves and their lives as happy, unhappy, or neither. Of course, we can and will continue to speak of the happy baby and the happy dog, but we should not take this too seriously, any more than we take seriously the remark that a stubborn horse 'has a will of its own', knowing full well that horses have no will (ratiocinative desire).

4. Although being pleased at things and taking pleasure in things are constitutive elements in a happy life or happy period of life, as well as essential elements in hours, days and nights of happiness, pleasure is readily distinguished from happiness. One *takes* pleasure in certain activities and receptivities, but one *finds* happiness in things. Hedonists pursue pleasure, but as we shall see, eudaimonists do not, in the same sense, pursue happiness. The forms of pleasure, viz. sensual, physical, aesthetic, and intellectual, are not forms of happiness, even though they may contribute to it. One can have a momentary pleasure, but there is no such thing as a momentary happiness. A hedonist aims at a life of pleasure, but that is not the same as a happy life, as is evident from the histories of roués (Casanova), from art

(Hogarth's *The Rake's Progress*), and the literature of libertinage (*The Picture of Dorian Gray*; *Les Liaisons dangereuses*).

There is, however, greater affinity between happiness and contentment, hence differentiating the two is more important from the point of view of contrastive analysis. One cannot be leading a happy life while simultaneously feeling serious discontent with some serious feature of one's life. For such discontent signifies something wanting in one's life that mars it. On the other hand, one may be contented with one's lot without being happy. One may lack the personal autonomy in one's life that is a prerequisite for happiness, as in the case of a slave to a good master (e.g. Cicero's faithful slave Tiro is a good example). One may sacrifice one's life for the happiness of another, as Sidney Carton does for Lucie Manet in *A Tale of Two Cities*, but not for her contentment. One may seek contentment in cultivating one's garden for the sake of other ends, for example, to reduce the stress that is deleteriously affecting one's health. But one cannot want to be happy for the sake of any further goal. Long-term happiness is never a means to some other end, although there are many other ends than happiness.

The epistemology of happiness is distinctive. First-person *utterances* (a term of art) *of happiness* are exclamations of joys of the passing moment, rather than evaluative descriptions or reflections on a phase of life. They are not truth-evaluable. Here *truthfulness guarantees truth*. The corresponding third-person *ascriptions* of happiness, by contrast, rest on behavioural manifestations (including utterances) of joy or delight in appropriate circumstances and are truth-evaluable and defeasible. The same applies to avowals and descriptions of unhappiness – they may be exaggerated, but not mistaken. First-person utterances of happiness over longer periods of time, such as 'I have never been so happy as with you these last weeks' or 'We have been so happy here' are similarly asymmetrical. Corresponding memory utterances, such as 'We were so happy there' or 'Those were the happiest days of my life' lie in an intermediate zone. They are indeed utterances, but they are susceptible to error, as one's memory paints the past in pink, and they are rich sources of self-deception. The case of judgements of happiness of one's life as a whole are more complex. The subject's judgement is an evaluation, an evaluation that things on balance went well, that all things considered one's goals and undertakings were worthwhile and achieved to a satisfactory degree, and so forth. These are the subject's evaluations, and as such have a privileged status. But that does not mean that they are the last word. For self-deception is possible and the judgement of others, who know one well, may override the subjective judgement.

5.   Happiness is a *scalar concept* in the sense that it makes sense to speak of greater and lesser degrees of happiness. One may have had a happier childhood than youth, or a happier old age than earlier ages in one's life. But such comparisons are severely circumscribed. They make sense in a subjective, personal context. But interpersonal comparisons of degrees of happiness are much more problematic. To be sure, one may readily say that Jill has a happier temperament than Jack, as one may aver that Jack was happier that day than Jill. But when it comes to comparing lives, things are more constrained. Of course, if lives are conducted within comparable parameters, comparisons make sense. Raphael certainly led a happier life than Michelangelo. But where what makes one person happy differs extensively from what makes another happy, comparisons are meaningless. It makes no sense to wonder whether Raphael led a happier life than Julius Caesar.

As is already clear, happiness is intrinsically related to the satisfaction or non-satisfaction of *needs* and *wants*. For their non-satisfaction is a source of discontent and frustration, and their satisfaction is normally a reason for being pleased and sometimes a source of pleasure that may contribute to happiness in one or another of its forms. We may distinguish *absolute needs*, that are part of the human condition, such as the need for healthy food and drink, clothing, and shelter, from *socially minimal needs* that are a function of the economic norms of one's society, and both from *agent relative needs* that are determined by agential goals.

Wanting takes many forms: wishing and hoping for something; felt desires, cravings and appetites; inclinations; reason-supported wanting; and goals and purposes pursued. Among the goals pursued one must distinguish between *targets* and *roundabouts*, that is between *terminative goals* that one may strive to achieve once and for all and *regulative goals* that have no terminus, for example, to be a good V-er (viz. to fulfil a role well) or a good human being (which is not a role).

It is not difficult to list the preconditions of a happy human life, that is to say: a set of *facilitative conditions* – not necessary or sufficient conditions, but conditions for the possibility of a happy life for human beings. They are conditions the non-satisfaction of which reduces the likelihood of happiness, although they do not preclude it. What *is* difficult is to avoid parochialism, on the one hand, and unqualified relativism, on the other. Such conditions are physical, psychological, pedagogical, social, economic, and political. Physical normality and good health are preconditions of happiness in as much as physical abnormalities constrain one's mobility or dexterity, limiting one's ability to engage in the activities of normal human beings and reducing the vital pleasures of childhood, youth and early adulthood. Similarly, deficiencies of personal appearance (especially facial features), of perceptual faculties or speech are limitative, as well as being sources of embarrassment, of unavoidable, even though unwarranted, shame (Somerset Maugham's Philip Cary in *Of Human Bondage*), as well as resentment and bitterness (Shakespeare's Richard III). Psychological preconditions have already been discussed: a happy temperament, cheerful disposition, and fortitudinous character make a happy life more likely for their possessors than the melancholia that afflicts those born under Saturn. Mental abnormalities are commonly debilitating, sorely limiting available opportunities, since opportunities are relative to abilities. Pedagogical preconditions are clear, both in the context of parental home and of formal education. A good education, relative to the times, gives one the knowledge and skills that are both intrinsically valuable in the culture in which one lives and instrumentally valuable in enhancing life opportunities. Equally crucial is the absence, both in pedagogical processes and in society at large, of discrimination, injustice, and unfairness. Socio-economic conditions include need satisfaction, labour opportunities, care for the sick and aged. Socio-political conditions include minimal criminality, security of life, limb and property, equality before the law, due process of law, personal liberty (no slavery or serfdom) as well as recognition of human dignity, formal respect for persons, and absence of humiliation (see Essay 13). Most importantly, the absence of the most diligently organised of all human social activities, namely war.

So much for connective and contrastive analysis.

6.   In philosophical reflection in the West, two traditions dominate thought on the Good of Man. First, the hedonic tradition according to which happiness is to be gained through the pursuit of pleasure or is identical with pleasure. Second is the Greek eudaimonic tradition, according to which living a worthy and worthwhile life, doing good and doing well, is the Good of Man. Each of these embraces a variety of conceptions.

Epicurean hedonism held that pleasure, or what Epicurus (341–270 BC) called 'natural pleasure', is predominantly privative.

It consists largely in the absence of pain and suffering, absence of hunger, thirst and cold, which are natural needs. The satisfaction of natural needs, coupled with justice and friendship, are sufficient for a happy life. Justice consists in abiding by the social contract, neither harming nor threatening others. Friendships are essential for human happiness. Other pleasures, such as eating or drinking to excess (the pleasures of the gourmand) or eating luxury foods and wines (the pleasures of the gourmet) do not correspond to natural needs and are not necessary. Sexual pleasures are indeed natural but produce no good and often produce harm. The pleasures of power, wealth, public honours, and intellect are neither natural nor necessary. They are not necessary in so far as their absence involves no pain or, alternatively, their presence is likely to cause pain. The wise will eschew such pleasures. There seems a curious inconsistency in as much as friendship, lauded by Epicurus, is the source of great pain – grief at the loss of a beloved friend or sorrow at the break-up of a friendship. Epicurean hedonism is a withdrawal into the inner citadel – the slings and arrows of outrageous fortune will break upon the walls. The less one demands of life, the less often will one be disappointed.

Epicurean minimalism was not the only hedonic doctrine in the ancient world. Cyrenaican hedonism, preached and practised by Aristippus the Elder (ca. 435–356 BC) advocated the pursuit of sensory and sensual pleasure. This, he held, is constitutive of a happy life, provided one does no harm to others.

Modern forms of hedonism are utilitarian in origin. In his *Introduction to the Principles of Morals and Legislation*, Bentham proclaimed that 'Nature has placed mankind under the governance of two sovereign masters, *pain* and *pleasure*. It is for them alone to point out what we ought to do, as well as determine what we shall do'. He did not distinguish between pleasure and happiness. Moreover, he held pleasure to be the polar opposite of pain, which is a mistake, in as much as some pains may be pleasurable and some pleasures painful. He conceived of both pleasure and pain as sensations. This was an egregious fault: physical pains are sensations, but pleasure is not, even though some sensations are pleasurable (see Essay 12). Roughly speaking, Bentham held that the only good reason for action is a present or future pleasure and the avoidance of a present or future pain. This was doubly erroneous. On the one hand, it screened out the manifold backward-looking reasons for action. One does not keep a promise because it will produce future pleasure, but because one made it. One does not strive to do right because it is the best thing to do in the circumstance in the currency of pleasure. On the other hand, it is a perniciously monist axiology, holding that all apparent values are reducible to pleasure alone. But, as we have seen in Essays 12 and 13, human beings are essentially and unavoidably axiological pluralists. The incommensurability of values and conflict of values is part of the human condition. To be sure, the pursuit of one's own pleasure is not, according to utilitarians, the *summum bonum*. The greatest good is to achieve by one's actions the greatest happiness for the greatest number. Notoriously, Bentham had difficulty reconciling his psychological hedonist account of motivation with his universalist doctrine of the greatest good.

The eudaimonic tradition in the ancient world was the dominant one, although it took different forms. It is important to bear in mind that what the ancients meant by *eudaimonia* is different from what the moderns mean by *happiness*. It meant, roughly speaking, a worthy and worthwhile life, or a successful and meritorious life – a combination of a life of virtue and a life characterized by good fortune. In general, the ancient Greeks had a tragic view of life, impressed, as they were, by the vicissitudes of fortune, the precariousness of health, the transitoriness of youth and beauty, the corruptibility of wealth and power, and the miseries of old age. It was in this historical context that debates on eudaimonia among poets and dramatists, no less than among philosophers, took place. Eudaimonists were not axiological monists. There are many values that human beings pursue other than eudaimonia: honour, fame, power, wealth, pleasure, not all of which are worthy of pursuit. But only eudaimonia is pursued for its own sake and not for the sake of some further goal. It is not a selfish, self-regarding goal, since the eudaimon is a person of virtue, courageous in holding his place in the hoplite shield-wall in defence of the polis, just and faithful to the laws of the polis, living in harmony with his fellow citizens, meticulous in avoiding the excesses of *hubris* that are offensive to the gods. Aristotle's discussion of the nature of eudaimonia is a high point of Greek moral philosophy, elaborated at the time in which its aptness for citizens of the polis was reaching its end, as the age of Macedonian empire displaced the age of the independent city-state. With the collapse of the polis, the ideal of the virtuous participant in a self-governing community fades. Virtuous private life becomes an option, and a corresponding change in the conception of eudaimonia occurs in the writings of the Stoics – a withdrawal into the inner citadel, comparable to the minimalist Epicureans. The role assigned to eudaimonia is no longer a combination of faring well and doing well, but rather *ataraxia* – equanimity or imperturbability in the face of ill-fortune. Taken to its extreme, as in the writings of Cicero and Seneca, the eudaimon's *ataraxia* must be sufficiently robust to withstand *all* suffering, no matter how dreadful. Here we have moved a very long way from the elaboration of the ideal form of life suited to mankind. With the subsequent rise of Christianity, happiness is, for some centuries, relegated to the next world, restricted to the obedient servants of God basking blissfully in the light of His glory and enjoying the delights of watching the torments of the damned in hellfire (a ghastly thought endorsed even by the gentle Aquinas).

7.   Our conception of happiness is far removed from the ancient conceptions of eudaimonia. It is not so closely bound up with the possession and exercise of virtues or with good judgement; it is not bound up with public service; nor is it required to be immune to ill hap. It is not restricted to the lives of the great and the good: being a farm labourer or factory worker, an artisan or tradesman, a clerk or banker does not exclude the possibility of happiness as we understand the term. What our idea of happiness requires by way of worthiness is primarily absence of serious vices, including folly. A happy person must want for nothing important, lack of which would make one unhappy and discontented, frustrated, miserable or wretched. Such a person must find reasonable fulfilment in their life, in the successful exercise of talents, in friendships and family relationships. Happy people must take pleasure and find enjoyment in some of their activities and receptivities. They must evaluate their activities and voluntary commitments as being worthwhile and think of themselves as achieving their goals and purposes to a reasonably satisfactory degree. To be sure, a happy life or period of life must be sufficiently robust to withstand the inevitable tragedies and sorrows of human life, the loss of parents or beloved siblings, the death of dear friends. It must also constitute something of a bastion against the occasional inevitable failures and disappointments.

   Like eudaimonia, happiness is never sought for the sake of any of the other ends of life. One may want to be wealthy, possess power, or achieve fame for the sake of being happy, but one cannot want to be happy in order to be wealthy, powerful, or famous. Although happiness is a feature of the Good of Man, it is often reasonable to sacrifice one's happiness or prospects of happiness for other ends – for the sake of one's vocation or for one's art, for the sake of one's country, for one's parents in their illness or dotage, for one's children, if their most urgent needs demand it, for ideals, such as justice or liberty, and for ideologies.

8.   It is a moot point whether the wicked and evil can enjoy happiness. That the wicked often prosper is evident, be they robber barons or bankers, corrupt leaders of corrupt regimes or wicked religious ideologues. As we saw in the previous essay, they may have lost their own soul, or destroyed it in the course of their evil-doings. Does this preclude happiness? One would like to think so, but it is not obvious. It is a subject worth investigating.

To be sure, if the wicked and evil-doers are, like Macbeth, racked with guilt and paranoia, they are not going to be leading happy lives. But one of the marks of many evil people is complete absence of guilt and remorse (none of the Nazi leaders at Nuremberg showed either guilt or remorse, save for Speer, who pretended remorse to save his skin; see Essay 14). They may indeed believe in their own evil ideology and be triumphant in their achievements (as were the great dictators of the twentieth century and the various *genocidaires* of the twentieth and twenty-first). To be sure, that does not amount to happiness. People who are truly wicked possess a panoply of interwoven and complementary vices: of cruelty, deceitfulness, disloyalty, treachery, arrogance, cunning, concupiscence, contempt for humanity, self-deception, and so forth (wonderfully depicted in Goya's hideous Black Paintings). They can, indeed, be said to have lost their soul, but they would not miss it. The absence of any moral sensibility is not something that they would even notice. The moot point is whether the possession of the vices of the wicked and evil-doers is compatible with happiness. Are such evil persons capable of genuine love and friendship, both of which require forms of selflessness and generosity? They may need love, demand it, and get it (Hitler, Mussolini), but are they capable of giving love? That seems more than doubtful.

PART IV

Methodology

16

On Method: Connective, Contrastive, and Contextual Analysis

> To set in order – That's the task
> Both Eros and Apollo ask;
> For Art and Life agree in this
> That each intends a synthesis,
> That order which must be the end
> [Of every thinking personage].
>   W. H. Auden, *The Double Man*

1. Methodology

The fifteen previous essays exemplify an array of methods of logico-linguistic analysis for solving, resolving and dissolving a variety of fundamental philosophical problems. They follow the dictum that the proof of the pudding is in the eating. The methodical characterization of the cooking should come after the meal. Talk of the mind, it was shown, is not talk about a kind of thing – the mind is not a something, but it is not a nothing either. Rather, talk of the mind is a form of representation: a way of presenting human intellectual powers and their exercise (Essay 1). The classical mind/body problem, on analysis, simply dissolves into nothing (Essay 2). The vexing puzzles concerning the nature of consciousness are solved by painstaking connective, contrastive, and contextual analysis (Essay3), and the egregious

Solving, Resolving, and Dissolving Philosophical Problems: Essays in Connective, Contrastive and Contextual Analysis, First Edition. P. M. S. Hacker.
© 2025 John Wiley & Sons Ltd. Published 2025 by John Wiley & Sons Ltd.

muddles about the what-its-likeness of experience and qualia were exposed and uprooted (Essay 4). The venerable bafflement about other minds and the possibility of knowing their contents are pernicious weeds and accordingly were extirpated, leaving behind the genuine problems of knowing other people, problems that are part of the human condition (Essay 5). Salient epistemological concepts were investigated, namely: knowledge, belief, memory, imagination, thinking, and dreaming (Essays 6–11). The domain of value is equally amenable to our analytic methods. The predicaments concerning the place of value in a world of facts were dissolved and the roots of value and the nature of moral goodness were laid bare, as were the roots and nature of evil (Essays 13–15). The indispensability of the notion of the human soul was clarified without recourse to religion or to misconceived notions about post-mortem survival (Essay 15).

Our results have, in a variety of ways, been striking and unexpected. But they are unexpected not in the sense that a great novel scientific theory (say, the theory of electricity) is unexpected. For while the response to a new scientific theory may well be 'Who would have thought that things are so?', the response to our analyses should uniformly be, 'I should have thought of that!' or 'Yes, of course! Why didn't I see that?'. For what we have been disclosing are features of our own conceptual scheme, features of the net with which we strive to capture reality – not the empirical fish that we capture with it. We have been disclosing conceptual truths by logico-linguistic analysis. It is now time to analyse our methods – to give a systematic overview of connective, contrastive, and contextual analysis in which we draw together a multitude of threads spun in the essays. To ward off misunderstandings: this is no more meta-analysis or meta-philosophy than the spelling of 'orthography' is meta-orthography – it is just more philosophical analysis.

2. The method of linguistic analysis

Our methods are forms of *logico-linguistic* analysis. We are engaged in examining linguistic usage, that is: how words are to be used in the practices of competent speakers of the language. We are not engaged in theory construction on the model of the manifold forms of theory construction characteristic of different empirical sciences. There is nothing new about the Way of Words: one of its greatest practitioners was Aristotle. Nor is there anything novel about the idea of analysis in one sense or another. So, we need to elucidate the various forms of analysis as practised in philosophy throughout the ages, by contrast with *logico-linguistic* analysis of the kind exemplified in this book. When this has been made clear, we may turn to the notion of *theory* to explain why we are not engaged in theory-construction on the model of the natural sciences.

The notion of analysis in philosophy has a variety of meanings and very different forms of analysis have been practised by great philosophers in the past. So we need to differentiate our forms of analysis from others. In the ancient world, Plato advocated analysis of instances of justice, courage, or piety (for example, a just act, a courageous man, or a pious custom) into timeless unchanging Ideas. The forms of analysis embraced in the early modern era are those most familiar to us today. Descartes was engaged in analysis of objects in reality into their constituent simple natures. Locke was engaged upon a different enterprise of analysing complex ideas into their simple indecomposable simple ideas. In modern times there was a recapitulation of classical empiricism in the Vienna Circle doctrine that all experience is to be analysed into sense-data and that the empirical world is reducible to sense-data.

The kind of analysis that we embrace is radically unlike the various classical and empiricist forms. It is rather connective, contrastive, and contextual analysis. The term 'connective analysis' is Peter Strawson's:

> let us imagine … the model of an elaborate network, a system, of connected items. Concepts, such that the function of each concept, could, from a philosophical point of view, be properly understood only by grasping its connections with others, its place in the system – perhaps better still, the picture of interlocking systems of such a kind. (*Analysis and Metaphysics: An Introduction to Philosophy* (Oxford University Press, 1992))

The nodes in the network are connected to other nodes by logical relations of implication, mutual implication, entailment and mutual entailment, exclusion and incompatibility, criteria of application, empirical and a priori probabilification, and presupposition. These logical connections constitute *the nature* of anything falling under the concept.

So, we distinguish between the *defining essence of* X, as given by an analytic definition in terms of necessary and sufficient conditions (on the Platonist model of geometry) or the *real essence* of X, on the one hand, and the *constitutive nature* of Xs, given by a description of linguistic usage, viz. connective analysis, on the other. Essentialism is a Platonist doctrine, linked to the purported differentiation of Real Definition (*definitio rei*) from Nominal Definition (*definitio nominis*). Its typical form is analytic definition in terms of genus and differentia, and decompositional analysis into constituent universals. It may also take the form of decomposition into constituent or integral parts on the model of the composition of a parallelogram out of two triangles. Hence, the seventeenth-century Port-Royale *Logic*, written by Antoine Arnauld (1612–94), argued that defining human beings as a composite of mind and body was a correct Real Definition. A Real Definition must make it possible for us to understand the essence or essential nature of anything it signifies and to account for its principal characteristics. It purported not to be concerned with mere words, which are, after all, arbitrary, but with real things – just as it was held that geometrical analysis is not concerned with the analysis of the word 'circle' (or the Greek word *kyklos*), but with the timeless and universal essence of circles. The notion of Real Definition persisted well into the nineteenth century. It fell out of fashion after powerful criticisms made by John Stuart Mill and Richard Whately (1787–1863), who held that all definition was nominal. It enjoyed a revival under a different name in the conception of natural kinds that pre-occupied many Anglophone philosophers in the wake of Hilary Putnam. It should be evident that our forms of analysis favour nominalism. We are examining word usage in order to solve, resolve and dissolve philosophical problems.

Contrastive analysis is complementary to connective analysis. To attain an overview of any problematic expression that gives rise to philosophical problems, confusions, and bafflement, we need not only to describe its connections with related terms, but also its manifold contraries and contradictories, and, in a looser sense, its opposites. This was patent in our examination of the varieties of goodness (Essay 12). For, as we have seen, a common failure in philosophical reasoning is to draw the wrong contrasts, to invoke misguided analogies. So, for example, philosophers have been prone to construe thought, emotion, perception, and volition as mental attributes and to contrast them with physical attributes, such as height, weight, and strength. Similarly, mental attributes, duly misconstrued, are commonly contrasted with behavioural attributes, unwarrantedly reduced to the mere of moving one's limbs, one's facial expressions, and physical interactions with the environment. But, as was demonstrated, the contrasts are misguided. What is needed to illuminate the problems of mind and body is the contrast between somatic attributes and non-somatic attributes (Essay 2). So too, it was crucial, for our epistemological investigations into the nature of knowledge to show that the analysis of knowledge as justified true belief is erroneous, in as much as the negation of A knows that p is not the tripartite disjunction: either it is false that p, or A does not believe that p, or A is not justified in believing that p (Essay 6).

Contextual analysis is also of crucial importance to our methodology. There are many expressions that can licitly be employed only if certain contextual preconditions are satisfied, and that in two different senses: sentential context and circumstantial context. So, for example, it only makes sense to claim that one is certain if it makes sense in that *sentential context*, to doubt. If doubt is logically excluded, as in the case of being in pain, then certainty too is excluded. For one role of the concept of certainty is to exclude doubt, but if doubt is *logically* excluded ('I don't know whether I have a severe pain or not. Maybe I do and maybe I don't.' is unintelligible.), then there is no work for certainty to do. Similarly, it only makes sense to talk of recognition, if misrecognition or failure of recognition are intelligible in a given *circumstantial context*. If that contextual requirement is not satisfied, then the question of recognition or failure of recognition cannot arise. One doesn't either recognize or fail to recognize one's wife whenever one looks at her while having breakfast together, but one might be said to recognize or fail to recognize her face in a crowd. Some differences between uses are highly context-sensitive. In most contexts, as we have seen, 'I think' and 'I believe' are inter-substitutable. But when it comes to a context in which we distinguish between hearsay and personal opinion, they are altogether different: 'I believe your roses are beautiful' is an expression of hearsay, whereas 'I think your roses are beautiful' is an expression of personal judgement after looking at the rose garden.

So, we distinguish between connective, contrastive, and contextual linguistic analysis. Words are our raw data. The OED is a treasure trove for a philosopher, both because of its plethora of examples, and because of its etymologies. It does not answer any philosophical questions: it provides the raw material on which to work. The only alternatives are recent publications, on the model of science, or one's intuitions. But the last decade of philosophical writings will do no more than enshrine current prejudices and preconceptions. Appeal to one's own intuitions is no more than an appeal to one's hunches and guesses that leave one unable to distinguish between a valid intuition and a false intuition. So intuitions leave one in the lurch. The OED, we have emphasized, solves nothing, but it provides one with the raw material on which to work. What has to be done is *to find* or *make* order in the mass of linguistic data, an order that will illuminate the problem at hand.

Are we then interested only in words and how they are used? Are we just glorified lexicographers? Are we suggesting that philosophy sheds no light on the nature of things? No. What we are suggesting is that the only way to shed light on the *logically constitutive nature* of things is to clarify the concepts of those things, and the only way to clarify concepts is to describe the usage of the words that express those concepts. I know of no better statement of this point than a passage from Wittgenstein's *Philosophical Investigations* §370:

> One ought to ask, not what images are or what goes on when one imagines something, but how the word "imagination" is used. But that does not mean that I want to talk only about words. For the question of what imagination essentially is, is as much about the word "imagination" as my question. And I am only saying that this question is not to be clarified – neither for the person who does the imagining, nor for anyone else – by pointing; nor yet by a description of some process. The first question also asks for the clarification of a word, but it makes us expect a wrong kind of answer.

Investigating the nature of X, investigating the concept of X, and investigating the use (the meaning) of the word 'X' are merely three different modes of engaging in the same investigation. For the most part, these are equivalent. There is no way in which the constitutive, logical, nature of X *can* be investigated other than by clarifying the concept of X, and there is no way of investigating the concept of X other than by examining the usage of 'X'. The alternatives are (i) theory-mongering, which we shall discuss later; or (ii) the bogus method of intuitions, which are no more than hunches or guesses that have no place in philosophy; or (iii) the method of scanning current writings on the model of the sciences, on the false assumption that the form of philosophy, like the form of the empirical sciences, is progress. But the form of philosophy is not progress at all, for there are long regressive periods in the history of Western philosophy, when great insights sink from view for centuries (like Aristotle's ethics) or when a whole epoch becomes caught in the vice of a misbegotten pivotal concept, as when the concept of an 'idea' dominated philosophical thought from the seventeenth century until Kant.

3. Conceptual analysis

So, our methods are logico-linguistic. Logico-linguistic analysis *is* conceptual analysis. We have touched on the matter in previous essays, but now is the place to elaborate. Many, but not all, kinds of words can be said to express concepts (proper names do not; nor do greetings such as 'Hello', drinking toasts such as 'Cheers', cries such as 'Tally-ho!', or incantations such as 'Abracadabra', which have meaning but do not have a meaning). All our talk of concepts is abstraction from specific languages in order to dissociate local grammatical features and idiom that are philosophically irrelevant. The differences between 'cause', 'la cause', 'Ursache', 'causa' may well be philosophically irrelevant, so talk of the concept of causation enables us to focus upon commonalities. Words (with the exception of the kinds of words cited previously) have meanings, concepts do not. Sentences consist of a word or words, and may express thoughts, that is, what we think. But thoughts do not consist of anything. Rather, one must have mastered the relevant concepts if one is to be able to think the thought. To possess a concept is to have mastered the use of a word or phrase that expresses it.

The problems we are dealing with are, for the most part, conceptual problems – problems about the net, not about the empirical fish that may be caught with it in our scientific investigations. They can be solved, resolved or dissolved *only* by conceptual analysis. Why 'for the most part'? Because, in some cases, to shed light upon our problems we need to consider very general and incontrovertible facts about the natural world we inhabit as well as very general and incontrovertible facts about human nature. This was evident, for example, in our investigations into morality and the nature of moral goodness in Essay 13. The upshot of our investigations often consists in conceptual truths, by contrast with empirical truths that are the product of successful scientific investigations. This was patent in our elucidation of the nature of the mind (Essay 1), in our dissolution of the mind/body problem (Essay 2), in the illumination shed by our investigations into the nature of dreaming (Essay 11). Conceptual truths of this kind were idiosyncratically characterized by Wittgenstein as 'grammatical propositions' – an intelligible usage, but one that has not caught on. Why the recurrent qualification 'often'? Because sometimes the upshot of our investigations consists in no more than untying knots in the web of words that were themselves the product of a misuse of words, or the employment of a misconceived analogy, or the spinning of a theory (of which more anon). Sometimes achievement consists in sweeping away misconceptions that stand in the way of apprehending obvious conceptual truths. For example, the answer to the question of how we know of the existence of objects in the world around us is: 'By the use of our eyes and ears' which is not news from The Transcendental Times. But dozens of misconceptions stand in the way of this grammatical triviality (confusions of about primary and secondary qualities, about private ownership of experience and private knowledge of experience, about doubt and certainty, about direct and indirect knowledge, about qualitative and numerical identity, and so forth). Similarly, the answer to the question of how we know what others are thinking or experiencing is: 'By reference to what they do and say', which is not news from The Metaphysical Gazette. But multitudinous misunderstandings stand in the way of apprehending this grammatical triviality (misunderstandings about the 'inner' and the 'outer', about introspection and self-ascription of experience, about the nature of the mind, about what counts as human behaviour, about the limits of possible pretence, and so forth). Moreover, in our investigations into moral goodness and the nature of evil, we often had to appeal to fundamental principles of value (e.g. of self-transcendence, of justice, kindness, and compassion) and fundamental norms of behaviour (e.g. the moral prohibition on humiliation and the need for formal respect), which are certainly not grammatical trivialities (but they are not theories either).

The claim that philosophical questions are characteristically conceptual rather than empirical and that their solution, resolution or dissolution is for the most part effected by conceptual, logico-linguistic analysis, is controverted by some leading twenty-first century Anglophone philosophers. One argument runs as follows: an example of an alleged conceptual truth is that red things are coloured. An alleged mark of a conceptual truth is universal assent. But this, it is argued, is mistaken. A speaker may learn the use of 'red' and 'coloured', but later decide that the word 'coloured' is so tainted by racist associations that it correctly applies to nothing. She refuses to call anything 'coloured'. She no longer assents to 'Red things are coloured', although she has not lost her understanding of the sentence and has no difficulty in following other speakers when they use the term 'coloured'. If there is one such dissident among English speakers, then 'Red things are coloured' fails the test of universal assent. Similar examples can be constructed for any other candidate for conceptual truth. So it is unclear whether any useful distinction between conceptual and non-conceptual truths can be drawn.[1]

This is mistaken. First, conceptual truths are marked by their *role*: they are rules for the use of the expressions they incorporate. In some cases, a given conceptual truth may be an inference licence. So, for example, 'Anything red is coloured' entitles one to infer from the fact that A is red that A is coloured without looking *de novo*. In other cases, a conceptual truth may in effect constitute an exclusionary rule. So, the statement 'Nothing can be simultaneously red all over and also green all over' excludes the sequence of words 'simultaneously red all over and green all over' from use. It is a meaningless sequence of words, as is 'round square', by contrast with 'red square'. Hence, secondly, conceptual truths have a role in teaching the use of words and in correcting misuses of words. If someone (a philosopher or cognitive neuroscientist) asserts that colours are sensations in the brain, one may remind him that colours are seen, not felt, whereas sensations are felt and not seen, and that while, as a matter of fact, there are no sensations in the brain, sensations in the head are called 'headaches', not 'colours'. These reminders are conceptual truths. Thirdly, among the marks of a conceptual truth are not universal assent, but rather speaker's and hearer's assent, coupled with their finding the negation of a patent logico-grammatical truth *unintelligible*. If someone were to assert that red things are *not* coloured, *we would not understand what they are saying* and would ask them to explain what they mean. Dissent in the case of the negation of a patent conceptual truth is a mark of incomprehension, not of denial of a possibility. Similarly, assent to a fully understood assertion of a conceptual truth is not assent to a matter of fact or theory. It is assent to a rule or norm of representation. Finally, the fact that an expression may be 'tainted' by offensive association does not imply that it does not apply correctly to its extension. The expression 'Jew' is tainted by centuries of Christian and Islamic anti-Semitism, but that does not imply that it is not correctly applied to Jews.

Incidentally, there is nothing odd about insisting that conceptual truths are expressions of rules and also claiming them to be true, for although rules are not true or false, the statement of a rule may be

---

[1] T. Williamson, *Philosophical Method: A Very Short Introduction* (Oxford University Press, Oxford, 2020), p. 42.

said to be true, for example, 'It is true that the chess king moves one square at a time'. What it means to ascribe truth to such a rule formulation is simply to affirm that the stated rule *is* a rule of the system. To say that it is true that anything red is coloured is simply to say that this is a rule of our colour grammar – a rule for the use of 'red' and 'coloured'. To be sure, the negation of a conceptual truth is not false (there are no false rules, although it may be false that such-and-such is a rule) but nonsense – a form of words that has no licit use in the language. The utterance 'Red is not a colour' would be met with incomprehension ('Say that again!') and a request for an explanation of what was meant ('What *do* you mean?').

Of course, numerous philosophical claims are not obvious nonsense at all. Philosophers have, for centuries, insisted that human beings are a combination of mind and body, and that the mind is the thinking part of a human being (Essays 1–2). We have shown that to be mistaken. For millennia, philosophers have insisted that memory is of the past. We have shown that to be confused, *conceptually* confused (Essay 8). Philosophers, psychologists, and cognitive neuroscientists insist that it is an obvious matter of fact that dreams occur during sleep. We have shown that while it is true that dreams occur during sleep, that is not a matter of fact at all, but a convention of representation (Essay 11). These mistaken ideas are not at all obviously incorrect – had they been obviously incorrect they would not have been advanced for so many centuries by so many brilliant thinkers. They are *unobviously* incorrect. That is why Wittgenstein was profoundly right in holding that one task of philosophy is to transform *latent nonsense* into *patent nonsense*. That task is anything but easy and straightforward. Again, as Wittgenstein noted, philosophical confusions are knots we have tied in our understanding, and in disentangling them, we have to make as many and as complex an array of movements of thought as is necessary to disentangle the knot.

4. Description not theory

Disentangling knots in our understanding, rendering implicit conceptual connections explicit and perspicuous, showing a wide variety of claims made by philosophers, psychologists, cognitive neuroscientists, physicists, and other scientists to be not empirically false but conceptually incoherent has been our objective throughout the essays of this book. Disabusing the proverbial 'Man on the Clapham Omnibus' of some of his conceptual confusions, both those of his own making and those that are consequences of back-seepage from confused science, theological incoherences, and bad philosophy has been no less important a purpose. Our aim, above all, is clarity, conceptual clarity. Our methods are painstaking descriptions of logico-linguistic rules elicited from linguistic practices of competent speakers of the language. We invoke no theories on the model of the empirical sciences. This is a source of contention and animus against logico-linguistic analysis. Contemporary Anglophone philosophy is much given to the claim that the task of philosophy is *theory construction* (Williamson, op. cit.). One contention is that theories advance answers to questions, philosophy advances answers to questions, therefore philosophy advances theories. This is patently an invalid inference, and doubtless unintended. What seems more serious are the claims that scientists sometimes have to compare different theories, and philosophers often compare philosophical theories (e.g. idealism as opposed to realism, transcendental idealism as opposed to empirical idealism, Platonism as opposed to nominalism); moreover, scientific theories are tested by empirical experiment, and philosophical theories are analogously tested by thought experiments.

However, thought experiments are no more experiments than monopoly money is money. They are at best intuitive endeavours to determine the limits of linguistic usage and the existence of borderline cases. At worst, they are science-fiction stories of the kind toyed with by Twin-Earth theorists (such as Hilary Putnam), teletransportational fantasies (such as Derek Parfit's (1942–2017)), and ill-thought-out speculations about 'zombies' (such as David Chalmers's (b. 1966)).

The expressions 'theory' and 'theoretical' have many different uses. Philosophical theories are radically unlike scientific theories. They are not confirmed or infirmed by an *experimentum crucis*. They are not validated by observation, but by argument and painstaking analysis. One can neither confirm nor infirm the philosophical theory that the mind is the brain by observation, and there is no experiment to validate the theories that colours are sensations in the mind or brain, that there are no material objects, or that the past does not exist and time is unreal. These are not false theories, they are 'theories' that on careful connective, contrastive, and contextual analysis are shown to make no sense. They are not false theories akin to the theory of phlogiston, to the geocentric theory of the solar system, or to evolutionary theories of design. They are logically incoherent in as much as they transgress the bounds of sense.

Philosophical questions are categorially unlike empirical questions. They are not like 'Where is the North Pole?' or even 'Where is El Dorado?', but more akin to 'Where is the East Pole?' (El Dorado, *as it happens*, does not exist, but *there is no such thing* as an East Pole. One may go on a futile expedition to El Dorado, but one cannot even go on a futile expedition to the East Pole.) 'What is the time?' is an empirical question; 'What is time?' is a philosophical one. We know how to find out what time it is, but it is far more problematic to find out what time is. As Augustine remarked, 'What, then, is time? I know well enough what it is, provided that nobody asks me; but if I am asked what it is and try to explain, I am baffled'.[2] For one does not have an overview, a surveyable representation, of one's own use of the word 'time' and of temporal expressions such as 'earlier', 'later', 'then', 'now', 'an hour', 'a day', 'a year', 'at the same time', and 'at a different time', and so forth.

Philosophical theories abound. But we need to disabuse ourselves of them. We need to dismantle them by analysis, showing how and why they are incoherent. Where we find theories in philosophy, we can learn much from their meticulous deconstruction. We have to replace them by logico-linguistic analysis and descriptions of the web of words.

5. Whose language and what evidence?

Linguistic data concerning the usage of words are the raw materials the gathering and ordering of which is the first step in all our logico-linguistic investigations. But how do we know what usage is? And whose usage are we to attend to? Should we not be engaging in social surveys about the uses of English? Should we not be scouring regional sociolects and attending to class differences in language use? Should we not investigate American English or Indian English no less than English English? Are we not laying ourselves open to the common accusation that all we are doing is giving priority to the English that is characteristic of Oxbridge senior common rooms? Are we not simply consulting our linguistic intuitions? And why should our linguistic intuitions be given preference over the linguistic intuitions of others?

These qualms are unwarranted. They rest on misunderstandings and misconceptions. Mastery of a language is a skill. Some people are

---

[2] Augustine, *Confessions* Book XI, section 14.

more skilful than others. That is why dictionaries compiled on historical principles are valuable resources for examples of usage, since they select dozens if not hundreds of examples from competent, often highly competent writers over many centuries. How can a philosopher, in his proverbial armchair, adjudicate upon usage and criticize misuses? Should he not be consulting others? Philosophers tend to be highly competent speakers of their language. They no more need engage in social surveys than a chess-master needs to consult hundreds of chess players to assure himself that the chess king moves one square at a time or is the piece that gets checked when threatened. Those who suppose that social surveys of linguistic use are necessary before any appeal to ordinary language is licit forget the knowledge the competent practitioner has of the practice of which he is a master. Here we might reply, 'I don't need a social survey, since I know how to play the game'. That does not mean that a competent speaker does not make mistakes in his description of usage – through oversight (Gilbert Ryle or J. L. Austin (1911–60) on voluntariness), or through lack of linguistic imagination. Above all, as we have stressed recurrently, mastery of use does not mean mastery of comparative use. Every English speaker has mastered the use of 'nearly' and the use of 'almost', but hardly anyone can answer the question of how their respective uses differ (they differ with respect to negation), since mastery of use does not require mastery of comparative use (no English speaker would say, 'There isn't almost enough sugar in the pudding'). Nor does mastery of use demand possession of an overview of use. That explains the widespread confusions over the relations between 'voluntary' and 'intentional', for example (that something may be voluntary without being intentional, and intentional without being voluntary). But, of course, once an error has been pointed out, a competent speaker will recognize his mistake or omission. If he does not, then that is a valuable datum for further exploration.

Of course, there may be different sociolects, regional, class, and national. But these only very rarely impact upon any serious philosophical question. In the rare cases in which they do, they are simply more grist for philosophical mills. I have yet to come across a philosophical question that turned on differences between various British regional sociolects. Should we not examine different languages, indeed radically different languages? Certainly, there may be great interest in doing so, in seeing how different cultures at different times and places have struggled to evolve useful linguistic instruments by the use of which they can grapple with the world. That is why we have often made brief forays into Latin, Greek, and ancient Hebrew, as well as Old English and Middle High German. Differences are more grist for our analytic mills. They may serve two invaluable purposes. First, they may disabuse us of any illusions we have that our concepts are uniquely matched to reality, if not in their surface grammar, then in their depth grammar. Secondly, they may offer us important clues for connective analysis, as we saw in our investigations into the etymologies of 'evil' in Essay 14.

6. Sources of philosophical problems

We have harped upon the linguistic sources of philosophical questions and of the logico-linguistic roots of conceptual entanglement. It is true that natural language is one great source of philosophical confusions. Expressions with the same use often look as if they were altogether different (e.g. 'That's true', 'That is the case', 'That's a fact', and 'Things are as they have been said to be'; 'A thought crossed his mind' and 'Something occurred to him'), and expressions with quite different uses often look as if they have the same use (e.g. 'I don't know what he thinks about such-and-such' and 'I don't know what I think about such-and-such'; 'is blue' and 'is true'; 'some tame tigers growl' and 'some tame tigers exist'; 'I have a pain' and 'I have a pin'). It is of paramount importance to realize that 'natural language' here is being contrasted with 'artificial language', that is, with logical calculi of various kinds. It is equally important to realize that *ordinary language*, to which we have often appealed in our investigations in philosophy of psychology and in epistemology, is to be contrasted with *technical language*, as is to be found in advanced sciences or in mathematics and formal logic. Philosophical confusions and unclarities arise out of ordinary language. But they commonly arise to no less a degree out of technical language. Quantum mechanics and transfinite arithmetic are sources of conceptual confusion no less than common or garden reflections on the mind and the body. For the technical expressions in these domains are equally subject to misuse and misunderstanding.

It would, however, be misleading to suggest that all philosophical questions are rooted in language. For there are numerous other sources of philosophical confusion. Religion and religious doctrine were and continue to be a great source of conceptual unclarity and confusion. Talk of the God of monotheism gave rise, in the fulness of time, both to attempts to prove by reason that an omnipotent, omniscient, and benevolent disembodied being exists beyond space and time, and to incoherent doctrines of the immortality of the soul and to post-mortem existence. Science, which replaced religion in the West as the primary explanation of natural phenomena, is no less a source of metaphysical confusion. This is patent in the domains of fundamental physics and cosmology, in cognitive neuroscience and neurology, in experimental psychology and psychoanalysis. But science is not merely a source of conceptual unclarities and confusions in specific sciences, it is also a source of scientism, that is: the attempt to extend science and scientific methods beyond their legitimate limits. This is patent in cognitive neuroscientific endeavours to show that free will is an illusion, that memory is stored at synaptic connections, that the brain thinks and understands, knows and believes, decides and wills. It is also evident in the contention that science is the measure of all things, of what is that it is and of what is not that it is not (Wilfred Sellars (1912–89)), thus excluding the manifold of explanations of human action and omission in terms of reasons and motives, inclinations and tendencies, goals and values, justifications and excuses by reference to which we render ourselves intelligible to ourselves and to others.

Purely intellectual, a priori advances often generate new philosophical problems, for example concerning the relations between logical calculi and human reasoning, or between being rational and being reasonable. The invention of geometry generated the problem of the logical status of geometry: whether it is a theory of space or a grammar of space – a problem that became acute with the invention of alternative geometries. Frege's and Russell's invention of the first-order predicate calculus with identity gave rise to the nagging problem of the relation between natural language and the calculus, in particular the relation between the logical connectives and quantifiers in the calculus and in ordinary speech. Technological advances are an equally fertile source of conceptual puzzlement and confusion. The invention of clockwork and of automata in the sixteenth and seventeenth centuries provided an irresistible analogy for construing nature in general and the human body in particular as divine clockwork. Similarly, the invention of computers offered the temptation to construe the brain on the model of a computer and the mind on the model of a computer program. It also raised the question of whether computers can think and whether future computers will be able to think better than human beings can – a question rendered even more urgent by the recent advances in artificial intelligence. Developments in the empirical sciences are likewise a seedbed of conceptual bafflement, as is patent in Newtonian kinematics, relativity theory, and quantum mechanics.

Of course, these multitudinous sources of bafflement are themselves expressed in natural or technical language, in extending the uses of expressions beyond their legitimate domains and in seizing upon misguided analogies (e.g. of clockwork, computers, and computer programs). But it would be misleading to say that language is the sole root of philosophical problems and conceptual confusions.

7. Therapeutics and description of the web

Our methods of connective, contrastive, and contextual analysis are often said to be no more than aspects of a singularly negative therapeutic conception of philosophy. All we do, it is sometimes said, is explode illusions and dispel confusions. But this accusation is unwarranted. The dialectic of philosophy, the systematic study of philosophical illusions and confusions, is but one part of the task of philosophy. It is indeed negative: the unravelling of knots we tie in our understanding. But complementary to the dialectic of philosophy is the analytic: the description of different parts of the web of words that constitutes our conceptual scheme.

In the course of the essays in this book, we have encountered a wide range of very difference kinds of concepts. Some are definable by analytic definitions in terms of necessary and sufficient conditions of application. But such are relatively rare outside the formal sciences of arithmetic, geometry, and logic. Family resemblance concepts are not uncommon. If Wittgenstein is right, then concepts such as proposition and number are family resemblance concepts, as are many psychological concepts, such as knowledge and understanding. We have come across focal concepts of the kind already identified by Aristotle, such as the concept of the health of a being. Going a step beyond Aristotle, we suggested that it is fruitful to systematize some concepts as multifocal. Seizing upon an unexploited suggestion in Wittgenstein, we also canvassed the notion of concepts that are centres of variation without any definite central concept around which other derivative concepts are arranged, and we also suggested the idea of concepts constituted by multiple centres of variation, such as consciousness or thinking. Our investigation into the concept of goodness revealed the character of variety-concepts as introduced by G. H. von Wright, an idea that seemed worth exploiting in the case of the concepts of truth and of existence. It must however be born in mind that there is nothing definitive about this classification of different kinds of concepts. These are merely organizational devices that help us to describe the logico-grammatical character of concepts that attract our interest for philosophical reasons.

Our analysis of any particular concept that needs clarifying in order to solve, resolve, or dissolve a philosophical problem requires us to put the problematic concept through its paces, as it were. With respect to any concept that concerns us in our philosophical investigations we must examine how it behaves under negation, carefully differentiating predicate negation, 'A does not have the property F' from propositional negation, 'It is not the case that A has the property F', which can sometimes be revealing. We must see whether the problematic concept has a contrary or contradictory or neither – despite one's initial intuitive reaction, 'pain', for example, is not the contradictory or contrary of 'pleasure' (since displeasure is not the contradictory of pleasure, and there are painful pleasures as well as pleasurable pains) and 'mental 'is not the contradictory of 'physical' (since getting married or running up debts are neither mental nor physical, but rather non-somatic attributes). We should investigate the forms of quantification it allows: 'much' or 'many'; 'a few' or 'a bit', numerical and ordinal quantification. If the concept is apparently a categorial one, such as 'state', 'event', 'process', 'substance', 'property', 'relation', 'act', 'activity', 'action', 'tendency', 'disposition', etc. we should pay very careful attention. These apparent categorials, as has been stressed, are far from being the hardest of the hard, akin to variables in a calculus, the substitution instances of which are the concepts they subsume. They were not designed by a divine Linnaeus for the classification of everything that exists. Many concepts may, from context to context, be subsumable under different categorials. So, for example, 'fear' may be used to characterize a current feeling, or a behavioural disposition. Other concepts may not be subsumable under any apparent categorial, for example 'belief' (see Essay 7). Others may merely have an *affinity* to some categorial, as 'knowledge' and 'understanding' have an affinity to ability and potentiality (see Essay 6).

There are numerous expressions that have a descriptive use in as much as they can occur in sentences that are rightly said to be descriptive. But we must be aware of the multivalence of the idea of a description. There are many different kinds of description, for example descriptions of perceptibilia, of past events, of mental states, of what one imagines, of what one remembers experiencing, of what one thought, of what one dreamt, and so on. Each of these have different logico-grammatical features. This becomes evident when one asks how one might improve a description of a given kind, and how one might verify a certain sort of description. In the case of perceptibilia one might, in some cases, look or listen again, improve observation conditions, ask someone else to look or listen too. But describing what one dreamt cannot be improved by looking again or asking someone else to look too. In other cases, one can improve one's description only by more refined reflection – as in describing one's plans. Describing the house one has built is one thing, describing the house one wants to build is something quite different.

With respect to any concept under investigation we should ask what we should lack if we did not have that concept in our linguistic toolbox. If we were unable to differentiate between the voluntary and the intentional, on the one hand, and between the involuntary and the unintentional, on the other, what difficulties would we have in distinguishing cases that need to be distinguished (we can see this vividly in Aristotle, who did indeed lack the means whereby to draw the distinctions). If, like the ancient Greeks and Romans, we had only natural numbers and no signed integers (hence no negative numbers), what would we not be able to do? If we lacked a first-person pronoun, how would this affect our discourse? And so on, and so forth.

We have recurrently emphasized that abstract nouns are a common source of conceptual confusion. We are all too prone to think abstract nouns stand for abstract objects. But we should bear in mind Wittgenstein's sapient remark that to say that a noun stands for an abstract entity amounts to little more than saying it looks as if it stands for some concrete item but it does not. Whenever possible, when faced with a problematic statement, replace abstract nouns by appropriate verbs, adjectives or adverbs. Instead of asking 'What is consciousness?', ask 'What is it for a creature to be conscious of something?' (Essay 3); instead of asking 'What is pleasure?', ask 'What is it to take pleasure in something?' and 'What is it to be pleased by something?'. Instead of asking 'What is memory?', ask 'What is it to remember something?' and 'What is it that one remembers when one remembers something?' (Essay 8).

We must attend to the tense differences and tense asymmetries of verbs, to asymmetries between first- and third-person uses of certain verbs, especially psychological and epistemic verbs. Groaning 'I am in pain' or 'It hurts' is an expression of pain, 'He is in pain' is not.

'I am going to London' is an expression of intention, 'He is going to London' is not. 'I don't know what I think' is an expression of indecision, 'I don't know what he thinks' is a confession of ignorance. We should note logical differences between kinds of verbs that are usually not noticed by grammarians, for example, between adverbial verbs, task verbs, achievement verbs, polymorphous verbs, action verbs, activity verbs, and so on.

When we have put a problematic expression through its paces, we shall have attained a reasonably good overview of its logico-grammatical character and have a reasonably good idea of its place in the web of words. That is precisely what is needed to solve, resolve, or dissolve philosophical problems.

Further Reading

The following lists for further reading do not aim to provide comprehensive reading lists for further study, but rather to indicate the immediate sources on which I drew in writing this volume on the exemplification of the methods of connective, contrastive, and contextual logico-linguistic analysis. In the tetralogy on human nature, on which this volume rests (save for essays 5 and 11), there are multitudinous references to all those to whom I am indebted for ideas and inspiration. Many of the other volumes cited here also provide a wide range of references in their footnotes to scholarly works for readers who wish to take matters further.

Essay 1: The Nature of the Mind

P. M. S. Hacker, *Human Nature: the Categorial Framework* (Blackwell, Oxford, 2007), chapters 8–10.
Bede Rundle, *Mind in Action* (Clarendon Press, Oxford, 1997), chapter 2.
A. J. P. Kenny, *Metaphysics of Mind* (Clarendon Press, Oxford, 1989), chapter 2.
Gilbert Ryle, *The Concept of Mind* (Hutchinson, London, 1949), chapters 1–2.
A. R. White, *The Philosophy of Mind* (Random House, New York, 1967), chapter 2.

Essay 2: The Nature of Our Body and the Mind/Body Relation

P. M. S. Hacker, *Human Nature: the Categorial Framework* (Blackwell, Oxford, 2007), chapter 9.

P. F. Strawson, *Individuals, An Essay in Descriptive Metaphysics* (Methuen, London, 1959), chapter 3.

Essay 3: What Is Consciousness?

P. M. S. Hacker, *The Intellectual Powers: A Study of Human Nature* (Wiley/Blackwell, Oxford, 2013), chapter 1

M. R. Bennett and P. M. S. Hacker, *Philosophical Foundations of Neuroscience*, 2nd edition (Wiley/Blackwell, Oxford, 2022), chapters 10–14.

A. R. White, *Attention* (Blackwell, Oxford, 1964), chapter IV.

Essay 4: Consciousness and Experience or 'What It Is Like to Be a Bat?' Revisited

Thomas Nagel, *Mortal Questions* (Cambridge University Press, Cambridge, 1979), chapter 12.

P. M. S. Hacker, 'Is there anything it is like to be a bat?', *Philosophy* 77 (2002), pp. 157–74.

P. M. S. Hacker, 'The sad and sorry history of consciousness: being among other things a challenge to the "consciousness studies community"', *Royal Institute of Philosophy, supplementary volume* 70 (2012), pp. 1–20.

M. R. Bennett and P. M. S. Hacker, *Philosophical Foundations of Neuroscience*, 2nd edition (Wiley/Blackwell, Oxford, 2022), chapter 11.

Essay 5: Other Minds and Other People

P. M. S. Hacker, 'Other Minds, Other People, and Human Opacity', *Ratio* 2022, pp. 1–12

Essay 6: Knowledge

P. M. S. Hacker, *The Intellectual Powers: A Study of Human Nature* (Wiley/Blackwell, Oxford, 2013), chapter 4.

Oswald Hanfling, *Philosophy and Ordinary Language* (Routledge, London, 2000), chapter 6.

A. R. White, *The Nature of Knowledge* (Rowman and Littlefield, Totowa, New Jersey, 1982).

Essay 7: Belief

P. M. S. Hacker, *The Intellectual Powers: A Study of Human Nature* (Wiley/Blackwell, Oxford, 2013), chapters 5–6.
Bede Rundle, *Mind in Action*, chapter 2, section 5, chapter 3, section 2.

Essay 8: Memory

P. M. S. Hacker, *The Intellectual Powers: A Study of Human Nature* (Wiley/Blackwell, Oxford, 2013), chapter 9.
L. R. Squire and E. R. Kandel, *Memory: From Mind to Molecules* (Scientific American Books, New York, 1999).
Bede Rundle, 'Memory and Causation', *Philosophical Investigations* 9 (1986), pp. 302–7.
M. R. Bennett and P. M. S. Hacker, *Philosophical Foundations of Neuroscience*, 2nd edition (Wiley/Blackwell, Oxford, 2022), chapter 6.

Essay 9: Imagination

P. M. S. Hacker, *The Intellectual Powers: A Study of Human Nature* (Wiley/Blackwell, Oxford, 2013), chapter 11.
A. R. White, *The Language of Imagination* (Blackwell, Oxford, 1990).
P. M. S. Hacker, *Wittgenstein: Meaning and Mind*, 2nd edition (Wiley/Blackwell, Oxford, 2019), Part I, the essays, Essay XII.
Arthur Koestler, *The Act of Creation* (Hutchinson, London, 1964).

Essay 10: Thinking

P. M. S. Hacker, *The Intellectual Powers: A Study of Human Nature* (Wiley/Blackwell, Oxford, 2013), chapter 10.
G. Ryle, *On Thinking* (Blackwell, Oxford, 1979).
B. Rundle, *Mind in Action* (Clarendon Press, Oxford,1997), chapters 4, 7, 8.
Arthur Koestler, *The Act of Creation* (Hutchinson, London, 1964).

Essay 11: On Dreams and Dreaming

Descartes, *Meditations on First Philosophy*, Meditation 1 and last paragraphs of Meditation 6.
Wittgenstein, *Philosophy of Psychology: a Fragment*, §§ 52–3, 320.
Lectures on Philosophical Psychology, p. 14.
Remarks on Philosophical Psychology I, §§ 101, 201, 374, 375–6, 934–5.
Severin Schroeder, 'The Concept of Dreaming', *Philosophical Investigations* vol. 20 (1997), 15–38.

Essay 12: The Place of Value in a World of Facts

P. M. S Hacker, *The Moral Powers: A Study of Human Nature* (Wiley/Blackwell, Oxford, 2021), chapters 1 and 8.

G. H. von Wright, *The Varieties of Goodness* (Routledge and Kegan Paul, London, 1963), chapters. I–V.

Lassi Jakola, *The Philosophy of* The Varieties of Goodness (1963), (Philosophical Studies from the University of Helsinki (54), Helsinki, 2023).

Essay 13: Morality and the Analysis of Moral Goodness

P. M. S. Hacker, *The Moral Powers: A Study of Human Nature* (Wiley/Blackwell, Oxford, 2021), chapters 1–2.

A. R. White, *Modal Thinking* (Blackwell, Oxford, 1975), chapter 10.

Essay 14: Badness, Wickedness, Evil and the Death of the Soul

P. M. S. Hacker, *The Moral Powers: A Study of Human Nature* (Wiley/Blackwell, Oxford, 2021), chapters 3–5.

John Kekes, *The Roots of Evil* (Cornell University Press, Ithaca, NY, 2005).

John Kekes, *Hard Questions* (Oxford University Press, Oxford, 2019), chapter 7.

Essay 15: Happiness

P. M. S. Hacker, *The Moral Powers: A Study of Human Nature* (Wiley/Blackwell, Oxford, 2021), chapter 9.

Aristotle, *The Eudemian Ethics.*

Rosanna Lauriola, 'From Eudaimonia to Happiness: Overview of the Concept of Happiness in Ancient Greek Culture', *Revista Éspaço Acadêmico* 59 (2006). https://periodicos.uem.br/ojs/index.php/EspacoAcademico/article/view/59422/751375152245

Essay 16: On Method: Connective, Contrastive, and Contextual Analysis

P. M. S. Hacker, *The Intellectual Powers: A Study of Human Nature* (Wiley/Blackwell, Oxford, 2013), chapter 10 and Appendix.

M. R. Bennett and P. M. S. Hacker, *Philosophical Foundations of Neuroscience*, 2nd edition (Wiley/Blackwell, Oxford, 2022), chapter 17 and Appendix 3.

A. R. White, *Methods of Metaphysics* (Croom Helm, London, 1987).

Index

Printed and bound by CPI Group (UK) Ltd, Croydon, CR0 4YY

07/07/2026

14916222-0004